HALLS OF FAME

A TRIBUTE TO AMERICA'S SPORTING SHRINES AND THE ATHLETES THEY HONOR

HALLS OF FAME

A TRIBUTE TO AMERICA'S SPORTING SHRINES AND THE ATHLETES THEY HONOR

Text by Merrell Noden

ISBN: 1-929049-42-0
Manufactured in the United States of America
First printing 2001

SPORTS ILLUSTRATED Director of Development: Stanley Weil

HALLS OF FAME

Editorial Director: Morin Bishop
  Writer: Merrell Noden
  Project Editor: John Bolster
  Managing Editor: Theresa M. Deal
  Researchers: Andrew Blais, Kate Brash, Ward Calhoun, Jeff Labrecque
  Copy Editor: Lee Fjordbotten
  Photography Editor: John S. Blackmar
Designers: Barbara Chilenskas, Jia Baek, Vincent Mejia

HALLS OF FAME was prepared by
Bishop Books, Inc.
611 Broadway
New York, New York 10012

TIME INC. HOME ENTERTAINMENT
President: Rob Gursha
Executive Director, Branded Businesses: David Arfine
Executive Director, Marketing Services: Carol Pittard
Director, Retail & Special Sales: Tom Mifsud
Director, Branded Businesses: Kenneth Maehlum
Product Manager: Dana Pecoraro
Associate Product Manager: Ann Gillespie
Assistant Product Manager: Virginia Valdes
Editorial Operations Director: John Calvano
Book Production Manager: Jessica McGrath
Associate Book Production Manager: Suzanne DeBenedetto
Assistant Fulfillment Manager: Tara Schimming
Executive Assistant: Mary Jane Rigoroso

We welcome your comments and suggestions about SPORTS ILLUSTRATED Books.
Please write to us at:
SPORTS ILLUSTRATED Books
Attention: Book Editors
PO Box 11016
Des Moines, IA 50336-1016

If you would like to order any of our
hardcover Collector's Edition books,
please call us at 1-800-327-6388.
(Monday through Friday, 7:00 a.m.– 8:00 p.m., or Saturday, 7:00 a.m.– 6:00 p.m.
Central Time).
Please visit our website at **www.TimeBookstore.com**

10   9   8   7   6   5   4   3   2   1

CONTENTS

INTRODUCTION

The National Baseball Hall of Fame and Museum opened in Cooperstown, N.Y., on June 12, 1939, and welcomed its first 13 inductees, 10 of whom were photographed at the ceremony. Along with the iconic Babe Ruth (seated, third from right) were (standing, l to r) Honus Wagner, Grover Cleveland Alexander, Tris Speaker, Nap Lajoie, George Sisler, and Walter Johnson. Seated to Ruth's right was Eddie Collins, and to his left, Connie Mack and Cy Young. At the Naismith Memorial Basketball Hall of Fame in Springfield, Mass., fans can revisit the extraordinary careers of NBA centers Kareem Abdul-Jabbar (below, left) and Wilt Chamberlain (below, right) as well as learn about pioneers like Naismith's "first team" and the Original Celtics.

Grover Cleveland Alexander was working as a greeter in a Springfield, Ill., bar when the invitation arrived, asking him to come to Cooperstown, N.Y., on June 12, 1939, for the National Baseball Hall of Fame and Museum's first induction ceremony. "The Hall of Fame is fine," the great pitcher grumbled to a reporter, "but it doesn't mean bread and butter. It's only your picture on the wall."

Alexander did go, and one assumes that, bibulous old codger though he was, he was pleased with that lovely little village in the rolling hills of central New York. Induction day in Cooperstown is still a day of magical memories, with picnics, ball games, toasts and misty-eyed nostalgia. It's hard to imagine any of today's well-paid players having the same reaction as Alexander, but in one way or another, we are still debating precisely what the Hall means.

Very few subjects stir up the same passions as the question of who should and shouldn't be honored. That should not surprise us, because most halls are started not by cold-blooded statisticians, but by passionate fans hoping to preserve some small piece of the past. What exactly is it that they are preserving? It's not only the accomplishments of a lucky few men and women who have been blessed by nature with athletic gifts and

worked hard to cultivate them. No, we are also preserving something in *us*—our memories of those men and women, the excitement we felt when we heard a home run call or watched a buzzer-beating, game-winning basket, our memories of where we were and who was with us when we witnessed those stirring moments.

The first Hall of Fame was started on the campus of New York University in 1900 (that is, if you exclude Poet's Corner in Westminster Abbey, for what is that enclave if not a writer's Hall of Fame?). The NYU Hall,

Legendary tennis rivals Martina Navratilova (far left) and Chris Evert are enshrined in Newport, R.I. Gordie Howe (left, sitting) may have had an inkling that 11-year-old Wayne Gretzky (left), who was already a highly touted player in Canada, would grow up to shatter all of Howe's scoring records and join him in the Hockey Hall of Fame.

a shrine to great Americans, did not include any sports figures, which probably made sense because organized national sports were still quite new (the U.S. Lawn Tennis Association held the first American national championship in a major sport in 1881), and there really wasn't much of a national media to spread the news.

But the sports boom was just around the corner, and by now, almost every athletic pursuit has its own Hall of Fame. There are Halls of Fame for wristwrestling (in Petaluma, Calif.), trapshooting (in Vandalia, Ohio), professional bass fishing (Hot Springs, Ark.) and marbles (Wildwood, N.J.). Next time you're in Knik, Alaska, be sure to visit the Dog Musher's Hall of Fame, though it's hard to imagine that many of its members really qualify as "famous" outside the community of dog mushers. There is even—we're not making this up—a National Jousting Hall of Fame, in Natural Chimneys Regional Park in Mount Solon, Va. There, you can read about Mary Lou Bartram, who jousted as the "Maid of Bartram Manor" and persuaded the Maryland legislature to adopt jousting as the state sport. And we thought it was lacrosse.

Many countries, cities, and states have sports halls and museums. So do universities, high schools, and ethnic and religious groups. Jack Nicklaus has his very own museum, in Dublin, Ohio (it cost $5 million!), as does, in a bit of redundancy, basketball inventor James Naismith, who you'd have thought was honored sufficiently by the Naismith Memorial Basketball Hall of Fame, in Springfield, Mass.

Most Hall of Fame arguments start, we think, because of that last, tricky word: Fame. Maybe if we renamed these shrines, called them Halls of High Quality or Galleries of Greatness, it would be a little easier to choose their members. Roger Maris, surely, is more famous than Eppa Rixey, George Kelly or Rick Ferrell, yet Maris is not in the Hall of Fame while those three are.

To what extent should character be a consideration? O.J. Simpson is still in the Pro Football Hall of Fame despite being found liable for the death of two people in a civil trial. Would he have been ousted if the verdict in his criminal trial had gone the same way?

And then there's the most recent Hall controversy: Is it fair to reject Pete Rose, whose 4,256 career hits certainly made him "famous" but who was found to have bet on sports, possibly including baseball, while managing the Cincinnati Reds? How about "Shoeless" Joe Jackson, whose lifetime average of .356 places him third all-time but who was banned from baseball—and from the Hall—because he and his Chicago White Sox teammates conspired with gamblers to throw the 1919 World Series? The case has been made that Jackson was a naive country boy and not really aware of what he was doing. He also hit .375 in the Series, hardly proof of a man tanking. And if we are to punish Rose and Jackson, what about Cobb, who everyone agrees was a virulent racist?

Some would argue for the use of formulas to determine who's in, who's out, though the experience of the LPGA stands as a cautionary tale against such a method. The LPGA decided to employ an objective formula, with the result that its Hall was the most exclusive of all, with only 14 members 32 years after its founding. Golf fans who longed to honor Amy Alcott, winner of five majors, were subjected instead to her extended struggle against younger players to secure her 30th career win.

When the formula was changed in 1999, Alcott was not the only one sprung from limbo: The Hall itself was, also, as many fans were beginning to consider it a tyrannical institution that punished some of the game's best players. It would not be difficult to devise objective points-based formulas for all the Halls, yet the prospect turns us off. Personally, we don't mind the vagueness of the word 'fame,' though let's err on the side of inclusion and let poor Roger Maris in.

BASEBALL

Baseball fans have always loved a good debate. Mays or Mantle? The Murderers' Row Yankees of the '20s or Cincinnati's Big Red Machine of the '70s? So there's nothing particularly sacrilegious about questioning the historical reasons for placing baseball's Hall of Fame in Cooperstown, N.Y., that lovely village on the northern tip of Otsego Lake, rather than, say, Hoboken, N.J., or Providence, R.I., or any of the other contending cities.

Cooperstown became the site largely because of the findings of the Mills Commission. Formed in 1905 by owner and sporting goods magnate Albert G. Spalding to research the game's origins, the commission spent three years evaluating the evidence, then declared that "the first scheme for playing baseball according to the best evidence obtainable to date, was devised by Abner Doubleday at Cooperstown, N.Y., in 1839."

The most compelling evidence for Doubleday was the testimony of Abner Graves, a mining engineer living in Denver. Graves had grown up in Cooperstown

Crowds flocked to Cooperstown, N.Y., for the opening of the National Baseball Hall of Fame and Museum on June 12, 1939 (above). After a day of food, festivities and speeches came a game of baseball, in which Babe Ruth, four years retired, belted a tremendous, towering . . . foul ball.

and claimed to have been present when his schoolmate Doubleday unveiled the rules that would distinguish baseball from the popular frontier game of Town Ball. According to Graves, Doubleday used a stick to scratch out a diamond on Elihu Phinney's cow pasture, set a limit on the number of players in the game, and added bases, forever differentiating baseball from its more wide open predecessor. When a battered baseball was discoverd in a trunk in Graves's attic 27 years later, it seemed to confirm Doubleday's role. The ball, known ever since as "the Doubleday baseball," now resides in the Hall.

Alas, subsequent research suggests that Doubleday, a hero at the Battle of Gettysburg, was almost certainly at West Point in 1839 and, further, that he was 20 years old that summer while Graves was only five, debunking Graves's story that they were school chums. The truth is that baseball, like America, has a melting-pot of origins. The game has no single "inventor," but the Doubleday myth was powerful enough to land the Hall of Fame in

Cooperstown. The moment you stroll down that village's leafy Main Street, though, you won't mind at all, for there could be no more perfect place for the Hall than Cooperstown. Named for the father of America's first popular novelist, James Fenimore Cooper, the town is a picturesque settlement of split rail fences, stone walls and red barns. The Iroquois nations held the spot sacred, and the Susquehanna River starts its journey south from Cooperstown. Cooper aptly called Otsego Lake "Glimmerglass" in his *Leatherstocking Tales* and the world mirrored there seems a shimmering reflection of some vanished time.

The push to create a permanent shrine to Doubleday and baseball came from many sources. In 1917 five men sitting around a cigar store near Cooperstown chipped in 25¢ apiece to start a fund to buy Phinney's pasture, which they did, building Doubleday Field there in 1920. In the mid-30s, Edward Clark, a Cooperstown resident who had inherited a portion of the Singer sewing machine fortune, bought the Doubleday ball with the idea of placing it in a national baseball museum. In 1935, with the game's mythical centenary approaching, Ford Frick, president of the National League, called for donations to create a National Baseball Hall of Fame; they poured in. The first class was elected in January, 1936, by the Baseball Writers Association of America, and it is the game's Rushmore: Babe Ruth, Ty Cobb, Honus Wagner, Walter Johnson and Christy Mathewson.

When the Hall opened on June 12, 1939, four of the five attended the ceremony—Mathewson had died in 1925—and were joined by seven players from subsequent classes. An ancient train track was refurbished for the occasion, and two special cars transported the honorees into town for a day of picnicking, speeches, toasts and, of course, a game of baseball at Doubleday Field.

The Hall now has 253 members, who must wait five years after they've retired from the game and then receive 75% of the vote to qualify. Included are not only players, but managers, executives, and even umpires,

Before they are done, both McGwire (above) and Griffey Jr. (below) may eclipse Aaron's hallowed career home run record of 755. Either way, they are both guaranteed to make the Hall of Fame, McGwire for his career power numbers, including a 70-homer season in 1998, and Griffey Jr. for his all-around brilliance.

temporarily forgiven their many transgressions. Not so lucky are "Shoeless" Joe Jackson, who is third alltime in lifetime batting average but tarnished forever as a member of the 1919 Chicago White Sox, who threw the World Series, and Pete Rose, the alltime hits leader with 4,256 but banished for betting on baseball while managing the Cincinnati Reds. Cooperstown seems to hold its members to a higher standard than other Halls, perhaps because of the lofty perch baseball occupies in American culture.

The Hall has more than 165,000 items in its collection, all of them donated by fans. And that figure does not include the more than half a million photos in the library collection. Many items are personal, such as Lou Gehrig's address book, Cobb's diary, Ruth's camelhair coat, Mathewson's checkers set and the dime-store pen Catfish Hunter used to sign the first free agent contract.

Baseball fans being a stat-obsessed (some would say nerdy) bunch, many of the items are linked to numbers. Among the milestones reified in leather, ash and flannel are bats (the one Henry Aaron used to hit his 714th homer); gloves (the one Willie Mays wore when he snagged Vic Wertz's drive to center in the 1954 World Series and the one Yogi Berra used to catch Don Larsen's perfect game in the 1956 World Series); and uniforms (the midget Eddie Gaedel's jersey with the ⅛ on the back). There are scripts, lockers, bleacher seats, Harry Caray's spectacles and Mel Ott's ashtray.

By now, the Hall has expanded several times, to accomodate exhibits on baseball movies, the old Negro Leagues and the evolution of equipment that includes the first catcher's mask, from 1876. Who'd have guessed "the tools of ignorance" originated at Harvard?

And just to remind us that baseball is a living, breathing game, there are exhibits on the current World Champs and other active greats sure to be honored soon, like home run kings Mark McGwire and Ken Griffey Jr. You can bet that on the day they are inducted, they too will feel the same magic we all do in that storied town.

HANK AARON

On April 8, 1974, Henry Aaron of the Atlanta Braves homered off the Dodgers' Al Downing to break perhaps the most cherished of major league records, Babe Ruth's 714 career home runs. It was only later, after finishing his 24-year career with records for homers (755), RBIs (2,297) and total bases (6,856), that Aaron spoke of what he'd endured when it became clear that he was going to break the beloved Babe's mark. There were threats on his life and hundreds of "Dear Nigger" letters. He kept the letters in a box as a kind of serum against the hatred in the world. "They remind me not to be surprised or hurt," Aaron explained. "They remind me of what people are really like."

Aaron's greatest achievement was to emerge from this ordeal with his humanity intact, determined to overcome the ugliness in society. Today, as an executive for the Braves, he is a tireless campaigner for minority hiring in baseball and a member of the boards of the NAACP and Morehouse College.

Aaron played his first pro ball with the Indianapolis Clowns of the Negro Leagues and retired in 1976 as the last alumnus of those leagues still playing in the majors. Though he is celebrated primarily for his home runs, Aaron was one of the

THE RECORD

YEAR	TEAM	G	R	HR	RBI	SB	AVG
1954	Mil-N	122	58	13	69	2	.280
1955	Mil-N	153	105	27	106	3	.314
1956	Mil-N	153	106	26	92	2	.328
1957	Mil-N	151	118	44	132	1	.322
1958	Mil-N	153	109	30	95	4	.326
1959	Mil-N	154	116	39	123	8	.355
1960	Mil-N	153	102	40	126	16	.292
1961	Mil-N	155	115	34	120	21	.327
1962	Mil-N	156	127	45	128	15	.323
1963	Mil-N	161	121	44	130	31	.319
1964	Mil-N	145	103	24	95	22	.328
1965	Mil-N	150	109	32	89	24	.318
1966	Atl-N	158	117	44	127	21	.279
1967	Atl-N	155	113	39	109	17	.307
1968	Atl-N	160	84	29	86	28	.287
1969	Atl-N	147	100	44	97	9	.300
1970	Atl-N	150	103	38	118	9	.298
1971	Atl-N	139	95	47	118	1	.327
1972	Atl-N	129	75	34	77	4	.265
1973	Atl-N	120	84	40	96	1	.301
1974	Atl-N	112	47	20	69	1	.268
1975	Mil-A	137	45	12	60	0	.234
1976	Mil-A	85	22	10	35	0	.229
TOTAL		**3,298**	**2,174**	**755**	**2,297**	**240**	**.305**

best all-around players the game has seen. He went about his business with a quiet dignity and efficiency. "Mays did everything with flair," said Aaron's teammate, Lew Burdette, "but he never made the perfect throws to the cutoff man the way Hank did. Hank was just so smooth about everything."

Even as a slugger Aaron sneaked up on people. He never hit more than 47 in a season and had the most productive five years of his career between the ages of 35 and 40. In the end, he extended the Babe's record to 755. Reggie Jackson once put that figure in context: "If you hit 35 home runs a year for 20 years, you're still 55 short."

But the true impact of Aaron's historic feat extended beyond sports. As former Atlanta mayor Andrew Young said, "You have to see Hank's achievement of 715 in the context of a sport that, until 1947, said that blacks were inferior and couldn't play this game. With that home run, Hank said that an individual could achieve greatness in America in spite of color and in spite of being born poor."

TIMELINE

1957
Aaron (right) led the league in runs (118), homers (44) and RBIs (132) while batting .322 and leading the Braves to the World Series. There, he batted .393 with three homers and seven RBIs as the Braves topped the mighty Yankees in seven games.

1966
Number 44 hit 44 home runs in a season four times in his career, including in 1966 (left), when he led the league in homers and RBIs (127). According to the *Total Baseball* rankings, Aaron was the top player in baseball from 1961 to 1990, and the fifth-best of all time, behind Babe Ruth, Nap Lajoie, Ty Cobb and Ted Williams.

1969
Another routinely excellent year for Aaron, who batted .300, drove in 97 runs, blasted 44 homers and led the Braves to the NLCS, where he hit a home run in every game and drove in a series-high seven runs but still couldn't prevent a Mets sweep.

1971
The 37-year-old Aaron was voted to the All-Star Game for the 17th consecutive year and finished the season with a career-high 47 homers, a .327 batting average, 118 runs batted in and a league-leading slugging percentage of .669.

1974
Crowning Glory: Aaron (right) broke baseball's most hallowed record in the fourth inning of the Braves' home opener, belting a 1–0 fastball from the Dodgers' Al Downing over the leftfield fence for the 715th home run of his career, one more than Babe Ruth's lifetime total of 714.

1907

As a 20-year-old, third-year outfielder, Cobb (right) enjoyed a breakout season, batting .350 with 119 RBIs and 49 stolen bases, all league-leading totals. He helped the Tigers to the 1907 World Series, where they lost to the Cubs in five games, one of which was a tie.

1911

The Georgia Peach, who once said, "I've got to be first at everything," nearly was in 1911, when he produced a season for the ages, winning the batting title with a whopping .420 average and leading the league in runs (147), hits (248), doubles (47), triples (24), stolen bases (83) and RBIs (127). Yet for all of Cobb's brilliance, the Tigers finished 13½ games behind Philadelphia in the American League.

1912

The major leagues may never have seen a more fearsome baserunner than Cobb (left), who often sharpened his cleats on the dugout steps—to make sure that fielders could see what he was doing—and routinely came in spikes-up. He was also speedy, with excellent timing, and he led the league in steals six times, including in 1912 when he swiped 61.

1914

His star on the rise, Cobb did promotional work (below) for a men's apparel company in 1914, which was, for him, an off year: He played only 98 games and his home run and RBI totals dropped off somewhat, but he still led the league in batting (.368) and slugging percentage (.513) and stole 35 bases.

TY COBB

Ty Cobb was, by just about any measure, the greatest ballplayer of his era; by some measures he remains the greatest ever. He still holds the career record for runs scored (2,246), and his record lifetime average of .366 looks more unapproachable every year. He won 12 American League batting titles and topped .400 in a season three times. When he retired in 1928 after 24 major league seasons, he held the records for hits (4,191), RBIs (1,937), total bases (5,854) and stolen bases (892).

Baserunning offered Cobb a special thrill, and he perfected the "fall away" slide to elude the tag of a baseman. He also often sharpened his cleats with a file on the dugout steps to give infielders reason to stay out of his way. He stole home 50 times, including once when he was 41 years old. In 1909, tired of hearing that he was only a singles hitter, Cobb began gripping the bat at the bottom and banged out nine homers, two more than anyone in either league.

His nickname was the Georgia Peach, but Cobb was anything but sweet. He fought with everyone and anyone, including a handicapped heckler he once waded into the stands to kick with his cleats. He feuded continually with teammates. One fellow once had the temerity to use the bathtub before Cobb: "I've got to be first at everything," Cobb explained to the man before laying him out with a punch.

Whatever propelled Cobb drove him mercilessly. Whether it was a true "persecution complex," as Tiger catcher Sam Crawford theorized, or just competitive instinct run amok, Cobb had a desperate need to prove his superiority, combined with an utter lack of what today we call political correctness. Standing on first base during the 1909 World Series, he shouted down to Honus Wagner, the Pirates' great shortstop: "Hey, Krauthead, I'm coming down." He did, and Wagner—to the delight of just about everyone—slapped the tag right on Cobb's mouth, relieving him of two teeth.

"He has such a rotten disposition that it was damn hard to be his friend," said teammate Davy Jones. So detested was Cobb that when he decided to sit out the final day of the 1910 season to preserve his lead in the race for the batting title, St. Louis manager Jack O'Connor ordered his third baseman to play back on the outfield grass to give Cleveland's Nap Lajoie the bunt hits he needed to sneak past Cobb. After Lajoie's 8-for-9 performance in the doubleheader sealed the batting title, eight players sent him a telegram of congratulations—and they were all teammates of Cobb's.

But no one underestimated Cobb's ferocious drive to win. As Connie Mack advised his Athletics, "Let him sleep, if he will. If you get him riled up, he will annihilate us."

In later years Cobb became wealthy from investments in Atlanta-based Coca-Cola. But he yearned for atonement. According to Yankee scout Paul Krichell, who spoke with Cobb late in his life, the once-combative Cobb expressed a sad wish: that "the fellows he played with and against would only accept him and talk to him today."

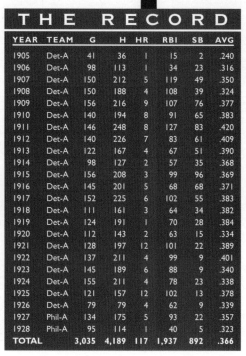

THE RECORD

YEAR	TEAM	G	H	HR	RBI	SB	AVG
1905	Det-A	41	36	1	15	2	.240
1906	Det-A	98	113	1	34	23	.316
1907	Det-A	150	212	5	119	49	.350
1908	Det-A	150	188	4	108	39	.324
1909	Det-A	156	216	9	107	76	.377
1910	Det-A	140	194	8	91	65	.383
1911	Det-A	146	248	8	127	83	.420
1912	Det-A	140	226	7	83	61	.409
1913	Det-A	122	167	4	67	51	.390
1914	Det-A	98	127	2	57	35	.368
1915	Det-A	156	208	3	99	96	.369
1916	Det-A	145	201	5	68	68	.371
1917	Det-A	152	225	6	102	55	.383
1918	Det-A	111	161	3	64	34	.382
1919	Det-A	124	191	1	70	28	.384
1920	Det-A	112	143	2	63	15	.334
1921	Det-A	128	197	12	101	22	.389
1922	Det-A	137	211	4	99	9	.401
1923	Det-A	145	189	6	88	9	.340
1924	Det-A	155	211	4	78	23	.338
1925	Det-A	121	157	12	102	13	.378
1926	Det-A	79	79	4	62	9	.339
1927	Phil-A	134	175	5	93	22	.357
1928	Phil-A	95	114	1	40	5	.323
TOTAL		3,035	4,189	117	1,937	892	.366

JOE DIMAGGIO

Grace is the quality most often accorded Joe DiMaggio. As the star centerfielder for 13 New York Yankees teams, nine of which were World Series champions, DiMaggio ruled Yankee Stadium's cavernous outfield with effortless elegance, giving the impression, as the poet Donald Hall put it, that "the game at last had grown unfairly easy."

Joltin' Joe made it look easy on offense, too. Along with his career batting average of .325, his homers-to-strikeouts ratio of 361 to 369 and his average of 118 RBIs per season, DiMaggio owns what many consider to be the most

untouchable record in baseball: his 56-game hitting streak during the 1941 season. He struck out only 13 times that season (while belting 30 home runs) and won the second of his three MVP awards.

Like Babe Ruth before him, DiMaggio became an icon, signifying something greater than his baseball skills. In 1936, when DiMaggio made his debut with the Yankees, Ruth had just retired and the nation was only beginning to shake off the Great Depression. DiMaggio became a reassuring symbol of classiness and quality. Thirty years later, in the middle of another turbulent decade, Paul Simon invoked DiMaggio as a symbol of stability and quiet heroism in the song "Mrs. Robinson."

DiMaggio's origins were quite humble. He was the eighth of nine children born to Joseph DiMaggio, a

San Francisco fisherman, and his wife, Rosalie. Though two of DiMaggio's older brothers, Vince and Dom, made the big leagues, Joe always insisted that the best ballplayer in the family had been Tom, who never tried for the majors. Still, young Joe was no slouch. In 1934, as a shortstop for the minor league San Francisco Seals, he hit safely in 61 straight games.

But unlike Ruth, DiMaggio was no extrovert; he was a laconic and private young man who wore his mantle stoically. The pressure of the streak gave him ulcers. "He knew he was Joe DiMaggio," said his teammate Lefty Gomez, "and he knew what that meant to the country." When DiMaggio married Marilyn Monroe in 1954, the match seemed the apex of glamour. But when they divorced just nine months later, the breakup offered a glimpse behind the glossy facades of two of America's most enduring icons.

THE RECORD

YEAR	TEAM	G	H	HR	RBI	SB	AVG
1936	NY-A	138	206	29	125	4	.323
1937	NY-A	151	215	46	167	3	.346
1938	NY-A	145	194	32	140	6	.324
1939	NY-A	120	176	30	126	3	.381
1940	NY-A	132	179	31	133	1	.352
1941	NY-A	139	193	30	125	4	.357
1942	NY-A	154	186	21	114	4	.305
1946	NY-A	132	146	25	95	1	.290
1947	NY-A	141	168	20	97	3	.315
1948	NY-A	153	190	39	155	1	.320
1949	NY-A	76	94	14	67	0	.346
1950	NY-A	139	158	32	122	0	.301
1951	NY-A	116	109	12	71	0	.263
TOTAL		1736	2214	361	1537	30	.325

TIMELINE

1936
Yankee legend Lou Gehrig (below, left) welcomed DiMaggio to New York; they would help the Yanks win the next three World Series.

1939
Joltin' Joe won the first of three MVP awards, leading the Yankees to a fourth straight title with a .381 batting average, 30 homers and 126 RBIs. In the World Series he went 5-for-16, hit a home run and drove in three runs as New York swept Cincinnati.

1941
On July 1 DiMaggio (above) tied Wee Willie Keeler's 44-year-old record of hitting safely in 44 games. He broke it with a home run the next day and would extend it to 56 games. DiMaggio beat out Ted Williams, who hit .406, for the MVP award that year.

1947
DiMaggio returned from military service in 1946 and hit a subpar (for him) .290, prompting talk that the Yankees would trade him to Boston for Ted Williams. The Yankee Clipper scotched those plans with the third MVP season of his career, batting .315 and belting two home runs in the World Series, which the Yankees won in seven games over Brooklyn.

1954
Power Couple: In a pairing of two of pop culture's brightest lights, DiMaggio wed Hollywood legend Marilyn Monroe (above). The media-ready match did not last though, as Monroe filed for divorce nine months later. DiMaggio spent much of his retirement as a commercial pitchman, most notably for a coffee-machine manufacturer.

LOU GEHRIG

It is surely baseball's cruelest irony: Lou Gehrig, the "Iron Horse" who played in 2,130 consecutive games, a record that would stand for 57 years, is immortalized as much for the awful disease that now bears his name as for his feats in pinstripes.

Gehrig was the backbone of the legendary Yankees teams of the '20s and '30s, which won seven World Series from 1925 to '39. Though he is often remembered as a foil to Babe Ruth, the game's greatest and most colorful player, it should be noted that in those Murderers Row lineups it was Gehrig who batted cleanup. The two were good friends and even roommates for part of their careers, despite the obvious differences in their personalities. As Gehrig once said, "I'm not a headline guy."

Much of his modesty came from his upbringing. Gehrig grew up in New York City, the son of hardworking German immigrants. He was an unusual major leaguer in

that he attended college, at New York's Columbia University, where he excelled in football and baseball.

Gehrig entered the big leagues in 1923, and after spending most of two seasons in the minors, he got his break on June 1, 1925, subbing for Wally Pipp. Poor Pipp never returned to the starting lineup. Over the next 13 seasons Gehrig averaged 139 runs scored and 147 RBIs per season. He won the Triple Crown in 1934. He retired in 1939 with 493 homers and a .340 career average.

Still, it was impossible to escape the Babe's wide shadow, though Gehrig never seemed to mind. We remember 1927 as the year that Ruth hit 60 homers, yet Gehrig won the MVP award that season.

When Gehrig's output diminished in the 1938 season it was chalked up to the inevitable effects of aging. But a visit to the Mayo clinic confirmed the awful truth: Gehrig had amyotrophic lateral

sclerosis, a horrifyingly debilitating disease of the nervous system. Such were his grace and courage that when he announced his retirement in front of more than 60,000 fans in Yankee Stadium on July 4, 1939, Gehrig said, "Today I consider myself the luckiest man on the face of the earth."

THE RECORD

YEAR	TEAM	G	H	HR	RBI	SB	AVG
1923	NY-A	13	11	1	9	0	.423
1924	NY-A	10	6	0	5	0	.500
1925	NY-A	126	129	20	68	6	.295
1926	NY-A	155	179	16	112	6	.313
1927	NY-A	155	218	47	175	10	.373
1928	NY-A	154	210	27	142	4	.374
1929	NY-A	154	166	35	126	4	.300
1930	NY-A	154	220	41	174	12	.379
1931	NY-A	155	211	46	184	17	.341
1932	NY-A	156	208	34	151	4	.349
1933	NY-A	152	198	32	139	9	.334
1934	NY-A	154	210	49	165	9	.363
1935	NY-A	149	176	30	119	8	.329
1936	NY-A	155	205	49	152	3	.354
1937	NY-A	157	200	37	159	4	.351
1938	NY-A	157	170	29	114	6	.295
1939	NY-A	8	4	0	1	0	.143
TOTAL		2,164	2,721	493	1,995	102	.340

TIMELINE

1923
The rookie Gehrig (above) spent most of his first season with the Yankees' farm club in Hartford, Conn., but in 26 major-league at bats that year, he hit .423 with nine RBIs. In his first full season, 1925, he rapped out 129 hits in 126 games.

1927
A benchmark year for the Yankees and for Gehrig, who led the league in doubles (52) and RBIs (175) while batting .373. In the World Series he smacked two triples and drove in four runs in the Yankees four-game sweep of the Pittsburgh Pirates.

1932
Gehrig belted four home runs in a game on June 3, but his feat was upstaged by manager John McGraw's retirement, which took place on the same day. In the World Series, Ruth hit his famous "called shot," overshadowing Gehrig's home run on the next pitch.

1938
Gehrig earned the nickname "Iron Horse" for his astounding durability. On May 31 the Yankee first baseman (left) suited up for his 2,000th consecutive game. He would play in 2,130 straight games, a record that stood until 1995.

1939
Stricken with the destructive disease amyotrophic lateral sclerosis, which is now commonly known as Lou Gehrig's Disease, Gehrig (above) announced his retirement to a packed house at Yankee Stadium on Independence Day, 1939, telling the crowd, "I may have been given a bad break, but with all this I have a lot to live for. I consider myself the luckiest man on the face of the earth."

WALTER JOHNSON

Walter Johnson was the best pitcher of his era, though there was nothing particularly subtle about his approach to his craft. Johnson was the original power pitcher, the "Big Train" who blew his fastball past hapless hitters. According to Birdie Cree of the New York Highlanders, the only way to time your swing properly when facing Johnson was to swing as the big pitcher's arm began its descent. "How do you know what Johnson's got?" sportswriter Grantland Rice memorably asked. "Nobody's seen it yet."

Johnson was born in Kansas but attended high school in Fullerton, Calif. He began his pro career in obscurity, playing for semipro Weiser in the Idaho State League, where he pitched 75 scoreless innings and averaged 15 strikeouts a game. An itinerant cigar salesman-turned-scout spotted Johnson and began to bombard Detroit Tigers owner Bill Yawkey with letters about this big kid in Idaho with the sensational fastball. When Yawkey didn't act, the cigar man contacted the Washington Senators, who snatched him up. Johnson made his major league debut late in the 1907 season, losing to Ty Cobb's Tigers who, discovering very quickly that they couldn't hit Johnson, beat him with six bunt singles. The following season, over one remarkable four-day weekend, he threw three straight complete-game shutouts against the New York Highlanders, yielding just 10 hits in 27 innings.

A fast worker who pitched nearly sidearm, Johnson led the American League in strikeouts 12 times, with a best of 313 in 1910. Eleven times his seasonal ERA was under 2.00, and his career ERA was 2.17 with a record of 417–279. In 1913, Johnson enjoyed what surely deserves consideration as the greatest season a pitcher has ever had, leading the league in wins (36), complete games (29), strikeouts (243), shutouts (11) and earned run average (1.14), and giving up only 38 walks in 346 innings.

Had Johnson pitched for a steady contender rather than reliably mediocre Washington ("first in war, first in peace and last in the American League," as the adage put it), one wonders what marks he might have left behind. As it is, Johnson still holds the major league record for shutouts—he also lost 20 1–0 games— and his 110 places him 20 ahead of runner-up Grover Cleveland Alexander.

Johnson was 36 and on the downside of his great career when Washington at last made it to the World Series. After losing two starts, Johnson made a relief appearance in the seventh game with the score tied. For four innings he held New York scoreless until a freak bounce in the 12th gave the Senators the only Series the franchise would ever win.

THE RECORD

YEAR	TEAM	G	W	L	ERA	IP	SO
1907	Wash-A	14	5	9	1.88	110⅓	71
1908	Wash-A	36	14	14	1.65	256⅓	160
1909	Wash-A	40	13	25	2.22	296⅓	164
1910	Wash-A	45	25	17	1.36	370	313
1911	Wash-A	40	25	13	1.90	322⅓	207
1912	Wash-A	50	33	12	1.39	369	303
1913	Wash-A	48	36	7	1.14	346	243
1914	Wash-A	51	28	18	1.72	371⅔	225
1915	Wash-A	47	27	13	1.55	336⅔	203
1916	Wash-A	48	25	20	1.90	369⅔	228
1917	Wash-A	47	23	16	2.21	326	188
1918	Wash-A	39	23	13	1.27	326	162
1919	Wash-A	39	20	14	1.49	290⅓	147
1920	Wash-A	21	8	10	3.13	143⅔	78
1921	Wash-A	35	17	14	3.51	264	143
1922	Wash-A	41	15	16	2.99	280	105
1923	Wash-A	42	17	12	3.48	261	130
1924	Wash-A	38	23	7	2.72	277⅔	158
1925	Wash-A	30	20	7	3.07	229	108
1926	Wash-A	33	15	16	3.63	260⅔	125
1927	Wash-A	18	5	6	5.10	107⅔	48
TOTAL		**802**	**417**	**279**	**2.17**	**5914⅓**	**3509**

TIMELINE

1912

Johnson (left) led the perennially cellar-dwelling Senators to their best season yet, going 33–12, with seven shutouts, to help Washington to 91 wins and a second-place finish in the American League, 14 games behind Boston. The following year Johnson was named MVP of the AL as he twirled 11 shutouts and went 36–7 with a record 1.14 ERA.

1924

At age 36, after 18 workhorse seasons and 376 victories in the major leagues, Johnson (right) won his second MVP trophy and finally reached his first World Series. He led the league in victories (23), ERA (2.72) and shutouts (6), and won a title at last as Washington prevailed over the Giants in seven close games.

1925

Johnson and the Senators made it back to the World Series and faced the Pirates. The Big Train blew past Pittsburgh in the opener, striking out 10 and giving up only five hits and one run as the Senators scored four. He returned to the hill in Game 4 and pitched a shutout to give Washington a 3–1 Series lead. But his teammates couldn't hold it, and when Johnson returned to the mound to pitch Game 7, his defense allowed four unearned runs and the Senators lost 9–7.

1927

The Big Train eased into retirement with 417 victories and a major league record 110 career shutouts, a landmark that is surely as untouchable as Cy Young's career record of 511 wins. A Senator for life, Johnson had almost signed with the Pirates after high school but decided against it when the club refused him a $9 signing bonus. Pittsburgh's parsimony was Washington's good fortune:

Twenty-nine years and 531 complete games later the rawboned youth the Senators had signed out of Fullerton, Calif., would join Babe Ruth, Ty Cobb, Honus Wagner and Christy Mathewson—"the Immortal Five"—in the Baseball Hall of Fame's first class.

1955

Koufax won only two decisions as a 19-year-old rookie (left), but the first was a gem that hinted at great things to come: On August 27, he struck out 14 Cincinnati Redlegs en route to a two-hit, 7–0 victory in Brooklyn.

1963

Koufax thoroughly dominated National League batters from 1962 to 1966, never more so than in '63 (right) when he went 25–5 with a 1.88 ERA. He twirled an astounding 11 shutouts that season and struck out a league-leading 306 batters to help the Dodgers to the NL pennant. Then he topped himself in the World Series, pitching two complete-game victories and fanning 23 Yankees as Los Angeles swept to the title in four games.

1965

Koufax developed arthritis in his pitching elbow in 1964 but still won 26 games the following season, including a perfect game on September 9 against the Cubs. After the game, a 1–0 Dodgers victory, Koufax (right) held up four baseballs with zeros painted on them to commemorate the four no-hitters of his career. He would lead the Dodgers in the '65 World Series against Minnesota and win the decisive Game 7 with a three-hit, 10-strikeout performance.

1966

Koufax led the league in ERA (1.73) for the fifth straight season, won 27 games and again led Los Angeles to the Series. After the Dodgers were swept by Baltimore, Koufax decided to retire, citing the severe arthritis in his pitching arm. In 1972 he became the youngest player ever elected to the Hall of Fame.

SANDY KOUFAX

Was ever a baseball career more clearly divided into two completely different halves than the one Sandy Koufax put together with the Brooklyn, then Los Angeles, Dodgers from 1955 to '66? For the first six of those years, Koufax was at best a mediocre pitcher, an erratic fastball specialist with a cumulative record of 36–40; for the final six he was the most consistently brilliant pitcher in modern baseball history, going 129–47 and winning five straight National League ERA titles, three Cy Young Awards (this in the years before there was both an AL and an NL Cy Young winner) and the 1963 MVP award.

Born Sanford Braun to a middle class family in Brooklyn, he became Sandy Koufax when, following his parents' divorce, his mother married Irving Koufax, a lawyer. Like many city boys, Koufax preferred basketball to baseball, and he accepted an athletic scholarship to the University of Cincinnati with the idea of paying for his education as an architect. Koufax was only dabbling in a second sport during the spring of 1954 when he caught the eye of baseball scouts by striking out 51 batters in 32 innings.

Impressed not only by his fastball but also by the fact that this local boy was good-looking and Jewish, the Dodgers saw Koufax as a great gate attraction. They offered him a bonus contract, which, under baseball rules then in effect, meant he could not be sent to the minors for the seasoning he desperately needed. So erratic was Koufax that the Dodger pitching coach let him warm up out of sight to spare him embarrassment. In 1958 Koufax walked 105 batters in 158⅔ innings and threw a league-leading 17 wild pitches. "Taking batting practice against him is like playing Russian roulette with five bullets," said Duke Snider. "You don't give yourself much of a chance."

But Koufax—who later admitted that as a young pitcher he had tried to throw every pitch harder than the last—learned to relax and take his time on the mound. "Wild-man Koufax tried to throw it by everyone," he once said. "Older and wiser Koufax pitches the ball, anticipating it will be hit at someone."

The first glimpse of the older and wiser Koufax came on August 31, 1959, when he whiffed 18 San Francisco Giants to tie Bob Feller's record for strikeouts in a game. This new Koufax was as overpowering as wild-man Koufax had tried to be: He pitched four no-hitters, including one perfect game, in four years and led the league in strikeouts four times. In 1965 he fanned 382 batters, the second-highest single-season total of the modern era. In each of his final two seasons he pitched a mind-boggling 27 complete games, which may explain why he pitched in constant pain and retired at 30, at the very top of his game. He had developed arthritis.

Famously inscrutable and aloof—"a damned hermit," according to one teammate—Koufax's reserve has only heightened in retirement. These days he rarely speaks to the media or, indeed, anyone else outside a small circle of confidants.

THE RECORD

YEAR	TEAM	G	W	L	ERA	IP	SO
1955	Bro-N	12	2	2	3.02	41⅔	30
1956	Bro-N	16	2	4	4.91	58⅔	30
1957	Bro-N	34	5	4	3.88	104⅓	122
1958	LA-N	40	11	11	4.48	158⅔	131
1959	LA-N	35	8	6	4.05	153⅓	173
1960	LA-N	37	8	13	3.91	175	197
1961	LA-N	42	18	13	3.52	255⅔	269
1962	LA-N	28	14	7	2.54	184⅓	216
1963	LA-N	40	25	5	1.88	311	306
1964	LA-N	29	19	5	1.74	223	223
1965	LA-N	43	26	8	2.04	335⅔	382
1966	LA-N	41	27	9	1.73	323	317
TOTAL		**397**	**165**	**87**	**2.76**	**2,324⅓**	**2,396**

WILLIE MAYS

More than 25 years after his retirement Willie Mays is still the man most likely to be named in response to the question, "Who is the greatest all-around player in baseball history?" As sportswriter Arthur Daley put it, "Willie Mays could do everything and do it better than anyone else [and] with a joyous grace."

Besides hitting for both average and power, Mays had speed on the basepaths and a strong, accurate arm. Of his defense in the outfield the saying went, "Willie Mays's glove, that's where triples go to die."

Very few players have made defensive plays so spectacular that they are a savored part of baseball lore. Mays made such plays almost routinely. In his rookie season of 1951, while sprinting madly towards the fence in deep center field, Mays realized the ball was tailing away from his glove hand, so he reached up on the dead run and speared it with his bare hand. His back-to-the-plate, over-the-shoulder grab of Vic Wertz's 440-foot blast in the 1954 World Series is the most celebrated defensive play in baseball history.

Mays was not naive about his own worth as an entertainer. He adopted the "basket catch" for routine flies, and wore a cap a few sizes too small so it would blow off his head when he ran and heighten the play's drama.

Born in rural Alabama, Mays played for the Birmingham Barons of the old Negro Leagues and then for minor league teams in Trenton, N.J., and Minneapolis, where he was such a hero that the Giants had to take out a full page ad apologizing for promoting him to the majors in 1951. He started his career with a 1-for-26 slump but recovered to win Rookie of the Year honors.

Mays spent the next two seasons in the service, missing years which might ultimately have pushed him past Ruth on the alltime homer list. As it happened, Mays retired second in career home runs (660), third in runs scored (2,062) and sixth in RBIs (1,903). He won two National League MVP awards and 11 Gold Gloves. About the only thing Mays couldn't do was remember names, and his nickname, "the Say-Hey Kid," came from the greeting he customarily gave. No one had any trouble remembering *his* name, though.

THE RECORD

YEAR	TEAM	G	H	HR	RBI	SB	AVG
1951	NY-N	121	127	20	68	7	.274
1952	NY-N	34	30	4	23	4	.236
1954	NY-N	151	195	41	110	8	.345
1955	NY-N	152	185	51	127	24	.319
1956	NY-N	152	171	36	84	40	.296
1957	NY-N	152	195	35	97	38	.333
1958	SF-N	152	208	29	96	31	.347
1959	SF-N	151	180	34	104	27	.313
1960	SF-N	153	190	29	103	25	.319
1961	SF-N	154	176	40	123	18	.308
1962	SF-N	162	189	49	141	18	.304
1963	SF-N	157	187	38	103	8	.314
1964	SF-N	157	171	47	111	19	.296
1965	SF-N	157	177	52	112	9	.317
1966	SF-N	152	159	37	103	5	.288
1967	SF-N	141	128	22	70	6	.263
1968	SF-N	148	144	23	79	12	.289
1969	SF-N	117	114	13	58	6	.283
1970	SF-N	139	139	28	83	5	.291
1971	SF-N	136	113	18	61	23	.271
1972	SF-N	19	9	0	3	3	.184
	NY-N	69	52	8	19	1	.267
	Yr.	88	61	8	22	4	.250
1973	NY-N	66	44	6	25	1	.211
TOTAL		**2,992**	**3,283**	**660**	**1,903**	**338**	**.302**

TIMELINE

1954
Mays (below) made the most famous catch in baseball history in Game 1 of the 1954 World Series against Cleveland, chasing down Vic Wertz's drive to center and latching onto the ball 440 feet from home plate.

1957
Producing perhaps his best all-around season to date, Mays won a Gold Glove and hit .333 with 35 homers, 97 RBIs, 20 triples and a league-leading 38 stolen bases. He also topped the league with a .626 slugging percentage.

1963
Mays (below) reached the 400-homer plateau in August and would finish the season with 38, third in the National League behind his teammate Willie McCovey and the Braves' Hank Aaron (tied with 44). Despite the power in its lineup, San Francisco finished third in the NL, 11 games off the pace.

1965
Exploding for a league-leading 52 homers, including an NL-record 17 in the month of August, Mays won his second MVP award. He also drove in 112 runs and led the league in on-base percentage (.399) and slugging percentage (.645).

1971
Though his primary offensive statistics were down, Mays (above) still led the National League in walks (112) and on-base percentage (.429) and helped the Giants to the NL West title. In the playoffs against Pittsburgh, he hit a homer and drove in three runs, but the Giants lost in four games.

BABE RUTH

In the early 1990s New York Yankee star Don Mattingly made an embarrassing confession: He had been well into adulthood before he understood that Babe Ruth was an actual flesh-and-blood man and not a cartoon character.

But Mattingly's mistake is understandable, for more than any other athlete, Ruth inhabits the same mythical world of outsized folk heroes as Paul Bunyan and John Henry. In that decade of giddy excess we know as the Roaring '20s, he stands unrivaled as the hungriest, most famous and best player in the game. "I swing as hard as I can, and I try to swing right through the ball," Ruth once said. "I hit big or I miss big. I like to live as big as I can."

Traded from the Boston Red Sox to the New York Yankees in 1920, and shifted from the pitcher's mound to the outfield so that his prodigious power would be in the lineup every day, Ruth hit very big

indeed. In 1920 he upped his single-season record from 29 to 54 home runs, 35 more than the runner-up, George Sisler, hit. The next year Ruth broke the record again, belting 59, and in 1927 he smacked 60, a record that stood for 34 years.

Excellent timing explains Ruth's popularity as well as his power. He resurrected baseball from the depths of its greatest scandal. To sports fans still reeling from the Black Sox Scandal of 1919, Ruth's Bunyanesque clouts were a godsend.

What couldn't the Babe do? He stole home 10 times (nine more times than Lou Brock did); he pitched 29 ⅔ scoreless World Series innings, a record that stood for more than 40 years; his career ERA was 2.28 and his lifetime pitching record was 94–46. He promised and delivered home runs for sick boys, he may have "called" a home run against the Cubs in the 1932 World Series, and he is surely the only pitcher ever to lead the majors in

home runs, a trick he turned in 1919 when he went 9–5 as a pitcher and hit 29 homers, 17 more than any other player. The Red Sox let him get away the following year, and they haven't won the World Series since.

THE RECORD

YEAR	TEAM	G	H	HR	RBI	SB	AVG
1914	Bos-A	5	2	0	2	0	.200
1915	Bos-A	42	29	4	21	0	.315
1916	Bos-A	67	37	3	15	0	.272
1917	Bos-A	52	40	2	12	0	.325
1918	Bos-A	95	95	11	66	6	.300
1919	Bos-A	130	139	29	114	7	.322
1920	NY-A	142	172	54	137	14	.376
1921	NY-A	152	204	59	171	17	.378
1922	NY-A	110	128	35	99	2	.315
1923	NY-A	152	205	41	131	17	.393
1924	NY-A	153	200	46	121	9	.378
1925	NY-A	98	104	25	66	2	.290
1926	NY-A	152	184	47	146	11	.372
1927	NY-A	151	192	60	164	7	.356
1928	NY-A	154	173	54	142	4	.323
1929	NY-A	135	172	46	154	5	.345
1930	NY-A	145	186	49	153	10	.359
1931	NY-A	145	199	46	163	5	.373
1932	NY-A	133	156	41	137	2	.341
1933	NY-A	137	138	34	103	4	.301
1934	NY-A	125	105	22	84	1	.288
1935	Bos-N	28	13	6	12	0	.181
TOTAL		**2,503**	**2,873**	**714**	**2,213**	**123**	**.342**

TIMELINE

1915
A second-year pitcher, Ruth (above) went 18–8 and helped Boston to the World Series, which it won in five games over Philadelphia. The next year he pitched the longest complete-game victory in World Series history, a 14-inning, 2–1 gem over Brooklyn.

1921
In his second year with the Yankees, Ruth smacked 59 homers, drove in 171 runs, batted .378 and attracted fans by the thousands, allowing New York to finance "The House that Ruth Built," a new, state-of-the-art stadium built in 1923.

1932
We will never know whether or not Ruth was calling his shot in Game 3 of the 1932 World Series (above), when he appeared to point at the centerfield bleachers on an 0–2 count in the fifth inning against the Cubs. Either way, the next pitch went over the wall in deepest centerfield, and the Yanks swept the Series the next day.

1935
It was nothing like his glorious 1927 season, in which he batted .356, belted 60 homers and drove in 164 runs, but Ruth's final year held one more flourish: a three-homer game in Pittsburgh, including the longest blast ever hit at Forbes Field.

1948
On June 13 Ruth made one last appearance at Yankee Stadium to help celebrate its 25th anniversary. Despite rainy weather, a crowd of 49,641 turned out to honor the legendary Yankee slugger, who stood near home plate as a band played "Auld Lang Syne." Two months later Ruth was dead. His lifetime slugging percentage of .690 remains baseball's highest.

TED WILLIAMS

1941

A banner year for batters, it included Joe DiMaggio's 56-game hitting streak and the Splendid Season for the Splendid Splinter (right), who batted .406 and also slugged the game-winning home run in the All-Star Game, a clout he later called the most memorable of his career.

1946

Back in the major leagues after spending three years as fighter pilot in World War II, Williams hit the first pitch he saw for a home run. He would slug 37 more that year and finish with 123 RBIs and a .342 average, leading the Sox to 104 victories and the American League title. He was also named MVP that season. In his first and only World Series, though, Williams faltered, going 5-for-25 as Boston lost to St. Louis in seven games. The following year Williams would win the second Triple Crown of his career (the first was in '42), batting .343 with 32 homers and 114 RBIs.

THE RECORD							
YEAR	TEAM	G	H	HR	RBI	SB	AVG
1939	Bos-A	149	185	31	145	2	.327
1940	Bos-A	144	193	23	113	4	.344
1941	Bos-A	143	185	37	120	2	.406
1942	Bos-A	150	186	36	137	3	.356
1946	Bos-A	150	176	38	123	0	.342
1947	Bos-A	156	181	32	114	0	.343
1948	Bos-A	137	188	25	127	4	.369
1949	Bos-A	155	194	43	159	1	.343
1950	Bos-A	89	106	28	97	3	.317
1951	Bos-A	148	169	30	126	1	.318
1952	Bos-A	6	4	1	3	0	.400
1953	Bos-A	37	37	13	34	0	.407
1954	Bos-A	117	133	29	89	0	.345
1955	Bos-A	98	114	28	83	2	.356
1956	Bos-A	136	138	24	82	0	.345
1957	Bos-A	132	163	38	87	0	.388
1958	Bos-A	129	135	26	85	1	.328
1959	Bos-A	103	69	10	43	0	.254
1960	Bos-A	113	98	29	72	1	.316
TOTAL		2292	2654	521	1839	24	.344

1952

A Marine captain, Williams (below) returned to the military to fight in Korea, where, on February 16, 1953, he crash-landed his F9F-5 Panther jet fighter, which had been hit and was on fire, at a U.S. forward base. He emerged from the wreckage unhurt.

1960

With a blast against the Cleveland Indians on June 17 Williams (below) joined the 500-homer club. He would turn 42 that season, his last, and belt 21 more home runs, including one in his last at bat, to finish the year with 29. He batted .316 in his final season.

No one who played against Ted Williams needed to be reminded of his extraordinary competitiveness. But they were reminded of it all the same, on the final day of the 1941 season, a season already momentous for having included Joe DiMaggio's 56-game hitting streak.

With his batting average at .39955 (which would be rounded up to .400 in the record books) and Boston scheduled to play an afternoon doubleheader against the A's in Philadelphia, Williams was invited by his manager, Joe Cronin, to protect that historic mark by sitting out that day. Williams refused. He played both games, going 6-for-8 and actually raising his average six points, to .406. Now that 60 years have passed and no one has gotten closer to .400 than Tony Gwynn's .394 in the strike-shortened 1994 season, Williams's decision to play looks even more courageous.

Born in San Diego to a portrait photographer and a Salvation Army missionary who cast a baleful eye on her son's new baseball associates, Williams showed up for Red Sox training camp in 1938 as a tall, skinny 19-year-old with a big ego and an even bigger mouth. "Wait 'til you see Jimmie Foxx hit!" one of the vets gushed. "Wait 'til Foxx sees me hit!" said Williams. He didn't make the team until the following year, but Williams promptly lit up the league's pitchers in 1939, batting .327 with 31 homers and 145 RBIs.

"All I want out of life," Williams told people, "is that when I walk down the street folks will say, 'There goes the greatest hitter who ever lived.' " No doubt he got his wish almost daily. His great rival, Joe DiMaggio, called him "absolutely the best hitter I've seen." Part of Williams's secret was his extraordinary eyesight (he supposedly could see a pitched ball spinning). He was also probably the most tireless student of the science of hitting.

Though that .406 looks more impressive with the passing years, Williams's career numbers point to his consistent brilliance. Not only did he win six batting titles, the last two at the ages of 39 and 40, but he also finished his 19-year career with a .344 lifetime average and 521 homers. His numbers would be even better—he might well have threatened Ruth's home run record—if Williams hadn't missed most of five seasons while serving as a Marine pilot in both World War II and the Korean War. He was such a force at the plate that Cleveland manager Lou Boudreau often employed the "Williams shift," a desperation maneuver in which the left-sided infielders were shifted to the right side of the diamond when Williams, a lefthanded pull hitter, came to bat.

When he was 41 Williams's batting average slipped below .300 (.254) for the first time in his career, so he returned for one more season, in order to leave on his terms. Sure enough, he hit .316 and provided the best coda he could, by homering in his final at bat.

CY YOUNG

If you are looking for the baseball record least likely to be broken, look no farther than the 511 games won by Cy Young from 1890 through 1911. Do the math: That's slightly more than 17 30-win seasons. Sure, Young's career ERA of 2.63 was helped by his having played in the era of "inside" baseball, when managers bunted and sacrificed for one or two cherished runs and single-digit totals often won the home run title. Nevertheless, compare his career record to his pitching peers in that offense-starved era, and you find that Young stands 94 wins ahead of the runner-up, Walter Johnson.

The Cy was for Cyclone, after the force with which he delivered his blinding fastball. Despite early problems with control, Young won his first game, giving up only three hits in a 3–1 win over the Chicago Colts. During the next 22 years, while pitching for five teams, Young had five 30-win years, including the 1892 season when he went 36–12. In 1901 he won the pitching Triple Crown, leading the American League in wins (33), strikeouts (158) and ERA (1.62). He still stands fourth on the alltime list for shutouts (77). He pitched three no-hitters, the last when he was 41 years old, and one perfect game, in 1904 against Connie Mack's Philadelphia Athletics. It was, said Mack, "the most perfect of perfect games" because Young threw every single pitch exactly where he wanted.

Young was a strapping 6' 2" and credited hard work on the family farm in Ohio during the off-season for his longevity and success. Living up to his all–American sounding Christian names, Denton True Young was a true gentleman, admired by teammates and rivals alike. In 1908 the American League players gave Young a loving cup on which these words were inscribed: "From the ball players of the American League to show their appreciation of Cy Young, as a man and as a ball player." To the chorus of voices praising Young, Ogden Nash added a verse: "Y is for Young/the Magnificent Cy;/People batted against him,/But I never knew why."

In 1911, when he finally retired, it was not, he said, because he could no longer pitch but because he could no longer field, and opponents were killing him with bunts. As a sendoff, he threw a magnificent dinner for his teammates at a Boston hotel; every dish was named for one of the players. "Far as I can see these modern pitchers aren't going to catch me," Young said of his career record for wins. Nearly a century later no one has come close.

THE RECORD

YEAR	TEAM	G	W	L	ERA	IP	SO
1890	Clev-N	17	9	7	3.47	147⅓	39
1891	Clev-N	55	27	22	2.85	423⅓	147
1892	Clev-N	53	36	12	1.93	453	168
1893	Clev-N	53	34	16	3.36	422⅔	102
1894	Clev-N	52	26	21	3.94	408½	108
1895	Clev-N	47	35	10	3.26	369⅔	121
1896	Clev-N	51	28	15	3.24	414⅓	140
1897	Clev-N	46	21	19	3.78	335⅓	88
1898	Clev-N	46	25	13	2.53	377⅔	101
1899	StL-N	44	26	16	2.58	369½	111
1900	StL-N	41	19	19	3.00	321⅓	115
1901	Bos-A	43	33	10	1.62	371⅓	158
1902	Bos-A	45	32	11	2.15	384⅔	160
1903	Bos-A	40	28	9	2.08	341⅓	176
1904	Bos-A	43	26	16	1.97	380	200
1905	Bos-A	38	18	19	1.82	320⅔	210
1906	Bos-A	39	13	21	3.19	287⅔	140
1907	Bos-A	43	21	15	1.99	343⅓	147
1908	Bos-A	36	21	11	1.26	299	150
1909	Clev-A	35	19	15	2.26	294½	109
1910	Clev-A	21	7	10	2.53	163⅓	58
1911	Clev-A	7	3	4	3.88	46⅓	20
	Bos-N	11	4	5	3.71	80	35
TOTAL		**906**	**511**	**316**	**2.63**	**7,356**	**2,803**

TIMELINE

1890

The 23-year-old Young (right) went 9–7 in his rookie year with the Cleveland Spiders, a record that looks more impressive when considered alongside the Spiders' 44–88 record that season, a performance that left the team 43½ games out of first place. Young's 1.83 walks-per-game average led the National League.

1902

Young (left) won 32 games for the Boston Somersets, but the team could do no better than third place in the AL. The following season, though, Boston, which changed its name to the Pilgrims, won the American League. Then, with Young pitching them to two victories, Boston took the inaugural World Series between the American and National League champions.

1908

After a pair of losing seasons that mirrored the downturn in the Pilgrims' fortunes, the 41-year-old Young bounced back with consecutive 21-win seasons. Incredibly, his ERA of 1.26 was only second-best in the American League. On June 30, against the New York Highlanders (who would later become the Yankees), Young pitched the third no-hitter of his career, an 8–0 Boston victory.

1911

On September 22, the 44-year-old Young blanked Pittsburgh 1–0 for the 511th and final victory of his extraordinary career. Now playing for the National League's dismal Boston franchise, which finished the year 44–107, Young's final outing was anticlimactic—he was shelled 13–3 by Brooklyn on October 6.

1932

Looking back on his career from the comfort of retirement on his farm in Ohio, Young (below) said that he didn't think any of the "modern" pitchers could catch his career win total, and how right he was: Rare is the contemporary pitcher who wins 300 games in a career, to say nothing of 500. If Young's record for victories is untouchable, his record for complete games is so far out of reach it's not even discussed: Young completed 749 of the 815 games he started. The modern award given to the top pitcher in each league is named for him.

NATIONAL BASEBALL
HALL OF FAME AND MUSEUM

President: Dale Petroskey
Vice President: Bill Haase
Vice President of Communications
and Education: Jeff Idelson
www.baseballhalloffame.org

P.O. Box 590/25 Main Street
Cooperstown, NY 13326
Telephone: (607) 547-7200

ENSHRINEES (PLAYERS ONLY)

NAME	POSITION	CAREER	INDUCTED	NAME	POSITION	CAREER	INDUCTED
Hank Aaron	OF	1954–76	1982	Kiki Cuyler	OF	1921–38	1968
Grover Alexander	P	1911–30	1938	Ray Dandridge*	3B		1987
Cap Anson	1B	1876–97	1939	George Davis	SS	1890–1909	1998
Luis Aparicio	SS	1956–73	1984	Leon Day*	P		1995
Luke Appling	SS	1930–50	1964	Dizzy Dean	P	1930–47	1953
Richie Ashburn	OF	1948–62	1995	Ed Delahanty	OF	1888–1903	1945
Earl Averill	OF	1929–41	1975	Bill Dickey	C	1928–46	1954
Frank Baker	3B	1908–22	1955	Martin Dihigo*	P-OF		1977
Dave Bancroft	SS	1915–30	1971	Joe DiMaggio	OF	1936–51	1955
Ernie Banks	SS-1B	1953–71	1977	Larry Doby	OF	1947–59	1998
Jake Beckley	1B	1888–1907	1971	Bobby Doerr	2B	1937–51	1986
Cool Papa Bell*	OF		1974	Don Drysdale	P	1956–69	1984
Johnny Bench	C	1967–83	1989	Hugh Duffy	OF	1888–1906	1945
Chief Bender	P	1903–25	1953	Johnny Evers	2B	1902–29	1939
Yogi Berra	C	1946–65	1972	Buck Ewing	C	1880–97	1946
Jim Bottomley	1B	1922–37	1974	Red Faber	P	1914–33	1964
Lou Boudreau	SS	1938–52	1970	Bob Feller	P	1936–56	1962
Roger Bresnahan	C	1897–1915	1945	Rick Ferrell	C	1929–47	1984
George Brett	3B	1973–93	1999	Rollie Fingers	P	1968–85	1992
Lou Brock	OF	1961–79	1985	Carlton Fisk	C	1969–93	2000
Dan Brouthers	1B	1879–1904	1945	Elmer Flick	OF	1898–1910	1963
Three Finger Brown	P	1903–16	1949	Whitey Ford	P	1950–67	1974
Jim Bunning	P	1955–71	1996	Bill Foster*	P		1996
Jesse Burkett	OF	1890–1905	1946	Nellie Fox	2B	1947–65	1997
Roy Campanella	C	1948–57	1969	Jimmie Foxx	1B	1925–45	1951
Rod Carew	1B-2B	1967–85	1991	Frankie Frisch	2B	1919–37	1947
Max Carey	OF	1910–29	1961	Pud Galvin	P	1879–92	1965
Steve Carlton	P	1965–88	1994	Lou Gehrig	1B	1923–39	1939
Orlando Cepeda	1B	1958–74	1999	Charlie Gehringer	2B	1924–42	1949
Frank Chance	1B	1898–1914	1946	Bob Gibson	P	1959–75	1981
Oscar Charleston*	OF		1976	Josh Gibson*	C		1972
Jack Chesbro	P	1899–1909	1946	Lefty Gomez	P	1930–43	1972
Fred Clarke	OF	1894–1915	1945	Goose Goslin	OF	1921–38	1968
John Clarkson	P	1882–94	1963	Hank Greenberg	1B	1930–47	1956
Roberto Clemente	OF	1955–72	1973	Burleigh Grimes	P	1916–34	1964
Ty Cobb	OF	1905–28	1936	Lefty Grove	P	1925–41	1947
Mickey Cochrane	C	1925–37	1947	Chick Hafey	OF	1924–37	1971
Eddie Collins	2B	1906–30	1939	Jesse Haines	P	1918–37	1970
Jimmy Collins	3B	1895–1908	1945	Billy Hamilton	OF	1888–1901	1961
Earle Combs	OF	1924–35	1970	Gabby Hartnett	C	1922–41	1955
Roger Connor	1B	1880–97	1976	Harry Heilmann	OF	1914–32	1952
Stan Coveleski	P	1912–28	1969	Billy Herman	2B	1931–47	1975
Sam Crawford	OF	1899–1917	1957	Harry Hooper	OF	1909–25	1971
Joe Cronin	SS	1926–45	1956	Rogers Hornsby	2B	1915–37	1942
Candy Cummings	P	1872–77	1939	Waite Hoyt	P	1918–38	1969

NAME	POSITION	CAREER	INDUCTED
Carl Hubbell	P	1928–43	1947
Catfish Hunter	P	1965–79	1987
Monte Irvin*	OF	1949–56	1973
Reggie Jackson	OF	1967–87	1993
Travis Jackson	SS	1922–36	1982
Ferguson Jenkins	P	1965–83	1991
Hugh Jennings	SS	1891–1918	1945
Judy Johnson*	3B		1975
Walter Johnson	P	1907–27	1936
Addie Joss	P	1902–10	1978
Al Kaline	OF	1953–74	1980
Tim Keefe	P	1880–93	1964
Willie Keeler	OF	1892–1910	1939
George Kell	3B	1943–57	1983
Joe Kelley	OF	1891–1908	1971
George Kelly	1B	1915–32	1973
King Kelly	C	1878–93	1945
Harmon Killebrew	1B-3B	1954–75	1984
Ralph Kiner	OF	1946–55	1975
Chuck Klein	OF	1928–44	1980
Sandy Koufax	P	1955–66	1972
Nap Lajoie	2B	1896–1916	1937
Tony Lazzeri	2B	1926–39	1991
Bob Lemon	P	1941–58	1976
Buck Leonard*	1B		1977
Fred Lindstrom	3B	1924–36	1976
Pop Lloyd*	SS-1B		1977
Ernie Lombardi	C	1931–47	1986
Ted Lyons	P	1923–46	1955
Mickey Mantle	OF	1951–68	1974
Heinie Manush	OF	1923–39	1964
Rabbit Maranville	SS-2B	1912–35	1954
Juan Marichal	P	1960–75	1983
Rube Marquard	P	1908–25	1971
Eddie Mathews	3B	1952–68	1978
Christy Mathewson	P	1900–16	1936
Willie Mays	OF	1951–73	1979
Tommy McCarthy	OF	1884–96	1946
Willie McCovey	1B	1959–80	1986
Joe McGinnity	P	1899–1908	1946
Bid McPhee	2B	1882–99	2000
Joe Medwick	OF	1932–48	1968
Johnny Mize	1B	1936–53	1981
Joe Morgan	2B	1963–84	1990
Stan Musial	OF-1B	1941–63	1969
Hal Newhouser	P	1939–55	1992
Kid Nichols	P	1890–1906	1949
Phil Niekro	P	1964–87	1997
Jim O'Rourke	OF	1876–1904	1945
Mel Ott	OF	1926–47	1951
Satchel Paige*	P	1948–65	1971
Jim Palmer	P	1965–84	1990
Herb Pennock	P	1912–34	1948
Tony Perez	1B	1964–86	2000
Gaylord Perry	P	1962–83	1991
Eddie Plank	P	1901–17	1946
Charley Radbourn	P	1880–91	1939
Pee Wee Reese	SS	1940–58	1984
Sam Rice	OF	1915–35	1963
Eppa Rixey	P	1912–33	1963
Phil Rizzuto	SS	1941–56	1994
Robin Roberts	P	1948–66	1976
Brooks Robinson	3B	1955–77	1983
Frank Robinson	OF	1956–76	1982
Jackie Robinson	2B	1947–56	1962

NAME	POSITION	CAREER	INDUCTED
Joe (Bullet) Rogan*	P		1998
Edd Roush	OF	1913–31	1962
Red Ruffing	P	1924–47	1967
Amos Rusie	P	1889–1901	1977
Babe Ruth	OF	1914–35	1936
Nolan Ryan	P	1966–93	1999
Ray Schalk	C	1912–29	1955
Mike Schmidt	3B	1972–89	1995
Red Schoendienst	2B	1945–63	1989
Tom Seaver	P	1967–86	1992
Joe Sewell	SS	1920–33	1977
Al Simmons	OF	1924–44	1953
George Sisler	1B	1915–30	1939
Enos Slaughter	OF	1938–59	1985
Duke Snider	OF	1947–64	1980
Warren Spahn	P	1942–65	1973
Al Spalding	P	1871–78	1939
Tris Speaker	OF	1907–28	1937
Willie Stargell	OF-1B	1962–82	1988
Turkey Stearns*	CF		2000
Don Sutton	P	1966–88	1998
Bill Terry	1B	1923–36	1954
Sam Thompson	OF	1885–1906	1974
Joe Tinker	SS	1902–16	1946
Pie Traynor	3B	1920–37	1948
Dazzy Vance	P	1915–35	1955
Arky Vaughan	SS	1932–48	1985
Rube Waddell	P	1897–1910	1946
Honus Wagner	SS	1897–1917	1936
Bobby Wallace	SS	1894–1918	1953
Ed Walsh	P	1904–17	1946
Lloyd Waner	OF	1927–45	1967
Paul Waner	OF	1926–45	1952
John Ward	2B-P	1878–94	1964
Mickey Welch	P	1880–92	1973
Willie Wells*	SS	1924–49	1997
Zach Wheat	OF	1909–27	1959
Hoyt Wilhelm	P	1952–72	1985
Billy Williams	OF	1959–76	1987
Ted Williams	OF	1939–60	1966
Vic Willis	P	1898–1910	1995
Hack Wilson	OF	1923–34	1979
Early Wynn	P	1939–63	1972
Carl Yastrzemski	OF	1961–83	1989
Cy Young	P	1890–1911	1937
Ross Youngs	OF	1917–26	1972
Robin Yount	SS	1974–93	1999

Note: Career dates indicate first and last appearances in the majors.
*Elected on the basis of his career in the Negro leagues.

PRO FOOTBALL

PRO FOOTBALL

A seven-foot bronze statue of Jim Thorpe greets visitors to the Pro Football Hall of Fame in Canton, Ohio. Clad in leather helmet and moleskin uniform, the great man appears to be feinting around some invisible tackler, the way he did on countless afternoons nearly a century ago.

Canton, a small, otherwise undistinguished city in northeastern Ohio, might seem an odd site for this monument to a game that, in the half century since Thorpe's death in 1953, has become both a billion-dollar business and, by many measures, the nation's most popular sport. With a population of slightly less than 100,000 and the Timken bearing and steel company reigning as the town's biggest business, Canton seems an underqualified host.

But nothing could be further from the truth. For starters, placing the Pro Football Hall of Fame in Canton is a good way to remind fans of the pro game's rustbelt roots. The 12 teams in the league's first season, 1920, all came from blue-collar factory towns spread around the Great Lakes, from Buffalo to Chicago. The

With its distinctive entry-way and roof, the Pro Football Hall of Fame in Canton, Ohio, is the most recognizable sporting shrine in the country. Opened in 1963, the Hall has been expanded three times and now houses the enshrinement busts of 212 members.

original 12 included two other franchises still in the league—Detroit and Cleveland—and a number of towns which, in sad testimony to the way American wealth has shifted, would have no prayer of winning an NFL team today: Muncie, Akron, Decatur, Hammond and, yes, Canton.

The Canton Bulldogs were pro football's first dynasty, going undefeated in both 1922 and '23. And Thorpe, who played a key role in the pro game's survival, had roots spread all over Canton. In those desperate early years, when new franchises were popping up and disappearing almost overnight and most decent folks looked on pro football as they would cockfighting today, the participation of the two-time Olympic gold medalist and national hero lent instant credibility to the enterprise. Thorpe played his first few pro seasons with the Bulldogs, attended the meeting in Canton in 1920 at which the first pro league, the American Professional Football Association, was founded, and served as the APFA's first president.

Next Stop, Canton: Rice (left), who leads all NFL receivers in career yards, receptions and touchdowns, and Sanders (right), who was 1,457 yards short of Walter Payton's career rushing record when he abruptly retired in 1999, will soon be enshrined in the Pro Football Hall of Fame. They will join such legendary predecessors as Don Hutson, Paul Warfield, Jim Brown and Gale Sayers.

None of these claims was lost on Canton's city fathers as football shed its back-alley image and emerged as a popular sport in the late 1950s. On Dec. 6, 1959, the *Canton Repository* editorialized passionately about the need for a Hall, under the headline PRO FOOTBALL NEEDS A HALL OF FAME AND LOGICAL SITE IS HERE. Canton's civic leaders took up the cause with enthusiasm.

But the city was not alone in seeking the Hall. Detroit made a strong bid, while Pittsburgh generously made the case for the neighboring town of Latrobe, which is generally accepted as the site of the first pro game. With the support of an enthusiastic Steering Committee, Canton's case was presented to the NFL by Timken executive William Umstattd in January 1961. Three months later Canton was awarded the Hall.

Following a fund-raising campaign that took in $378,026, NFL Commissioner Pete Rozelle held the shovel in the groundbreaking ceremony in August 1962. The Hall opened slightly more than a year later. A distinctive, circular stone building, the Pro Football Hall of Fame is instantly identifiable for the massive, white football that protrudes from its roof. Seventeen men were in the Hall's inaugural class, including Don Hutson, Bronko Nagurski, Red Grange and, of course, Thorpe. Key figures in the game's growth such as Chicago owner George (Papa Bear) Halas and league president Joe Carr, who replaced Thorpe and served from 1921 to '39, were also enshrined.

Thirty-six men serve on the Hall's Board of Selectors, including 30 newspapermen from NFL cities, one representative from the Pro Football Writers of America, and five at-large voters. To be eligible, players must wait five years after retirement, while coaches qualify the moment they retire. To win membership, nominees need approximately 80% of the vote, which is conducted on the Saturday prior to the Super Bowl.

The Hall has undergone three major expansions, the first in 1971 and most recent in 1995. The building now includes two theaters, one of which shows *Championship Chase*, a look at a season from training camp to Super Bowl. Among the items on display are the faded blanket emblazoned with a "C" that kept Thorpe warm on the sidelines, Joe Namath's knee brace, William (the Refrigerator) Perry's size-23 Super Bowl ring and club-footed kicker Tom Dempsey's half shoe.

Maybe it's those helmets, which obscure football players' identities more than those of their baseball or basketball counterparts, or maybe it's in keeping with the hard-nosed nature of the sport, but football seems to have more deserving players get passed over for the ultimate honor than any other sport. "People do get confused between very good players and great players," said Don Smith, the Hall's vice president. "It's very subjective and a matter of opinion."

All true, but it's hard to imagine what has kept certain worthies waiting so long. The great tight end John Mackey, for instance, was denied again and again before finally winning election in 1992—perhaps because of his role in organizing the players union. Both Lynn Swann, whose acrobatic catches helped the Steelers win two Super Bowls, and Paul Krause, whose 81 interceptions are still the NFL career record, waited 14 years to get in. A more recent controversy was the case of Lawrence Taylor. Considered by many the greatest linebacker of all time, Taylor has a history of problems with drugs. After a long and apparently heated closed-door discussion, he was admitted on the first vote.

The actual enshrinement ceremony takes place at the end of "Football's Greatest Weekend," during which parades, fireworks, street fairs and the annual Hall of Fame game are prelude to the induction ceremony. Hall of Fame shoo-ins who are still active (such as receiver Jerry Rice or running back Emmitt Smith) or only recently retired (like running back Barry Sanders or quarterback Dan Marino) have a wonderful few days to look forward to, when Canton proves the NFL chose well back in 1963.

JIM BROWN

THE RECORD

YEAR	TEAM	G	ATT	YDS	AVG	TD
1957	Clev	12	202	942	4.7	9
1958	Clev	12	257	1,527	5.9	17
1959	Clev	12	290	1,329	4.6	14
1960	Clev	12	215	1,257	5.8	9
1961	Clev	14	305	1,408	4.6	8
1962	Clev	14	230	996	4.3	13
1963	Clev	14	291	1,863	6.4	12
1964	Clev	14	280	1,446	5.2	7
1965	Clev	14	289	1,544	5.3	17
TOTAL		118	2,359	12,312	5.2	106

It usually took at least two tacklers to stop Jim Brown, and very often it took three, four or five. But it required just one man to take football's greatest running back out of the game for good, and that was Brown himself, who stunned everyone in the summer of 1966 by announcing his retirement, from a movie set in Europe. Though Brown had always been fiercely independent, no one had expected this from a man who, after all, was still only 30 and had been the league's MVP the previous season.

Brown's announcement brought an end to an extraordinary career. In nine seasons as fullback for the Cleveland Browns, he had won eight rushing titles and averaged 5.2 yards a carry, still a record. He produced 58 100-yard games and scored 126 touchdowns, 106 of them rushing. Four times he was named Player of the Year.

Brown could run around defenders, but often he simply ran over them. "I keyed on Brown every play," said Sam Huff, the New York Giants' Hall of Fame linebacker. "And when the ball was spotted at the hashmark, we would flop all of our best linemen to the wide side of the field, knowing just where Brown would have to run. And he'd still get five yards or more. There was just no stopping him."

Despite the gang tackling he endured every Sunday, Brown played in 118 straight games. Said Art Modell, the former owner of the Browns, "I do not recall him ever even missing a down in the five years that he played for me."

Standing a thickly muscled 6' 2", 228 pounds, Brown was probably the best all-around athlete to play football. Born in Georgia, he had grown up in Manhasset, Long Island, where as a high school senior he averaged 38 points a game in basketball and 14.9 yards per carry in football. At Syracuse University he was an All America in both football and lacrosse, and he is often mentioned as the greatest player ever in the latter.

Brown has not wasted his retirement. Though he has proven to be a surprisingly good actor, he has impressed people more with his tireless, uncompromising work on behalf of America's often-ignored inner city communities, and gang members especially. "What a man," marveled Ron Wolfley, Brown's former teammate. "If we all could do what he does, we'd have a pretty great country."

TIMELINE

1957
Fresh from his unanimous All-America selection as a senior for Syracuse, Brown (above, with ball) was the unanimous NFL rookie of the year, leading the league in rushing and helping Cleveland, which had been 5–7 the previous season, to a 9-2-1 record and the Eastern Conference title.

1958
Four news services picked Brown as the NFL's most valuable player after a season in which he gained 1,527 yards—the highest single-season total in NFL history at the time—while averaging a thoroughly dominating 5.9 yards per carry.

1964
Brown (above) won his eighth rushing title in eight years and led Cleveland (10-3-1) back to the top of the Eastern Conference. In the NFL title game against the heavily favored Colts, Brown broke open a 46-yard run to set up Cleveland's first TD en route to a 27–0 upset and the fullback's first and only championship.

1965
With career highs in yards (1,544) and touchdowns (17), Brown won another rushing title and helped Cleveland return to the NFL championship game, where it bogged down on a muddy Lambeau Field against the Packers, losing 23–12.

1966
From the London set of the Robert Aldrich film *The Dirty Dozen,* Brown (above) called a lunchtime press conference and shocked the U.S. sporting world by announcing his retirement, at the age of 30, after one of the best seasons of his career. He had been voted MVP of the league by a landslide in his final season.

DICK BUTKUS

Dick Butkus once said that his goal as a football player was to hit a ball-carrier so hard the man's head came off. Anyone who saw Butkus play in his nine seasons with the Chicago Bears must be relieved—and a little surprised—that he never achieved his goal, though he came close the time he hit St. Louis running back Johnny Roland so hard he shattered Roland's face mask with his own.

"More than any player ever, Dick Butkus made defense a mentality," wrote SPORTS ILLUSTRATED's Peter King. Indeed, it was Butkus whose vicious tackles persuaded statisticians to start counting them. In the nine seasons he played middle linebacker for the Bears, Butkus averaged 12.6 tackles per game; nowadays, 10 tackles makes a sensational game. Sacks were not kept as an official stat in Butkus's time, but the Bears counted them anyway. In 1967 Butkus had 18.

Teams soon learned to avoid Butkus, who earned the ultimate compliment from Packers coach Vince Lombardi. "Whenever we played the Bears," said Green Bay guard Fuzzy Thurston, "the game plan was to run away from Butkus. That was the only case in which Lombardi would make that kind of adjustment."

Born to a large Lithuanian family in Chicago, Butkus was in the fifth grade when he set his sights on pro football. "If I was smart enough to be a doctor, I'd be a doctor," he once said. "But I ain't. So I'm a football player." At Vocational High School he was named the Associated Press High School Player of the Year. In college at Illinois, he finished third in the Heisman Trophy voting as a senior and led the Illini to a 17–7 victory over Washington in the Rose Bowl.

A workout fanatic, Butkus invented his own "City of Big Shoulders" regimen. In the off-season he would load a beat-up old car with the heaviest objects he could find and then push the whole contraption up and down the hills near his house, rain or shine.

When bad knees ended his career in 1973, Butkus surprised people by choosing to be an actor and a sports commentator instead of a coach. "The attitude of many of the players entering the league when I was finishing up bothered me," he said. "I just felt I would have a very difficult time coaching these types of players because of their attitude and practice habits. I would have expected them to be like me."

That would have been asking a lot.

THE RECORD

YEAR	TEAM	G	INT	YDS	TD
1965	Chi	14	5	84	0
1966	Chi	14	1	3	0
1967	Chi	14	1	24	0
1968	Chi	13	3	14	0
1969	Chi	13	2	13	0
1970	Chi	14	3	0	0
1971	Chi	14	4	9	0
1972	Chi	14	2	19	0
1973	Chi	9	1	0	0
TOTAL		**119**	**22**	**166**	**0**

TIMELINE

1963
Butkus (above) was named first-team All-America in his junior year at Illinois, when the Illini finished 8-1-1, won the Rose Bowl and ranked third in the nation in the final Associated Press poll.

1964
As co-captain of the Illini, Butkus once again was named to the All-America team and would be taken in the first round of the NFL draft by the Chicago Bears. In 1985 an award for the top college linebacker in the nation was established in his name.

1965
The ferocious, 6' 3", 245-pound Butkus (above) had little trouble adjusting to the pro game. He started all 14 games his first year, picked off five passes and narrowly lost the rookie-of-the-year vote to his teammate, running back Gale Sayers.

1967
Despite the presence of the fearsome Butkus in the middle of their defense, the Chicago Bears finished below .500 more often than not during his nine-year career with the team, and they never made the playoffs. In '67, though, Chicago finished second in the NFL's Central division with a 7-6-1 record.

1969
Butkus (below) was his usual All-Pro self—Detroit G.M. Russ Thomas called him "an annihilating S.O.B."—but the Bears hit their nadir, going a miserable 1–13.

1950

After four years—and four titles—in the upstart AAFC, Graham (60) and the Browns joined the NFL to an overwhelming chorus of skeptical snickers. They began the season with a 35–10 rout of the NFL's defending champion Eagles and finished it with an MVP trophy for Graham and a 30–28 win over the Rams in the title game.

1952

Graham led the NFL in passing attempts, completions, yards and touchdown passes and helped the Browns to an 8–4 record and the American Conference title. In the NFL title game—Cleveland's third straight since joining the league—the Browns were stopped 17–7 by Detroit and quarterback Bobby Layne.

1954

The Lions had defeated Cleveland in the previous two NFL championship games, but the Browns got their revenge and then some, reaching the title game for the fourth time in as many seasons and routing Detroit 56–10 as Graham (above) ran for three touchdowns and passed for three more.

1955

With a 50-yard pass to Dante Lavelli in the second quarter, two rushing touchdowns in the third quarter and a 35-yard touchdown pass to Ray Renfro in the fourth, Graham (above, with ball) closed out his career in storybook fashion, leading the Browns to a 38–14 pasting of the Rams in the NFL championship game.

OTTO GRAHAM

If winning is the one true measure of athletic greatness, then Otto Graham is the greatest of all quarterbacks. In 10 seasons with Cleveland, Graham led the Browns to the championship game 10 times, winning seven titles and amassing a record of 114-20-4.

Graham could throw with the best of them, and his running, while never flashy, was surprisingly effective. If he is often the forgotten man when talk turns to the great quarterbacks, it may be because so few of his games were caught on film or because his worth is diluted by the constellation of stars he played among on those great Browns teams— Lou Groza, Marion Motley and Dante Lavelli, to name a few.

Graham grew up in Waukegan, Ill., where—in a nod not to Waukegan's Jack Benny but to his own dad, a music teacher at the local high school—he studied the piano, violin and french horn. Basketball was Graham's best sport, and he went to Northwestern intending to play basketball and study music. But when a coach spotted him playing football in an intramural game, Graham was persuaded to come out for the team. He starred at tailback for three seasons and was named All-America in his senior year in both football and basketball.

YEAR	TEAM	G	ATT	COMP	COMP%	YDS	TD	INT	RATING
1946*	Clev	14	174	95	54.6	1,834	17	5	112.1
1947*	Clev	14	269	163	60.6	2,753	25	11	109.2
1948*	Clev	14	333	173	52.0	2,713	25	15	85.6
1949*	Clev	12	285	161	56.5	2,785	19	10	97.5
1950	Clev	12	253	137	54.2	1,943	14	20	64.7
1951	Clev	12	265	147	55.5	2,205	17	16	79.2
1952	Clev	12	364	181	49.7	2,816	20	24	66.6
1953	Clev	12	258	167	64.7	2,722	11	9	99.7
1954	Clev	12	240	142	59.2	2,092	11	17	73.5
1955	Clev	12	185	98	53.0	1,721	15	8	94.0
TOTAL		126	2,626	1,464	55.8	23,584	174	135	86.6

*AAFC

Graham was the first man signed by Paul Brown in 1946, when he began to assemble those dynastic Browns. He was an odd choice, with no experience in a T offense, but Brown waved away this shortcoming. "Poise, ballhandling and leadership," insisted Brown. "Otto has the basic requirements of a T quarterback."

Graham and the Browns ripped up the All America Football Conference, a rival league to the NFL, losing only four games in four seasons— and redeeming each of those losses with four straight league titles. Still, they got no respect from fans of the older and supposedly superior NFL. When Cleveland joined the NFL in 1950, it faced a tough test in its first game, against the defending champion Philadelphia Eagles and their league-leading defense. Graham threw for three TDs and the Browns romped 35–10. They would win the NFL title that year. In the 1954 title game against the Detroit Lions, Graham ran for three touchdowns, passed for three more and handed off for another two as Cleveland trounced the Lions, 56–10.

"He is a pure passer," said Brown upon his star's retirement the following year. "He has a natural gift for throwing a pass that is straight, soft, and easy to catch. He seems to pull the string on the ball and set it down right over the receiver's head."

RED GRANGE

To Damon Runyan, that stylish chronicler of the 1920s, the Golden Age of Sport, Red Grange was "three or four men and a horse rolled into one. He is Jack Dempsey, Babe Ruth, Al Jolson, Paavo Nurmi and Man o' War."

The versatile, elusive Grange was also the Galloping Ghost, the Wheaton Iceman and the Illinois Cyclone. But his greatest contribution to football was to almost singlehandedly ensure the survival of the professional game by staking the glowing reputation he'd built as a college golden boy on the future of a struggling and plainly disreputable league.

Grange grew up in the Chicago suburb of Wheaton, where his father was police chief. He honed his skill at evading tacklers by playing a schoolyard game called "Run, sheep, run" and built his strength through summer jobs lugging 100-pound blocks of ice up and down stairs. Not particularly large at 5' 10", 170 pounds, Grange possessed fantastic moves. He ran, wrote Grantland Rice, "as a shadow flits and drifts and darts."

Playing for coach Bob Zuppke at the University of Illinois, Grange ran for three touchdowns in his varsity debut, against Nebraska, and at season's end was named to Grantland Rice's All-America team. The following year against Michigan, Grange returned the opening kickoff 95 yards for a touchdown then ran for scores of 67, 56 and 44 yards—all in the first quarter. He later added a fifth running touchdown and passed for a sixth in the Illini's 39–14 victory. The rapturous home crowd of 67,000 gave him a five-minute standing ovation. Against mighty Pennsylvania the following season he rushed for 363 yards. He made All-America three straight years, during which he ran for 3,637 yards and scored 31 touchdowns in 20 games.

College football ruled the day in the '20s. The NFL was so disdained by respectable people that Zuppke was among those expressing their fervent hope that Grange would not sully himself by signing on with the ragtag outfit. But a dapper movie-theater magnate known as C.C. (Cash and Carry) Pyle promised Grange $100,000 if he joined the league, and Grange ignored whatever qualms he had. During a barnstorming tour that lasted 66 punishing days, Grange played 19 games before wildly enthusiastic sellout crowds across the country. By the end of the coast-to-coast tour, Grange had played before 400,000 fans—including 75,000 at the L.A. Coliseum—forcing the nation to take the pro game seriously.

Never again would Grange gallop with the same brilliance, as injuries and exhaustion took their toll. But there is no underestimating the mark he made on the game. Said George Halas, the great Bears' coach, "[Grange's signing was an event] comparable to the national televising of games."

THE RECORD						
YEAR	TEAM	G	ATT	RUSH YDS	AVG	TD
1925	Chi B	5	—	—	—	3
1927	NYY	13	—	—	—	1
1929	Chi B	14	—	—	—	2
1930	Chi B	14	—	—	—	8
1931	Chi B	13	—	—	—	7
1932	Chi B	12	57	136	2.4	7
1933	Chi B	13	81	277	3.4	1
1934	Chi B	12	32	156	4.9	3
TOTAL		96	170	569	3.3	32

TIMELINE

1923

The multitalented Grange (right) led Illinois to an 8-0-0 record and the national title, doing everything asked of him and doing it well, including kicking, running, passing and playing defensive back. In 20 college games he scored 31 touchdowns. Grange was named to the All-America team for three consecutive seasons.

1925

On December 5 Grange (above, with ball) and the Bears met the New York Giants at the Polo Grounds and attracted 73,000 fans, the largest crowd to date for a pro football game. As always, Grange played on offense and defense, returning an interception 35 yards for a touchdown during Chicago's 19–7 victory.

1926

Hollywood was quick to capitalize on Grange's national celebrity during the Golden Age of Sport, casting him in the silent film *One Minute to Play*, a football drama based on the exploits of one "Red Wade," a speedy halfback. The following year Grange starred in *A Racing Romeo*, and in 1931 he played himself in the biopic *The Galloping Ghost*.

1932

Perhaps worn out by the grueling tour of 1925, Grange took intermittent years off from professional football before returning to play regularly for the Bears in 1929. In '32, Chicago went 7-1-6 and Grange caught the winning touchdown pass in the championship game. The following season, in the first official NFL Championship Game, Grange made a game-ending tackle to preserve Chicago's 23–21 triumph over the Giants.

JOE GREENE

The Pittsburgh Steelers were a woeful team at the end of the 1960s, going 2-11-1 in 1968 and 1–13 in '69. Not even the most optimistic of their long-suffering fans had an inkling of the glory soon to be theirs, of their four Super Bowl wins from 1975 to '80. Pittsburgh fans found it maddening when the Steelers, who desperately needed a quarterback, wasted their first pick in the 1969 draft on an unknown defensive end from obscure North Texas State named Joe Greene. Heck, the Steelers' own scouts had said of Greene: "I would question taking a boy like this in the first round as he could turn out to be a big dog."

Of course big dogs often have nasty bites, and that quickly proved to be the case with this quiet, intense rookie. In one early practice drill Greene was ordered to fight his way through two veterans, center Ray Mansfield and guard Bruce Van Dyke, to reach the quarterback. The two vets relished the chance to put the newcomer in his place. "The play starts," Mansfield recalled, "and Joe grabbed Bruce by the neck and me by the shoulder pads. We were gone, and it took him about half a second to get to the quarterback. We all just looked around and realized: Hey, we've got a player who's head and shoulders above everyone. It was like having a big brother around when the bullies were coming to fight you."

Quiet and intelligent off the field, Greene was the embodiment of controlled, perfectly focused rage on it, earning the nickname, Mean Joe Greene. At the end of the 1969 season, despite the Steelers' awful record, Greene was named Defensive Rookie of the Year. During the next decade he would become the unyielding linchpin of the Steelers' famed Steel Curtain defense, which, during one astounding nine-game stretch at the end of the 1976 season, gave up only 28 points. In a 1972 game against Houston that the Steelers needed to win to clinch the AFC Central division title, Greene blocked a field goal attempt, recovered a fumble and made five sacks. Pittsburgh won 9–3. Greene won the Defensive Player of the Year award in both 1972 and '74 and made the Pro Bowl 10 times.

"The Steelers have a number of stars and leaders of various kinds, but Greene is their sun," reported Roy Blount Jr., who spent the 1973 season with the Steelers on assignment for SPORTS ILLUSTRATED. "The main strength of the team is the defense, of the defense the front four, of the front four, Greene. There may never have been a lineman at once so smart, strong, fiery and, especially, quick as Greene when he is inspired."

THE RECORD

Sacks were not an official statistic during Mean Joe Greene's career, but according to the Pittsburgh Steelers, Greene made 66 of them in 181 regular-season games from 1969 to 1981. He also recovered 16 fumbles, including five in one season, and made one interception. Most of what Greene did for Pittsburgh didn't show up in the official box score, but anyone who saw him play knew that Greene was the cornerstone of the mid-'70s Steeler dynasty. An All-America at North Texas State in 1968, Greene was named NFL Defensive Player of Year in 1972 and '74 and played in 10 Pro Bowls, four Super Bowls and six AFC title games.

TIMELINE

1968

Though he was a consensus All-America at North Texas State, Greene (75) was unknown to most NFL teams prior to the 1969 draft. New Pittsburgh coach Chuck Noll, however, had been scouting Greene for three years, and liked what he saw.

1975

Greene (75) celebrated the Steelers' first Super Bowl victory with fellow defensive lineman Earnie Holmes (63). The trademark of the Pittsburgh dynasty was defense, and stalwarts like Greene, Holmes, linebackers Jack Ham and Jack Lambert and defensive back Mel Blount contributed mightily to the Supe IX triumph over Minnesota. The Steelers held the heavily favored Vikings scoreless until the fourth quarter and came away with a 16–6 victory in New Orleans. Greene intercepted a pass and recovered a fumble.

1979

In an instant-classic television commercial, Greene (below) limps down the tunnel toward the locker room after a tough Steelers loss. A young boy, gaping in awe as the big lineman passes, tentatively offers Greene a sip of cola. After gruffly accepting, Greene continues his pained journey toward the locker room—only to stop after a few steps, turn and say, "Hey Kid." When the youngster looks up, Greene tosses his Steelers game jersey into the boy's waiting arms.

1980

With a 31–19 victory over the Rams in Super Bowl XIV in Pasadena, the Steelers became the first team to win four Super Bowls (1975, '76, '79 and '80). Greene, who had seen the franchise progress from doormat to dynasty during his career—and played a prominent role in that turnaround—would retire after the following season. Former Pittsburgh linebacker Andy Russell would say of him, "He was unquestionably the player of the decade. There was no player who was more valuable to his team."

DON HUTSON

Just as Babe Ruth's tape-measure home runs changed baseball forever from a game of stingy strategy to one in which raw power could rule the day, so Don Hutson's incredible catches woke people up to the wonders of the forward pass in football. For a professional game still struggling to rise from the primordial ooze, this was a great leap forward. At a time when the forward pass was widely viewed as a risky trick play, Hutson was a streak of pure light, a revolutionary thinker who invented the basic repertoire of pass routes—buttonhooks, Z-outs and quits.

"I don't think there's any doubt that Don Hutson was the greatest receiver ever," wrote Washington Redskins coach George Allen in 1982. "He improvised moves and devised patterns that have been copied ever since."

And Hutson had the raw tools to capitalize on his leap of the imagination. He could run the 100-yard dash in 9.7 seconds (the world record was 9.5), making him a darting Ariel among the lumbering Calibans of the NFL. "He was the only man I ever saw who could feint in three directions at once," said Eagles coach Greasy Neale.

Hutson grew up during the Depression, in Pine Bluff, Ark., and showed his ambition when he became his state's first Eagle Scout. He played his college ball at Alabama, where he and quarterback Dixie Howell worked on their new-fangled aerial obsession. "I just ran like the devil and Dixie Howell got the ball there," said Hutson later. Together they led the Crimson Tide to a three-year record of 24-3-1, the highlight of which came at the 1935 Rose Bowl. Hutson caught two touchdown passes—as well as the eye of Green Bay Packers coach Curly Lambeau—in Alabama's 29–13 victory over Stanford.

Lambeau intended to pass and he found his receiver in Hutson. The 6' 1", 180-pound Hutson led the league in receiving for eight of his 11 seasons. Like Ruth, his numbers dwarfed those of his peers. Hutson caught 74 passes in 1942, 47 more than his nearest competitor. In one burst of compressed genius he caught four touchdown passes and kicked five extra points to score 29 points in a single quarter, still a record. When he retired after the 1945 season, he held the career records for receptions (488), receiving yards (7,991) and average (16.4 yards), and receiving touchdowns (99). Though it had to fall in the pass-happy era Hutson ushered in, his record for touchdown catches stood a staggering 44 years.

THE RECORD						
YEAR	TEAM	G	REC	YDS	AVG	TD
1935	GB	9	18	420	23.3	6
1936	GB	12	34	536	15.8	8
1937	GB	11	41	552	13.5	7
1938	GB	10	32	548	17.1	9
1939	GB	11	34	846	24.9	6
1940	GB	11	45	664	14.8	7
1941	GB	11	58	738	12.7	10
1942	GB	11	74	1,211	16.4	17
1943	GB	10	47	776	16.5	11
1944	GB	10	58	866	14.9	9
1945	GB	10	47	834	17.7	9
TOTAL		116	488	7,991	16.4	99

TIMELINE

1934
Hutson (above), who attended Alabama on a baseball scholarship and also starred in track, led the Crimson Tide to a 10–0 record. In the Rose Bowl on January 1, 1935, he caught six passes for 165 yards and scored twice, on receptions of 59 and 54 yards, as the Tide rolled over Stanford, 29–13 .

1936
Topping the NFL in receptions, yards and touchdown catches, Hutson helped Green Bay (10-1-1) to the Western Division title and the NFL championship game, in which he scored the Packers' first touchdown in their 21–6 triumph over Boston.

1938
Hutson (above, with ball) and the Packers returned to the NFL title game and met the Giants in front of 48,120 fans at the Polo Grounds. Despite outgaining New York 378 yards to 212, the Packers lost 23–17 as Hutson was kept out of the end zone.

1939
On October 22 in Green Bay, two Detroit Lions—look closely—weren't enough to prevent Hutson (below, right) from making the catch. In a play that typified his career, he corraled the ball and ran 40 yards for a score. The Packers won 26–7.

1939
Green Bay avenged its loss to New York in the previous year's championship game with a 27–0 thrashing of the Giants for the NFL title. Hutson, who had averaged a career-high 24.9 yards per catch during the season, failed to score, as heavy winds and double-coverage limited the Packers offense to 10 passes.

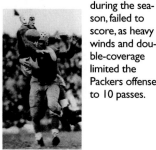

JOE MONTANA

Joe Montana came into this world with a name out of a dime store thriller, a name that promised ruggedness and reliability, a gunslinger's name. Montana delivered on that promise throughout a long career, first at Notre Dame and then with the San Francisco 49ers, by calmly guiding his teams to one fourth-quarter comeback after another, 31 in his NFL career. Montana led San Francisco to victory in four Super Bowls from 1982 to '90, winning the MVP award in three of them. His signature moments, though, were those brilliant fourth-quarter rallies, one of which came in Super Bowl XXIII against Cincinnati. "He's like Lazarus," marveled Montana's teammate Tim McKyer. "You roll back the stone, Joe limps out—and throws for 300 yards."

Montana hailed from a world short on miracles: the bleak coal country of western Pennsylvania, where the boys who were lucky might enjoy a brief flicker of sports greatness before heading down into the mines; and a few very lucky ones—with names like Namath, Marino, Lujack and Blanda—got to escape that dark world forever. Tall and skinny as a kid, Montana was a great all-around athlete, pitching three perfect games in Little League, high jumping 6' 9" at Ringgold High and starring in basketball and of course football.

He went to Notre Dame, where he first demonstrated his knack for high-pressure heroics in his sophomore year, coming off the bench late in the fourth quarter against North Carolina to bring the Irish back from a 14–6 deficit with two touchdowns. Though Montana would show his cool genius in game after game, leading Notre Dame to the 1977 national title, he saved his best for the 1979 Cotton Bowl, which happened to be his last game for Notre Dame. Battling the flu, he marched the Irish back from a 34–12 deficit with eight minutes remaining, completing a touchdown pass with two seconds left for an improbable 35–34 win.

Drafted by San Francisco in the third round, Montana guided the once-woeful 49ers to a 13–3 record and their first NFL title in his third season. In 1987 he completed 22 straight passes, still a record, in two games against Cleveland and Green Bay. Late in the 1981 NFC title game against Dallas, Montana calmly did his part in the play that has passed into NFL lore as "The Catch," Dwight Clark's soaring, end-zone grab of a pass Montana had lobbed before getting buried by an avalanche of Cowboys. The consummate big-game player, Montana completed 68% of his passes in four Super Bowl appearances, with no interceptions. "You knew you had to win, and you'd deal with it," he once shrugged. No big deal to Joe Cool.

THE RECORD

YEAR	TEAM	G	ATT	COMP	COMP%	YDS	TD	INT	RATING
1979	SF	16	23	13	56.5	96	1	0	81.1
1980	SF	15	273	176	64.5	1,795	15	9	87.8
1981	SF	16	488	311	63.7	3,565	19	12	88.4
1982	SF	9	346	213	61.6	2,613	17	11	88.0
1983	SF	16	515	332	64.5	3,910	26	12	94.6
1984	SF	16	432	279	64.6	3,630	28	10	102.9
1985	SF	15	494	303	61.3	3,653	27	13	91.3
1986	SF	8	307	191	62.2	2,236	8	9	80.7
1987	SF	13	398	266	66.8	3,054	31	13	102.1
1988	SF	14	397	238	59.9	2,981	18	10	87.9
1989	SF	13	386	271	70.2	3,521	26	8	112.4
1990	SF	15	520	321	61.7	3,944	26	16	89.0
1991	DNP								
1992	SF	1	21	15	71.4	126	2	0	118.4
1993	KC	11	298	181	60.7	2,144	13	7	87.4
1994	KC	14	493	299	60.6	3,283	16	9	83.6
TOTAL		**192**	**5,391**	**3,409**	**63.2**	**40,551**	**273**	**139**	**92.3**

TIMELINE

1979
Against the University of Houston in the Cotton Bowl, Montana (left, with ball) overcame the flu, icy weather conditions and a 34–12 deficit with fewer than eight minutes to play, leading Notre Dame to a stunning 35–34 comeback victory. The legend of Joe Cool was born.

1982

Chapter Two in the Book of Montana: In the NFC title game following the 1981 season, with his Niners trailing Dallas 27–21 with 4:54 to play and the ball on the San Francisco 11-yard line, Joe calmly led an 89-yard march for the winning score, which came on a now-legendary catch by Dwight Clark (right). "I was very confident in the huddle," said Montana, who completed six of eight passes on the drive. The 49ers won 28–27 and advanced to the first Super Bowl in franchise history. They won that as well, defeating Cincinnati 26–21 in Pontiac, Mich.

1985
Leading one of the best teams in football history—the Niners went 15–1 and put 10 players in the Pro Bowl—before a partisan crowd at Stanford Stadium in Palo Alto, Calif., Montana won his second Super Bowl MVP award, throwing three touchdown passes and running for one score as San Francisco blew out Miami 38–16 in Supe XIX.

1989
With 3:20 left in Super Bowl XXIII and San Francisco trailing Cincinnati 16–13, Montana (below) did it again: He completed eight pinpoint passes during an 11-play, 92-yard drive for the winning touchdown, which came on a 10-yard strike over the middle to Niners wideout John Taylor. Final score: San Francisco 20, Cincinnati 16.

WALTER PAYTON

Long before he gained fame darting and hurdling over and around the man-mountains of the NFL, Walter Payton was a dancer on *Soul Train*. Payton's specialty was dancing on his hands, which may help explain how a man who stood only 5' 10" and weighed only 202 pounds survived 13 seasons in the NFL and retired as the game's alltime leading rusher, with 16,726 yards. Payton was fast and strong, but above all he possessed superb balance, an instinct for staying on his feet and driving forward.

Payton was among the smallest of the great pro backs, but he was, in the words of SPORTS ILLUS-TRATED's Peter King, a "baby sledgehammer." Payton's nick-name was Sweetness—after his demeanor off the field and some of his moves on it—but make no mis-take, Payton was as tough as they come. Playing all of his 13 seasons in Chicago, he did that legendarily gritty city proud, missing only one game, in his rookie year, and carry-ing the ball a Herculean 3,838 times. After arthroscopic surgery on both knees in the 1983 off-season, he played four more years.

Payton's one concession to self-preservation was a straightarm, which he says he developed to keep kids from messing up his clothes on the sandlots of Columbia, Miss. Payton didn't begin playing football until his junior year at Columbia High, but he made up for lost time by running 65 yards for a touchdown on his first carry. When Columbia merged with an all-white school in the early '70s, Payton was on the front line of integration, using his gridiron skills to persuade folks to look past his skin color and see only the superb player he was. Recruited by a number of schools, he chose Jackson State in order to play with his brother, Eddie. His coach there, Bob Hill, boosted Payton's work ethic, telling him, "If you're going to die, you should die hard, never die easy." As a college player Payton scored 464 points, and the Bears were impressed enough to take him fourth in the 1975 NFL draft.

Payton gained an NFC-leading 1,390 yards in his first full season and just kept rolling. He led the NFC in rushing five straight seasons, from 1976 to 1980. He holds NFL records for rushing attempts (3,838), seasons rushing 1,000 yards (10), and most 100-yard games (77). His 275 yards on the ground against the Minnesota Vikings' vaunted Pur-ple People Eater defense on November 20, 1977, stood unapproached as the single-game rushing record for 23 years, until Corey Dillon broke it in 2000, gaining 278 yards against the Denver Broncos.

Life, which seems to love irony, handed Payton a rare liver disease in 1998. The great running back lost 65 pounds, wasting away to less than what he'd weighed in sixth grade. Still he hung on, dignified as he announced his illness to the public. He died on November 1, 1999.

THE RECORD

YEAR	TEAM	G	ATT	YDS	AVG	REC	YDS	AVG	TD
1975	Chi	13	196	679	3.5	33	213	6.5	7
1976	Chi	14	311	1,390	4.5	15	149	9.9	13
1977	Chi	14	339	1,852	5.5	27	269	10.0	16
1978	Chi	16	333	1,395	4.2	50	480	9.6	11
1979	Chi	16	369	1,610	4.4	31	313	10.1	16
1980	Chi	16	317	1,460	4.6	46	367	8.0	7
1981	Chi	16	339	1,222	3.6	41	379	9.2	8
1982	Chi	9	148	596	4.0	32	311	9.7	1
1983	Chi	16	314	1,421	4.5	53	607	11.5	8
1984	Chi	16	381	1,684	4.4	45	368	8.2	11
1985	Chi	16	324	1,551	4.8	49	483	9.9	11
1986	Chi	16	321	1,333	4.2	37	382	10.3	11
1987	Chi	12	146	533	3.7	33	217	6.6	5
TOTAL		**190**	**3,838**	**16,726**	**4.4**	**492**	**4,538**	**9.2**	**125**

TIMELINE

1977
On November 20 against the Vikings, Payton (left) put the Bears on his back and carried them to vic-tory, rushing 40 times for a record 275 yards and one touchdown in the Bears' 10–7 home win over Minnesota. Chicago—which threw only seven passes in the game, completing four—would win their next four games to clinch a spot in the playoffs.

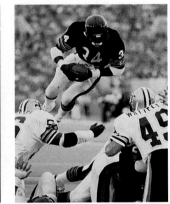

1984
Against the New Orleans Saints on October 7 Pay-ton (above, with ball) gained the 12,313th yard of his career to eclipse Jim Brown as the NFL's alltime leading rusher. Payton would extend the record, which still stands, to 16,726 yards before his retire-ment three years later.

1986
In his 11th year in the league, Payton won a well-deserved championship as the Bears romped to a 15–1 record, the NFC Central title and a 46–10 shellacking of the Patriots in Super Bowl XX (below). Payton carried the ball 22 times for 61 yards in the big game.

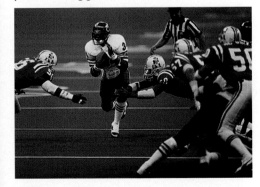

1987
For only the third time in his 13-year career Payton failed to average at least four yards per carry and decided to announce his retirement. Chicago coach Mike Ditka called Payton "without a doubt the most complete football player I've ever seen."

LAWRENCE TAYLOR

"We gotta go out there like a bunch of crazed dogs!" yelled Lawrence Taylor at his defensive mates on the New York Giants, in a statement picked up by television microphones. This was Taylor, stripped down to his competitive essence. He was attitude incarnate, backed up by a combination of physical abilities rarely found in one man. At 6' 3", 240 pounds, Taylor was big and strong enough to run through linemen and fast enough to catch running backs.

Taylor made 10 Pro Bowls in his 13-year career, and in 1986 when he led the league with 20.5 sacks, he became only the fourth defensive player to win the league MVP award. He had at least 10 sacks for seven straight seasons (1984–90). When he retired in 1993 Taylor had amassed 132.5 sacks, second in NFL history at the time. In 2000 Taylor was named to the NFL's Alltime Team.

Taylor always believed—and his coach, Bill Parcells, agreed—that his best game probably came against New Orleans in 1988. Playing with a torn pectoral muscle that had to be supported by a harness, he made 10 tackles and three sacks, and forced two fumbles in the Giants' 13–12 win. "It was his finest hour from a courage standpoint," said Parcells.

Growing up in Newport News, Va., where his father was shipyard supervisor, Taylor starred on both sides of the ball to lead his high school to the state championship. At the University of North Carolina, where he was ACC Player of the Year in 1980, he was given the nickname "Kamikaze" for his ability to dive over players to block punts.

The Giants selected Taylor with the second overall pick in the 1981 draft, hoping he would bring much-needed energy to a team that had not made the playoffs in 17 years. It was instantly clear they'd chosen well. Taylor made 133 tackles, 10.5 sacks and one interception in '81, and was named Rookie of the Year as well as AP Defensive Player of the Year. With Taylor, the Giants made the playoffs eight times, winning the Super Bowl in 1986 and 1990.

Since he retired, Taylor has brought trouble on himself, getting arrested several times for drug offenses and tax evasion. He also accepted $1 million to wrestle a 360-pound pro grappler named Bam Bam Bigelow. But it is a measure of Taylor's on-field dominance that in 1999, despite his recent problems, he was elected to the Hall of Fame on the first ballot.

THE RECORD

YEAR	TEAM	G	INT	YDS	TD	SACKS
1981	NYG	16	1	1	0	—
1982	NYG	9	1	97	1	7.5
1983	NYG	16	2	10	0	9
1984	NYG	16	1	-1	0	11.5
1985	NYG	16	0	—	—	13
1986	NYG	16	0	—	—	20.5
1987	NYG	12	3	16	0	12
1988	NYG	12	0	—	—	15.5
1989	NYG	16	0	—	—	15
1990	NYG	16	1	11	1	10.5
1991	NYG	14	0	—	—	7
1992	NYG	9	0	—	—	5
1993	NYG	16	0	—	—	6
TOTAL		184	9	134	2	132.5

TIMELINE

1981
A true impact player, Taylor (above) helped the Giants to a 9–7 record and a berth in the playoffs in his rookie season, one year after the team had gone 4–12. The Giants beat Philadelphia 27–21 in their first-round playoff game but were stopped in the next round by San Francisco.

1984
With Taylor spearheading their D, the Giants went 9–7 and returned to the playoffs for the first time in three years. They beat the Los Angeles Rams 16–13 but were again eliminated in the divisional playoffs by the 49ers, who won 21–10.

1987
New York won the 1986 NFC East title with a 14–2 record and Taylor enjoyed the best season of his career, making 20.5 sacks and leading the Giants in New York's 39–20 rout of John Elway and the Broncos in Super Bowl XXI (below) in January '87.

1989
Big Blue returned to the top of the NFC East with a 12–4 record as Taylor produced 15 sacks. The division title excused the Giants from the wild-card round, but they were upset 16–13 by the Los Angeles Rams in the divisional playoffs.

1991
"No other team ever hit me this hard," said Buffalo receiver Andre Reed after facing Taylor (above) and the rest of the Giants defense in Super Bowl XXV in Tampa. When the final whistle sounded, LT celebrated another championship: The Giants won 20–19 as a 47-yard field goal attempt by Buffalo's Scott Norwood sailed wide right in the game's final seconds.

JOHNNY UNITAS

Johnny Unitas had one of those wonderful names that used to fill up rosters in football's hardscrabble early days. It blends the jaunty optimism of youth with the promise of mature leadership, two qualities its owner demonstrated regularly in the late 1950s, when football was becoming a national obsession.

Unitas was the best quarterback of his generation, and he starred in what some still consider the greatest football game ever played, the Baltimore Colts' 23–17 overtime defeat of the New York Giants in the 1958 NFL title game. He also set NFL career passing records for attempts (5,186) completions (2,830), yardage (40,239 yards) and touchdowns (290). He was named Player of the Year three times.

But Unitas's march to the Hall of Fame was anything but straight. He was, quite literally, the beneficiary of other people's bad breaks, beginning at St. Justin's High in Pittsburgh, when the starting quarterback's broken ankle gave Unitas the job. After a good but hardly brilliant career at the University of Louisville, Unitas was drafted in the ninth round by his hometown Steelers.

Cut in the preseason, Unitas worked on a construction crew while playing weekends for a semipro team. He wound up in Baltimore as backup to George Shaw, the 1955 Rookie of the Year. Shaw injured *his* leg early in the season, providing Unitas another chance. Hardly an instant success, he had his first pass intercepted, his first handoff fumbled. But the next week Unitas engineered an upset over the Packers, and though no one knew it then, he was on his way to the NFL pantheon.

But nothing Unitas did rivaled his heroic game-tying and game-winning drives in that stirring 1958 NFL title game, which was played before a television audience—an NFL first that boosted the profile of the league, and Unitas, immeasurably.

YEAR	TEAM	G	ATT	COMP	COMP%	YDS	TD	INT	RATING
1956	Balt	12	198	110	55.6	1,498	9	10	74.0
1957	Balt	12	301	172	57.1	2,550	24	17	88.0
1958	Balt	10	263	136	51.7	2,007	19	7	90.0
1959	Balt	12	367	193	52.6	2,899	32	14	92.0
1960	Balt	12	378	190	50.3	3,099	25	24	73.7
1961	Balt	14	420	229	54.5	2,990	16	24	66.1
1962	Balt	14	389	222	57.1	2,967	23	23	76.5
1963	Balt	14	410	237	57.8	3,481	20	12	89.7
1964	Balt	14	305	158	51.8	2,824	19	6	96.5
1965	Balt	11	282	164	58.2	2,530	23	12	97.4
1966	Balt	14	348	195	56.0	2,748	22	24	74.0
1967	Balt	14	436	255	58.5	3,428	20	16	83.6
1968	Balt	5	32	11	34.4	139	2	4	30.1
1969	Balt	13	327	178	54.4	2,342	12	20	64.0
1970	Balt	14	321	166	51.7	2,213	14	18	65.1
1971	Balt	13	176	92	52.3	942	3	9	52.3
1972	Balt	8	157	88	56.1	1,111	4	6	70.8
1973	SD	5	76	34	44.7	471	3	7	40.0
TOTAL		211	5,186	2,830	54.6	40,239	290	253	78.2

THE RECORD

TIMELINE

1957
In his first full season in the NFL, Unitas (below) won the Jim Thorpe Trophy as the league MVP. He led the league in touchdown passes and helped the Colts, who were 5–7 in 1956, improve to 7–5.

1958
Unitas marched the Colts to a game-tying field goal with seven seconds left in regulation of the NFL title game, then led the thrilling, game-winning drive in overtime, capped by Alan Ameche's famous one-yard TD plunge. The nationally televised game remains an NFL landmark.

1959
The Colts and Giants returned to the NFL title game, but on this occasion overtime was unnecessary: Baltimore exploded for 24 points in the fourth quarter to win 31–16. The Colts simply had too many weapons for New York, including Unitas (19), who capped one of his best seasons by passing for two touchdowns and running for another in the title game.

1964
Baltimore ran away with the NFL's Western Conference, going 12–2 as Unitas led the league in yards per passing attempt (9.26) and threw 19 touchdown passses. Heavily favored in the NFL championship game, the Colts were flattened 27–0 by the Cleveland Browns.

1971
The 38-year-old Unitas shared the Baltimore quarterback job with Earl Morrall, and the platooning veterans led the Colts to a 10–4 record and second place in the AFC East. In the playoffs, Johnny U got the call, and he passed Baltimore to a 20–3 rout of the Browns in the first round but lost to Miami 21–0 in the second.

PRO FOOTBALL
HALL OF FAME

ENSHRINEES (PLAYERS ONLY)

NAME Pos. (YR. OF INDUCTION)	D.O.B. D.O.D.	CAREER SPAN
Herb Adderley DB (1980)	b. 6-8-39	1961–72
Lance Alworth WR (1978)	b. 8-3-40	1962–72
Doug Atkins DE (1982)	b. 5-8-30	1953–69
Morris (Red) Badgro OE/DE (1981)	b. 12-1-02 d. 7-13-98	1927–36
Lem Barney DB (1992)	b. 9-8-45	1967–77
Cliff Battles DB/RB (1968)	b. 5-1-10 d. 4-28-81	1932–37
Sammy Baugh QB/DB/P (1963)	b. 3-17-14	1937–52
Chuck Bednarik LB (1967)	b. 5-1-25	1949–62
Bobby Bell LB (1983)	b. 6-17-40	1963–74
Raymond Berry WR (1973)	b. 2-27-33	1955–67
Fred Biletnikoff WR (1988)	b. 2-23-43	1965–78
George Blanda QB/K (1981)	b. 9-17-27	1949–75
Mel Blount DB (1989)	b. 4-10-48	1970–83
Terry Bradshaw QB (1989)	b. 9-2-48	1970–83
Jim Brown RB (1971)	b. 2-17-36	1957–65
Roosevelt Brown OT (1975)	b. 10-20-32	1953–65
Willie Brown DB (1984)	b. 12-2-40	1963–78
Buck Buchanan DT (1990)	b. 9-10-40	1963–75
Nick Buoniconti LB (2001)	b. 12-15-40	1962–76
Dick Butkus LB (1979)	b. 12-9-42	1965–73
Earl Campbell RB (1991)	b. 3-29-55	1978–85
Tony Canadeo RB/DB (1974)	b. 5-5-19	1941–52
Guy Chamberlin DE/RB (1965)	b. 1-16-1894 d. 4-4-67	1920–27
Jack Christiansen DB/RB (1970)	b. 12-20-28	1951–58
Earl (Dutch) Clark DB/RB (1963)	b. 10-11-06 d. 8-5-78	1931–38
George Connor OT/LB/DT (1975)	b. 1-21-25	1948–55
Jimmy Conzelman RB/DE (1964)	b. 3-6-1898 d. 7-31-70	1920–29
Lou Creekmur OT/DT (1996)	b. 1-22-27	1950–59
Larry Csonka RB (1987)	b. 12-25-46	1968–79
Willie Davis DE/OT (1981)	b. 7-24-34	1958–69
Len Dawson QB (1987)	b. 6-20-35	1957–75
Eric Dickerson RB (1999)	b. 9-2-60	1983–93
Dan Dierdorf OT (1996)	b. 6-29-49	1971–83
Mike Ditka TE (1988)	b. 10-18-39	1961–72
Art Donovan DT/OT (1968)	b. 6-5-25	1950–61
Tony Dorsett RB (1994)	b. 4-7-54	1977–88
John (Paddy) Driscoll RB/QB (1965)	b. 1-11-1895 d. 6-28-68	1921–29
Bill Dudley RB/DB (1966)	b. 12-24-19	1942–53
Albert Glen (Turk) Edwards OT/DT (1969)	b. 9-28-07 d. 1-12-73	1932–39
Tom Fears WR/DB (1970)	b. 12-3-23	1948–55
Len Ford DE/OE (1976)	b. 2-18-26 d. 3-13-72	1948–58
Dan Fortmann OG/LB (1965)	b. 4-11-16 d. 5-24-95	1936–43
Dan Fouts QB (1993)	b. 6-10-51	1973–87
Frank Gatski C/LB (1985)	b. 3-18-22	1946–57
Bill George LB/OG (1974)	b. 10-27-29 d. 9-30-82	1952–66
Frank Gifford RB/DB (1977)	b. 8-16-30	1952–64
Otto Graham QB (1965)	b. 12-6-21	1946–55
Harold (Red) Grange RB/DB (1963)	b. 6-13-03 d. 1-28-91	1925–34
Joe Greene DT (1987)	b. 9-24-46	1969–81
Forrest Gregg OT/OG (1977)	b. 10-18-33	1956–71
Bob Griese QB (1990)	b. 2-3-45	1967–80
Lou Groza K (1974)	b. 1-25-24	1946–67
Joe Guyon RB (1966)	b. 11-26-1892 d. 11-27-71	1920–27
Jack Ham LB (1988)	b. 12-23-48	1971–82
John Hannah OG (1991)	b. 4-4-51	1973–85
Franco Harris RB (1990)	b. 3-7-50	1972–84
Mike Haynes DB (1997)	b. 7-1-53	1976–89
Ed Healey T/G/E (1964)	b. 12-28-1894 d. 12-10-78	1920–27
Mel Hein C/LB (1963)	b. 8-22-09 d. 1-31-92	1931–45
Ted Hendricks LB (1990)	b. 11-1-47	1969–83
Wilbur (Pete) Henry T (1963)	b. 10-31-1897 d. 2-7-52	1920–28
Arnie Herber RB/QB/DB (1966)	b. 4-2-10 d. 10-14-69	1930–45
Bill Hewitt OE/DE (1971)	b. 10-8-09 d. 1-14-47	1932–39
Clarke Hinkle RB/DB (1964)	b. 4-10-09 d. 11-9-88	1932–41
Elroy (Crazylegs) Hirsch WR (1968)	b. 6-17-23	1946–57
Paul Hornung RB/QB (1986)	b. 12-23-35	1957–66
Ken Houston DB (1987)	b. 11-12-44	1967–80
Cal Hubbard WR/DE (1963)	b. 10-31-00 d. 10-17-77	1927–36
Sam Huff LB (1982)	b. 10-4-34	1956–69
Don Hutson WR (1963)	b. 1-31-13 d. 6-26-97	1935–45
Jimmy Johnson DB (1994)	b. 3-31-38	1961–76
John Henry Johnson RB/DB (1987)	b. 11-24-29	1954–66
Charlie Joiner WR (1996)	b. 10-14-47	1969–86
David (Deacon) Jones DE (1980)	b. 12-9-38	1961–74
Stan Jones OG/DT (1991)	b. 11-24-31	954–66
Henry Jordan DT (1995)	b. 1-26-35 d. 2-21-77	1957–69
Sonny Jurgensen QB (1983)	b. 8-23-34	1957–74
Leroy Kelly RB (1994)	b. 5-20-42	1964–73
Walt Kiesling G/T (1966)	b. 3-27-03 d. 3-2-62	1926–38
Frank (Bruiser) Kinard T (1971)	b. 10-23-14 d. 9-7-85	1938–47
Paul Krause DB (1998)	b. 2-19-42	1964–79
Jack Lambert LB (1990)	b. 7-8-52	1974–84
Dick (Night Train) Lane DB (1974)	b. 4-16-27	1952–61
Jim Langer C (1987)	b. 5-16-48	1970–81
Willie Lanier LB (1986)	b. 8-21-45	1967–77
Steve Largent WR (1995)	b. 9-28-54	1976–89
Yale Lary DB (1979)	b. 11-24-30	1952–64
Dante Lavelli OE/DE (1975)	b. 2-23-23	1946–56
Bobby Layne QB (1967)	b. 12-19-26 d. 12-1-86	1948–62
Alphonse (Tuffy) Leemans RB/DB (1978)	b. 11-12-12 d. 1-19-79	1936–43
Bob Lilly DT (1980)	b. 7-26-39	1961–74
Larry Little OG/T (1993)	b. 11-2-45	1967–80
Howie Long DE/NT (2000)	b. 1-6-60	1981–93
Ronnie Lott DB (2000)	b. 5-8-59	1981–94
Sid Luckman QB (1965)	b. 11-21-16 d. 7-5-98	1939–50
William Roy (Link) Lyman T (1964)	b. 11-30-1898 d. 12-16-1972	1922–34

2121 George Halas Drive NW
Canton, OH 44708
Telephone: (330) 456-8207
Executive Director: John Bankert
Vice President of Public Relations: Joe Horrigan
www.profootballhof.com

NAME POS. (YR. OF INDUCTION)	D.O.B. D.O.D.	CAREER SPAN
Tom Mack OG (1999)	b. 11-1-43	1966–78
John Mackey TE (1992)	b. 9-24-41	1963–72
Gino Marchetti DE (1972)	b. 1-2-27	1952–66
Ollie Matson RB (1972)	b. 5-1-30	1952–62
Don Maynard WR (1987)	b. 1-25-35	1958–73
George McAfee RB/DB (1966)	b. 3-13-18	1940–50
Mike McCormack OT/DT (1984)	b. 6-21-30	1951–62
Tommy McDonald WR (1998)	b. 7-26-34	1957–68
Hugh McElhenny RB (1970)	b. 12-31-28	1952–64
Johnny (Blood) McNally RB (1963)	b. 11-27-03 d. 11-28-85	1925–38
Mike Michalske G/T/LB (1964)	b. 4-24-03 d. 10-26-83	1927–37
Wayne Millner OE/DE (1968)	b. 1-31-13 d. 11-19-76	1936–45
Bobby Mitchell WR (1983)	b. 6-6-35	1958–68
Ron Mix OT/OG (1979)	b. 3-10-38	1960–71
Joe Montana QB (2000)	b. 6-11-56	1979–94
Lenny Moore RB (1975)	b. 11-25-33	1956–67
Marion Motley RB (1968)	b. 6-5-20 d. 6-27-99	1946–55
Mike Munchak OG (2001)	b. 3-5-60	1982–93
Anthony Munoz OT (1998)	b. 8-19-58	1980–92
George Musso G/T (1982)	b. 4-8-10 d. 9-5-2000	1933–44
Bronko Nagurski RB/LB/T (1963)	b. 11-3-08 d. 1-7-90	1930–43
Joe Namath QB (1985)	b. 5-31-43	1965–77
Ernie Nevers RB (1963)	b. 6-11-03 d. 5-3-76	1926–31
Ozzie Newsome TE (1999)	b. 3-15-56	1978–90
Ray Nitschke LB (1978)	b. 12-29-36 d. 3-8-98	1958–72
Leo Nomellini DT/OT (1969)	b. 6-19-24	1950–63
Merlin Olsen DT (1982)	b. 9-15-40	1962–76
Jim Otto C (1980)	b. 1-5-38	1960–74
Steve Owen DT (1966)	b. 4-21-1898 d. 5-17-64	1924–33
Alan Page DT (1988)	b. 8-7-45	1967–81
Clarence (Ace) Parker RB/DB/QB (1972)	b. 5-17-12	1937–46
Jim Parker OT/OG (1973)	b. 4-3-34	1957–67
Walter Payton RB (1993)	b. 7-25-54 d. 11-1-99	1975–87
Joe Perry RB/DB (1969)	b. 1-27-27	1948–63
Pete Pihos OE/DE (1970)	b. 10-22-23	1947–55
Mel Renfro DB (1996)	b. 12-30-41	1964–77
John Riggins RB (1992)	b. 8-4-49	1971–85
Jim Ringo C (1981)	b. 11-21-31	1953–67
Andy Robustelli DE (1971)	b. 12-6-25	1951–64
Bob St. Clair OT (1990)	b. 2-18-31	1953–63
Gale Sayers RB (1977)	b. 5-30-43	1965–71
Joe Schmidt LB (1973)	b. 1-19-32	1953–65
Lee Roy Selmon DE (1995)	b. 10-20-54	1976–84
Billy Shaw OG (1999)	b. 12-15-38	1961–69
Art Shell OT (1989)	b. 11-26-46	1968–82
O.J. Simpson RB (1985)	b. 7-9-47	1969–79
Mike Singletary LB (1998)	b. 10-9-58	1981–92
Jackie Slater OT/OG (2001)	b. 5-27-54	1976–93

NAME POS. (YR. OF INDUCTION)	D.O.B. D.O.D.	CAREER SPAN
Jackie Smith TE (1994)	b. 2-23-40	1963–78
Bart Starr QB (1977)	b. 1-9-34	1956–71
Roger Staubach QB (1985)	b. 2-5-42	1969–79
Ernie Stautner DT/DE/OG (1969)	b. 4-20-25	1950–63
Jan Stenerud K (1991)	b. 11-26-42	1967–85
Dwight Stephenson C/OT (1998)	b. 11-20-57	1980–87
Ken Strong RB/DB (1967)	b. 8-6-06 d. 10-5-79	1929–45
Joe Stydahar T (1967)	b. 3-17-12 d. 3-23-77	1936–46
Lynn Swann WR (2001)	b. 3-7-52	1974–82
Fran Tarkenton QB (1986)	b. 2-3-40	1961–78
Charley Taylor WR (1984)	b. 9-28-41	1964–77
Jim Taylor RB (1976)	b. 9-20-35	1958–67
Lawrence Taylor LB (1999)	b. 2-4-59	1981–93
Jim Thorpe RB/WR (1963)	b. 5-28-1887 d. 3-28-53	1920–28
Y.A. Tittle QB (1971)	b. 10-24-26	1948–64
George Trafton C (1964)	b. 12-6-1896 d. 9-5-71	1920–32
Charley Trippi RB/QB/DB (1968)	b. 12-4-22	1947–55
Emlen Tunnell DB (1967)	b. 3-29-22 d. 7-23-75	1948–61
Clyde (Bulldog) Turner LB/OT (1966)	b. 11-10-19 d. 10-30-98	1940–52
Johnny Unitas QB (1979)	b. 5-7-33	1956–73
Gene Upshaw OG (1987)	b. 8-15-45	1967–81
Norm Van Brocklin QB (1971)	b. 3-15-26 d. 5-2-83	1949–60
Steve Van Buren RB (1965)	b. 12-28-20	1944–51
Doak Walker RB (1986)	b. 1-1-27 d. 9-27-98	1950–55
Paul Warfield WR (1983)	b. 11-28-42	1964–77
Bob Waterfield QB (1965)	b. 7-26-20 d. 3-25-83	1945–52
Mike Webster C (1997)	b. 3-18-52	1974–90
Arnie Weinmeister DT/OT (1984)	b. 3-23-23	1948–53
Randy White DT/DE (1994)	b. 1-15-53	1975–88
Dave Wilcox LB (2000)	b. 9-29-42	1964–74
Bill Willis DT/OG (1977)	b. 10-5-21	1946–53
Larry Wilson DB (1978)	b. 3-24-38	1960–72
Kellen Winslow TE (1995)	b. 11-5-57	1979–87
Alex Wojciechowicz C/LB (1968)	b. 8-12-15 d. 7-13-92	1938–50
Willie Wood DB (1989)	b. 12-23-36	1960–71
Ron Yary OT (2001)	b. 8-16-46	1968–82
Jack Youngblood DE (2001)	b. 1-26-50	1971–84

BASKETBALL

One controversy that routinely dogs other sports does not affect basketball, for the game's origins are quite clear. We know precisely when and where basketball was invented: in December of 1891, in a shoebox of a gym on the campus of the International YMCA Training School in Springfield, Mass. We know who invented it: a young gym teacher named James Naismith, whose Scottish Calvinist roots had persuaded him that sports offered a glorious path to God. And we know why he invented it: in a last ditch effort to bring order to a class of 18 rowdy young men who were studying to be YMCA executive secretaries.

Cabin fever had set in, and the 18 teenagers, mostly football and rugby types, were beginning to chafe against the tired old indoor recreations of the day, including leapfrog, Indian clubs and tumbling. "Those boys simply would not play drop the handkerchief," Naismith said.

After spending its first 17 years on the campus of Springfield College, the Naismith Memorial Basketball Hall of Fame (above) moved to its current quarters on West Columbus Avenue in Springfield. A new Hall is set to open in 2002.

The young Phys. Ed. teacher recalled duck on a rock, a game he and his childhood friends had played in rural Ontario. It involved placing a good-sized rock atop a boulder and then trying to knock it off by throwing smaller stones at it. Naismith wanted to use boxes for goals, but the school janitor could find only peach baskets, which Naismith nailed to the railing of the gym balcony, exactly 10 feet above the floor. Shortly before class on Dec. 21, 1891, he posted his new game's 13 rules on two neatly typed sheets and divided the class into two nine-man teams. We know that a man named William Chase scored basketball's first—and this historic game's only—basket, a toss from 25 feet away.

Those future executive assistants took to the new game enthusiastically, and when they completed their training and returned home, they spread basketball around the world. After some fine-tuning—the original

You won't find the legendary Johnson (32) or the incomparable Michael Jordan (23) in the following pages—or in the Basketball Hall of Fame. Outrageous? No, the two stars have not been retired from the game for the required five years. Johnson becomes eligible in 2002 and Jordan, provided he doesn't return to the hardwood, in 2004. You can bet they'll both be admitted on the first ballot.

13 rules had made no mention of dribbling, which was codified in the 1920s—basketball was added to the Olympic program in the 1936 Games. Its proud inventor made the long trek to Berlin to watch his game played on an outdoor tennis court of clay and sand that turned to a quagmire when it rained. He presented the gold medals to the winning U.S. team.

When Naismith died in 1939 at age 79, his admirers decided to create the Basketball Hall of Fame to honor him. At first it was mostly a local project, and World War II stalled planning, but the idea gained momentum in 1949 with the appointment of Edward Hickox, then the basketball coach at Springfield College, as executive secretary of the nascent Hall. After a decade of fundraising, the Naismith Memorial Basketball Hall of Fame inducted its first class, led of course by its namesake, in 1959. Yet there was still literally no Hall to house the inaugural enshrinees. Finally, after the city of Springfield got involved in the mid-60s, the Basketball Hall of Fame found a home, a small, red-brick building on the Springfield College campus. It opened to the public on Feb. 17, 1968.

An egalitarian spirit has always pervaded this Hall, whose modest original building was disparaged by critics as "Naismith Tool & Dye." Members of that first class were, with the exception of Naismith, Phog Allen and Amos Alonzo Stagg (he made basketball a five-man game) a relatively anonymous bunch. They included Naismith's deadline-setting boss, Luther Gulick; early sharpshooters John Schommer of the University of Chicago and Chuck Hyatt of the University of Pittsburgh; and William Chase and his 17 stir-crazy classmates, inducted simply as "First Team."

Expanding along with the game's history, the Hall moved into a new three-story building in downtown Springfield on June 30, 1985. Currently, another, newer Hall is being built as part of a $103 million redevelopment of the Springfield waterfront. It is expected to open just in time to welcome the class of 2002, which will include Magic Johnson.

Centerpiece of the Hall is surely the Honors Court, which pays tribute to the 238 individuals and teams enshrined in Springfield. In keeping with the Hall's egalitarian spirit, they include not only U.S. pro players like Wilt Chamberlain and Larry Bird, but also international greats like Kresimir Cosic, four-time Olympian with the former Yugoslavia, and other, lesser-known contributors like Danny Biasone, who invented the 24-second clock. Clair Bee, author of the *Chip Hilton* young-readers series, is in, and so is Chuck Taylor, who persuaded Converse to make the first shoes specifically for basketball, which the company named after him.

Along with the sort of memorabilia you'd expect—Bob Lanier's size-22 sneakers, for example, and the jersey Wilt Chamberlain wore on May 2, 1962, when he scored 100 points for the Warriors against the Knicks—there are more esoteric gems like the fishbowl used to select the picks in the NBA draft lottery. At the entrance you'll find what is best described as a basketball fountain, which showers basketballs down, and elsewhere a Shoe Tunnel containing thousands of shoes.

More than most other halls, the Naismith shrine encourages fan participation. In the Shoot Out Hall you can take shots at baskets set at any height. Every basket a visitor makes is numbered, whether it's a soaring dunk or a two-handed set shot, as part of a running total.

A genuine grassroots tribute to Naismith's brainchild, the Basketball Hall of Fame celebrates the professional game as well as the international, college and high school versions. In it you'll find both 2000 inductee Isiah Thomas, who won two NBA titles with the Detroit Pistons, and the Ida Grove High School girls team, which won back-to-back Iowa state titles in 1928 and '29. One suspects that Dr. Naismith, who saw his game as an educational tool rather than the billion-dollar industry it's become, would have applauded this spirit of inclusion.

KAREEM ABDUL-JABBAR

THE RECORD

YEAR	TEAM	G	FG %	FT %	REB	AST	PTS	PPG	RPG
1969–70	Mil	82	.518	.653	1,190	337	2,361	28.8	14.5
1970–71	Mil	82	.577	.690	1,311	272	2,596	31.7	16.0
1971–72	Mil	81	.574	.689	1,346	370	2,822	34.8	16.6
1972–73	Mil	76	.554	.713	1,224	379	2,292	30.2	16.1
1973–74	Mil	81	.539	.702	1,178	386	2,191	27.0	14.5
1974–75	Mil	65	.513	.763	912	264	1,949	30.0	14.0
1975–76	LA	82	.529	.703	1,383	413	2,275	27.7	16.9
1976–77	LA	82	.579	.701	1,090	319	2,152	26.2	13.3
1977–78	LA	62	.550	.783	801	269	1,600	25.8	12.9
1978–79	LA	80	.577	.736	1,025	431	1,903	23.8	12.8
1979–80	LA	82	.604	.765	886	371	2,034	24.8	10.8
1980–81	LA	80	.574	.766	821	272	2,095	26.2	10.3
1981–82	LA	76	.579	.706	659	225	1,818	23.9	8.7
1982–83	LA	79	.588	.749	592	200	1,722	21.8	7.5
1983–84	LA	80	.578	.723	587	211	1,717	21.5	7.3
1984–85	LA	79	.599	.732	622	249	1,735	22.0	7.9
1985–86	LA	79	.564	.765	478	280	1,846	23.4	6.1
1986–87	LA	78	.564	.714	523	203	1,366	17.5	6.7
1987–88	LA	80	.532	.762	478	135	1,165	14.6	6.0
1988–89	LA	74	.475	.739	334	74	748	10.1	4.5
TOTAL		1,560	.559	.721	17,440	5,660	38,387	24.6	11.2

Kareem Abdul-Jabbar's weapon of choice was the skyhook, which made perfect sense, since the man—like his unstoppable shot—approached the earth from an otherworldly angle. Perhaps his aloofness was a natural consequence of the estrangement big men feel in the world, but it seemed exaggerated in Abdul-Jabbar, even cultivated. "I've always been cautious and secretive, so of course people thought I was strange," he said.

Extraordinary is more like it: After 20 NBA seasons, he had played in more games and scored more points than any player in NBA history. He had won six NBA titles with two teams, a record six regular-season MVP awards and two Finals MVP trophies.

Known as Lew Alcindor until 1971, when his conversion to Islam prompted the name change, Abdul-Jabbar was used to standing out. He was 6' 3" at age 12, and nearly 7 feet by the time he graduated from Manhattan's Power Memorial High, which he led to three city titles before taking his game west to UCLA. He announced his arrival by leading the freshman team to a 15-point victory over the varsity, which happened to be the reigning national champs. With Abdul-Jabbar lobbing in those majestic hooks, the Bruins rolled to three more NCAA titles.

As great a pro player as Abdul-Jabbar was, basketball was only one part of a life that seemed an ongoing quest. He read voraciously, collected jazz albums, meditated and joined political causes.

Pride was always his greatest motivation. After a weak opening game of the '85 NBA Finals against Boston, Abdul-Jabbar was dressed down by coach Pat Riley. He responded by leading the Lakers back to win the series 4–2, averaging 30.2 points in those four victories and winning his second MVP award, 14 years after he'd won his first.

TIMELINE

1968
Known as Lew Alcindor at the time, Abdul-Jabbar (above, with ball) led UCLA past Houston and into the NCAA final, in which it routed North Carolina 78–55. Alcindor was named MVP of the Final Four in '67, '68 and '69.

1971
Having drafted Abdul-Jabbar the previous year, the Bucks traded for veteran guards Oscar Robertson and Lucius Allen. The result: Milwaukee won 66 games, and the NBA title. Abdul-Jabbar was named MVP of the season and the Finals.

1982
The Lakers recovered from the turmoil of coach Paul Westhead's early-season ouster to win 57 games under new coach Pat Riley. They peaked in the playoffs, sweeping past Phoenix and San Antonio to meet Philadelphia in the Finals. Abdul-Jabbar (above) savored his third NBA crown as the Lakers won in six games.

1988
Though pushed to the maximum seven games by both Utah and Dallas in the playoffs, Abdul-Jabbar and the Lakers made good on Pat Riley's outrageous promise that they would repeat as champs, defeating Detroit in seven games in the Finals.

1989
Determined to send Abdul-Jabbar, now the NBA's alltime leading scorer, into retirement with a third straight title, the Lakers swept their way to the Finals. But team injuries and the tough Pistons provided Abdul-Jabbar a somber sendoff instead, as Detroit won in four games.

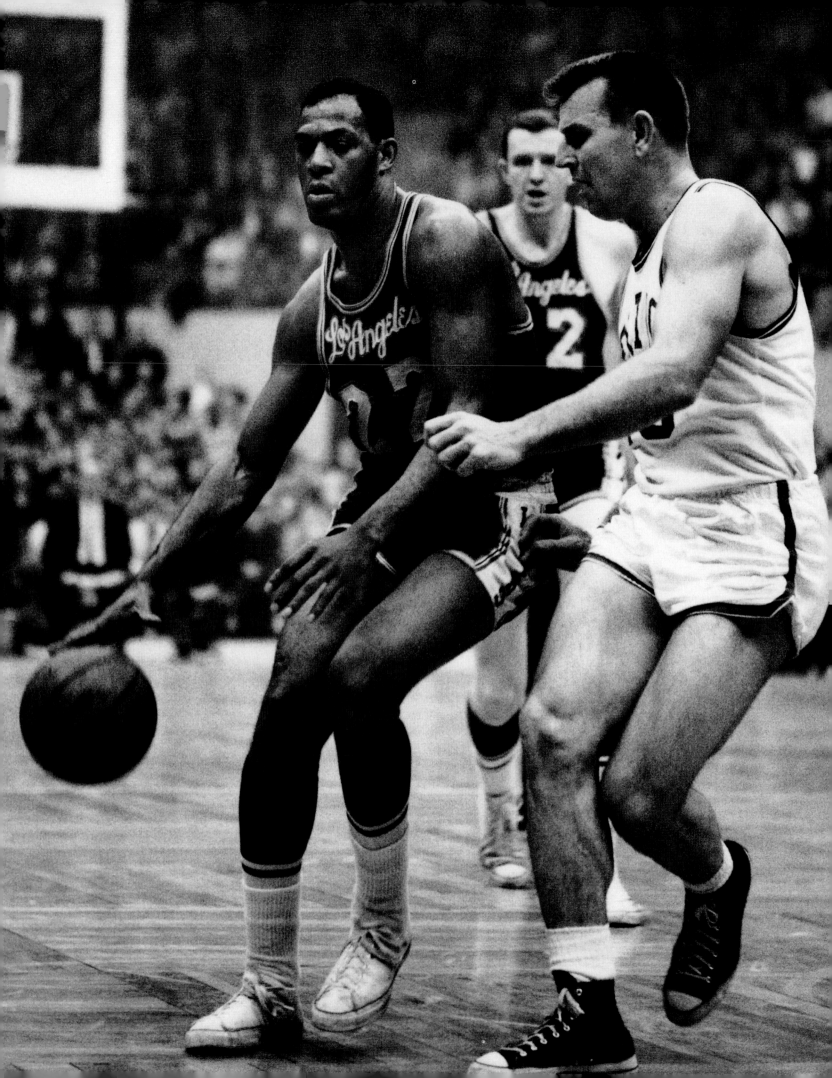

ELGIN BAYLOR

In basketball's evolution skyward, the game's first flyer was Elgin Baylor, the prototype for all subsequent flyers from Dr. J to Michael Jordan to Vince Carter. Baylor was endlessly elusive. He could cut, slither, feint, twist in the air. He got off astonishing shots. "Either he's got three hands or two basketballs," said New York Knicks guard Richie Guerin. "Guarding Baylor is like guarding a flood."

Water is the perfect image for Baylor because he was all supple grace, flowing through whatever crannies the defense gave him. "Watching Elgin Baylor on a basketball court was like watching Gene Kelly in the rain," wrote *Los Angeles Times* columnist Jim Murray. What made Baylor's grace all the more impressive was that at 6' 5", 225 pounds, he was not built like a dancer but more like the football player he had once been.

Baylor's unusual first name came from the watch his father glanced at to pinpoint his son's arrival in this world. He grew up in Washington, D.C., where the public playgrounds were closed to African Americans until Baylor was in his 14th year. Though he once scored a city-record 68 points in a high school game and became the first black player to make all-metro, weak grades kept Baylor from any big-time programs. He followed a neighborhood friend to the College of Idaho, to play football first, with basketball almost an afterthought. After a radio broadcast of the 1955 NCAA title game whet his appetite for a greater stage, Baylor transferred to Seattle University. He led the Chieftains to the 1958 NCAA championship game and scored 25 points in an 84–72 loss to Kentucky.

Drafted by the miserable Minneapolis Lakers, Baylor saved the franchise from bankruptcy with his magnificent play, averaging 24.9 points per game to win the Rookie of the Year award. The Lakers moved to Los Angeles in 1960, and Baylor only got better. He averaged more than 34 points per game for three consecutive seasons and set NBA single-game records by scoring 64 points in 1959 and 71 in 1960. Despite severe knee injuries that hobbled him in the latter half of his 14-year career, Baylor averaged 27.4 points per game, the highest average by a forward in the NBA's 55-year history.

It is one of the saddest injustices of sport that Baylor never won an NBA title. Eight times his Lakers reached the finals, losing to the mighty Celtics in seven of those championship series. Baylor's knees gave out nine games into the 1971–72 season. One wonders how he felt at the end of that season, congratulating the Lakers on winning without him the title they couldn't win with him.

THE RECORD

YEAR	TEAM	G	FG %	FT %	REB	AST	PTS	PPG	RPG
1958–59	Minn	70	.408	.777	1,050	287	1,742	24.9	15.0
1959–60	Minn	70	.424	.732	1,150	243	2,074	29.6	16.4
1960–61	LA	73	.430	.783	1,447	371	2,538	34.8	19.8
1961–62	LA	48	.428	.754	892	222	1,836	38.3	18.6
1962–63	LA	80	.453	.837	1,146	386	2,719	34.0	14.3
1963–64	LA	78	.425	.804	936	347	1,983	25.4	12.0
1964–65	LA	74	.401	.792	950	280	2,009	27.1	12.8
1965–66	LA	65	.401	.739	621	224	1,079	16.6	9.6
1966–67	LA	70	.429	.813	898	215	1,862	26.6	12.8
1967–68	LA	77	.443	.786	941	355	2,002	26.0	12.2
1968–69	LA	76	.447	.743	805	408	1,881	24.8	10.6
1969–70	LA	54	.486	.773	559	292	1,298	24.0	10.4
1970–71	LA	2	.421	.667	11	2	20	10.0	5.5
1971–72	LA	9	.433	.815	57	18	106	11.8	6.3
TOTAL		846	.431	.780	11,463	3,650	23,149	27.4	13.5

A first-team All-America at Seattle, Baylor (22) averaged 32.5 points per game and almost singlehandedly took the Chieftains to the NCAA title game. Though Seattle lost to Kentucky in the championship game, Baylor was named MVP of the Final Four, in which he averaged 24.0 points and 20.5 rebounds per game.

1959

Picking up where he left off in college, Baylor put the Minneapolis Lakers, which had been a horrendous 19–53 the previous season, on his back and carried them to the NBA Finals. Baylor averaged 24.9 points and 15.0 rebounds a game, was named rookie of the year and made the All-NBA team. His presence in the lineup improved the Lakers' record by 14 games. Little did he know it at the time, but his rookie season provided a glimpse of what almost every year of his career held in store for him: a spectacular regular season followed by a brilliant playoff run—and a loss to the Celtics in the Finals.

1963

Los Angeles won a second consecutive Western division title and made a second straight appearance in the NBA Finals (left), where they once again played the Brooklyn Dodgers to the Boston Celtics' New York Yankees, falling in six games. The Celtics' victory was the fifth of what would be eight straight NBA titles for them.

1968

There have been superstars who performed brilliantly for years without winning a title. Dan Marino, Charles Barkley, and Patrick Ewing come to mind. But is there any player in any sport who was as vexed and taunted by fate as the great Baylor? He played in eight championship series and four Game 7s (three of which were decided in the final seconds) without bringing home a ring. In the '68 Finals (right), it was Boston in six.

LARRY BIRD

Larry Bird was the unlikeliest-looking of NBA superstars, not only because he was ghostly white in a predominantly black league, but also because he was gawky, wasn't particularly fast and couldn't jump a lick. "A piece of paper couldn't be slipped under my sneakers when I jump," Bird once cracked.

Yet with vision, guile and smarts Bird became arguably the best forward ever. "If I had to start a team, the one guy in all history I would take would be Larry," said Boston G.M. Red Auerbach, who might have been expected to name his perennial meal ticket, Bill Russell. "He's the greatest to ever play the game."

Hailing from French Lick, Ind., Bird was the son of a waitress and an alcoholic father who committed suicide when his son was 18. Bird shot baskets as therapy. "Basketball was never recreation for me," he said. "It was something I fell in love with."

He attended Indiana University briefly, then junior college, then landed back in French Lick, working on a garbage truck. Bird returned to school in 1975, to Indiana State, and in his senior year he took the Sycamores to the NCAA final, where they lost to Michigan State and the man who would become Bird's foil and friend, Magic Johnson.

With his once mighty Celtics ailing, Auerbach wanted Bird so desperately he drafted the player in his junior year, knowing Bird wouldn't turn pro until after graduation. The rookie Bird led the Celtics from worst to first in the Atlantic Division. A year later Boston won the NBA championship. The Celtics and the Lakers would dominate the 1980s, with Bird and L.A.'s Johnson ruling the NBA. Bird was the league MVP for three straight seasons (1984 to '86) and led the Celtics to five finals and three championships.

Shy off the court, he had attitude to burn on it. Bird once greeted the entrants in the NBA 3-point shooting contest with, "All right, who's playing for second?" "The game is all confidence," he said, "and sometimes it's scary: When I'm at my best, I feel like I'm in total control of everything."

THE RECORD

YEAR	TEAM	G	FG %	FT %	REB	AST	PTS	PPG	RPG
1979–80	Bos	82	.474	.836	852	370	1,745	21.3	10.4
1980–81	Bos	82	.478	.863	895	451	1,741	21.2	10.9
1981–82	Bos	77	.503	.863	837	447	1,761	22.9	10.9
1982–83	Bos	79	.504	.840	870	458	1,867	23.6	11.0
1983–84	Bos	79	.492	.888	796	520	1,908	24.2	10.1
1984–85	Bos	80	.522	.882	842	531	2,295	28.7	10.5
1985–86	Bos	82	.496	.896	805	557	2,115	25.8	9.8
1986–87	Bos	74	.525	.910	682	566	2,076	28.1	9.2
1987–88	Bos	76	.527	.916	703	467	2,275	29.9	9.3
1988–89	Bos	6	.471	.947	37	29	116	19.3	6.2
1989–90	Bos	75	.473	.930	712	562	1,820	24.3	9.5
1990–91	Bos	60	.454	.891	509	431	1,164	19.4	8.5
1991–92	Bos	45	.466	.927	434	306	908	20.2	9.6
TOTAL		**897**	**.496**	**.886**	**8,974**	**5,695**	**21,791**	**24.3**	**10.0**

TIMELINE

1979
Bird (above, with ball) protested that his Indiana State teammates were as responsible for the Sycamores' run to the NCAA final as he was, but the following year, with Bird in the NBA and four starters back at ISU, the Sycamores went 16–11.

1980
With the rookie Bird in the lineup, Boston improved by 32 games, going from 29–53 in '79 to 61–21. The Celtics swept Houston in the first round of the playoffs but were bounced out of the conference finals by Julius Erving and Philadelphia.

1981
With the frontcourt additions of Robert Parish (via a laughably one-sided trade with Golden State) and Kevin McHale (through the draft), Bird (33) and the Celtics edged Erving (6) and the 76ers in a seven-game thriller in the Eastern Conference finals then went on to defeat Houston in six games for the NBA title.

1984
Four seasons into their pro careers, Magic and Bird met in the NBA Finals for the first time. Los Angeles took Game 1 but blew a late lead in Game 2, which Boston won in overtime. The Celtics grabbed an OT win again in Game 4 and took the series in seven.

1987
Together, Bird (33) and Johnson (32) revitalized the NBA in the 1980s, attracting legions of new fans and ushering in the league's international-profile Jordan era. Their teams would meet in the Finals three times, with Magic's Lakers winning twice, including in '87 (above), when L.A. won in six.

Though it served him brilliantly on the court, Wilt Chamberlain's size worked against him in the imaginations of basketball fans. "Nobody roots for Goliath," said Wilt, who was as impressive for his intelligence and wide-ranging curiosity as he was for his physical attributes.

While Bill Russell, the game's other dominant center in Chamberlain's era, was 6' 9½", Chamberlain towered at 7' 1". He also carried 300 pounds of lean muscle on his frame, making him the strongest player in the league as well as the tallest. When 6' 10", 270-pound Bob Lanier was asked for the most indelible memory of his career, he said, "When Wilt Chamberlain lifted me up and moved me like a coffee cup so he could get position."

When he retired in 1974 Chamberlain held or shared 43 NBA records, some of which may last forever. Contemplate these numbers: Chamberlain averaged 50.4 points a game in the 1961–62 season. He grabbed 22.9 rebounds per game for his career and once corralled 55 in a game—against the great Russell, no less.

On March 2, 1962, Chamberlain scored 100 points against the Knicks.

Chamberlain always stood out. By the time he entered Philadelphia's Overbrook High at age 15, he stood 6' 11" and excelled in track and field as well as basketball. At the University of Kansas, he scored 52 points in his first game. After a year with the Harlem Globetrotters, Chamberlain joined the NBA in 1959 and, like Gulliver among the Lilliputians, easily won the scoring title (37.6) and the MVP award.

Still, Chamberlain never shook his reputation as a loser, which was undeserved. He won titles with Philadelphia in 1967 and Los Angeles in '72, when he was named Finals MVP. The obstacle for Chamberlain was always Russell, the consummate winner. So let Russell deliver the final verdict: "Chamberlain is the greatest basketball player alive, no doubt about that. He has set standards so high, his point totals are so enormous, that they've lost their impact."

THE RECORD

YEAR	TEAM	G	FG %	FT %	REB	AST	PTS	PPG	RPG
1959–60	Phil	72	.461	.582	1,941	168	2,707	37.6	27.0
1960–61	Phil	79	.509	.504	2,149	148	3,333	38.4	27.2
1961–62	Phil	80	.506	.613	2,052	192	4,029	50.4	25.7
1962–63	S.F.	80	.528	.593	1,946	275	3,586	44.8	24.3
1963–64	S.F.	80	.524	.531	1,787	403	2,948	36.9	22.3
1964–65	S.F.-Phil	73	.510	.464	1,673	250	2,534	34.7	22.9
1965–66	Phil	79	.540	.513	1,943	414	2,649	33.5	24.6
1966–67	Phil	81	.683	.441	1,957	630	1,956	24.1	24.2
1967–68	Phil	82	.595	.380	1,952	702	1,992	24.3	23.8
1968–69	L.A.	81	.583	.446	1,712	366	1,664	20.5	21.1
1969–70	L.A.	12	.568	.446	221	49	328	27.3	18.4
1970–71	L.A.	82	.545	.538	1,493	352	1,696	20.7	18.2
1971–72	L.A.	82	.649	.422	1,572	329	1,213	14.8	19.2
1972–73	L.A.	82	.727	.510	1,526	365	1,084	13.2	18.6
TOTAL		1,045	.540	.511	23,924	4,643	31,419	30.1	22.9

TIMELINE

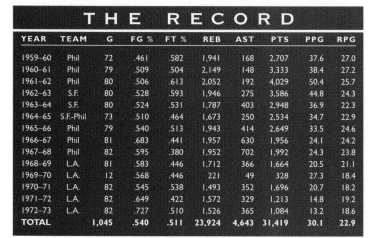

1958
One year after making it to the NCAA title game, which they lost to North Carolina, 54–53 in triple overtime, Chamberlain (12) and the Jayhawks finished 18–5 and did not receive an NCAA bid—despite their 61–44 rout of Kansas State, a team that would reach the Final Four.

1960
Chamberlain joined the NBA and became the first player to win both the rookie of the year and most valuable player awards. He led the league in scoring and rebounding, but Philadelphia lost to Boston in the second round of the playoffs.

1962
On March 2, Chamberlain (above) poured in 100 points against the Knicks. Normally a mediocre free-throw shooter, Wilt the Stilt was 28 of 32 from the line that night. He netted 31 points in the fourth quarter, and four of his teammates scored in double figures as Philadelphia won 169–147.

1972
With Chamberlain (right) dominating the pivot, the Lakers reeled off 33 straight victories en route to an unprecedented 69–13 regular-season record. They dispatched the Knicks in five games in the Finals to deliver Wilt his second NBA title.

BOB COUSY

Bob Cousy was not only the diminutive seed from which all those great Boston Celtics teams of the 1950s and '60s grew. He was also the game's first true showman, a backcourt wizard who perfected the whole bag of hyphenated tricks that still spice up the NBA: the behind-the-back dribble, the no-look pass and the reverse dribble. "The only kick I have with Cousy," said Boston coach Red Auerbach, "is that he makes practice sessions hard on a coach. All the other players just want to stand still and watch him."

Cousy had to prove himself to people for his entire career. The son of Alsatian immigrants, he spoke French until he was 10 and only picked up his strong New York accent when the family moved to New York City. Cousy did not make the basketball team at Andrew Jackson High in Queens until midway through his sophomore year, when, hearing that the coach was looking for a lefty guard, he practiced obsessively enough to pass—and we do mean pass—as one.

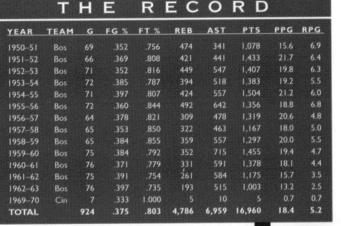

THE RECORD

YEAR	TEAM	G	FG %	FT %	REB	AST	PTS	PPG	RPG
1950–51	Bos	69	.352	.756	474	341	1,078	15.6	6.9
1951–52	Bos	66	.369	.808	421	441	1,433	21.7	6.4
1952–53	Bos	71	.352	.816	449	547	1,407	19.8	6.3
1953–54	Bos	72	.385	.787	394	518	1,383	19.2	5.5
1954–55	Bos	71	.397	.807	424	557	1,504	21.2	6.0
1955–56	Bos	72	.360	.844	492	642	1,356	18.8	6.8
1956–57	Bos	64	.378	.821	309	478	1,319	20.6	4.8
1957–58	Bos	65	.353	.850	322	463	1,167	18.0	5.0
1958–59	Bos	65	.384	.855	359	557	1,297	20.0	5.5
1959–60	Bos	75	.384	.792	352	715	1,455	19.4	4.7
1960–61	Bos	76	.371	.779	331	591	1,378	18.1	4.4
1961–62	Bos	75	.391	.754	261	584	1,175	15.7	3.5
1962–63	Bos	76	.397	.735	193	515	1,003	13.2	2.5
1969–70	Cin	7	.333	1.000	5	10	5	0.7	0.7
TOTAL		**924**	**.375**	**.803**	**4,786**	**6,959**	**16,960**	**18.4**	**5.2**

Though Cousy became an All-City guard, he was, in his own words, "deluged by all of two college [scholarship] offers." He settled on Holy Cross, a small, academically rigorous Jesuit school in Worcester, Mass. In his first year on the varsity Cousy was the backup point guard on the Crusaders team that won the 1946–47 NCAA championship. Though Holy Cross didn't win another title, with Cousy pulling the strings, they wowed their fans with their razzle-dazzle style.

After his college career, which included another Final Four appearance, in 1948, Cousy was determined to play for the Celtics. But Auerbach was not impressed. "Am I supposed to win," he asked, "or please the local yokels?" Cousy went to the Chicago Stags, who folded before he could play a single game. He was placed, along with the Stags' other two guards, in a supplemental draft. When the New York Knicks and the Philadelphia Warriors passed him over, Auerbach reluctantly made Cousy a Celtic.

The Boston G.M. quickly saw the error of his initial judgment. Cousy could sometimes lead a team to victory by himself—witness his 50 points, including 17 of the Celtics' final 21, against Syracuse in the 1953 NBA playoffs—but as the Celtics acquired other stars with complementary talents, Cousy settled into his role as the league's premier playmaker. And Boston, with players like Bill Russell, Tom Heinsohn and K.C. Jones, came into its own, winning six NBA championships in Cousy's career. Cousy's great gift was moving the ball, either by dribbling or by passing. He had 28 assists in one game—an NBA record that stood until 1978—and led the league in assists from 1953 to '60. He was elected to the Hall of Fame in 1970.

TIMELINE

1950
With the slick ballhandler Cousy (17) running the show, Holy Cross played a Showtime style three decades before the L.A. Lakers did. After winning the national title in 1947, the Crusaders finished third in '48 and lost to North Carolina State in the East regional semifinal in '50, Cousy's senior year.

1952
In his second year in the league, Cousy helped Boston to a 39–27 record and finished second in the NBA in assists and third in scoring. The Celtics made the playoffs but were eliminated by the New York Knicks in a best-of-three first-round series, dropping Game 3 88–87 in double overtime.

1962
Cousy (below) and the Celtics defeated Jim Krebs (32) and the Lakers in an epic seven-game series for the NBA title, Boston's fourth straight and fifth in six years. With the series tied at two games apiece, Los Angeles

forward Elgin Baylor scored 61 points to lead the Lakers to a 126–121 victory and a 3–2 series lead. With a golden chance to wrap up the series and dethrone the mighty Celtics, the Lakers lost Game 6 at home, 119–105. Back in Boston, Game 7 went to overtime when an attempted buzzer-beater by L.A.'s Frank Selvy rimmed out, and Cousy and the Celtics won it 110–107 in the extra period.

1963
On March 17, a tearful Cousy (below) said goodbye to the Boston Garden crowd after his final regular-season home game. He ended his 13-year Celtics career on a high note as Boston again defeated Los Angeles in the NBA Finals, winning four games to two. Cousy woud make a brief comeback in 1969, playing seven games with Cincinnati and fellow Hall of Famer Oscar Robertson.

1975

The three-point shot, the red-white-and-blue ball and the high-flying, Afro-wearing Dr. J (right) were the symbols of the free-wheeling American Basketball Association, which operated from 1967 to '76. In five ABA seasons, Erving averaged 28.7 points per game, won three MVP awards and two titles, including the one in '76, the league's final year of existence.

1977

The ABA's Denver Nuggets, New York Nets, San Antonio Spurs and Indiana Pacers jumped to the NBA for the 1976–77 season, and Erving (left)

jumped to the Philadelphia 76ers. He promptly delivered an Atlantic Division title and a berth in the NBA Finals to the City of Brotherly Love, but after he and the Sixers grabbed Games 1 and 2 from the Portland Trailblazers, they lost four straight and failed to bring home the championship.

1980

Erving had the best offensive season of his NBA career, finishing fourth in the scoring race, and the Sixers returned to the NBA Finals, knocking off Washington, Atlanta and Boston to get there. They fell short again, though, losing to Magic Johnson and the Lakers in a tense six-game series.

1982

With Dr. J averaging 24.4 points per game, Philadelphia clawed its way back to the NBA Finals but lost to Los Angeles again, four games to two.

1983

To the delight of basketball fans everywhere, except perhaps Los Angeles, Erving (left, dunking) and the 76ers finally broke through and won the NBA title. They did so in convincing fashion, going 65–17 during the regular season, winning 12 of 13 playoff games and sweeping the Lakers in the Finals.

JULIUS ERVING

Honored as we are to include him in our book, Julius Erving could just as easily figure in a history of aviation, side by side with dreamers like Icarus and the Wright brothers, for it was Erving who added flight to the game of basketball. With his highlight-reel dunks and his spectacular ability to hang in the air, Erving opened up a third dimension, verticality, in a game that hitherto had been played on a flat surface, back and forth.

To Pat Williams, the Philadelphia 76ers' G.M., Erving was "the Babe Ruth of basketball." Just as Ruth's clouts distracted fans from the sordid revelations of the Black Sox Scandal, so Erving appeared when fans were growing bored with the run-and-gun offenses then dominating the pro game. Erving presented a whole new world of possibilities. Even his hair elevated in those days, rising off his head in a massive Afro. And he certainly had the game's best nickname, Dr. J, bestowed upon him by a friend whose fondness for argument had led Erving to christen him the Professor.

A late bloomer, Erving didn't start on his Roosevelt (Long Island) High School team until his senior year, when he blossomed into a 6' 3" all–Long Island guard. Beseiged by scholarship offers, he chose the University of Massachusetts, reasoning that his game would develop faster if he went to an obscure school where he could play immediately rather than to a powerhouse where he would probably ride the pine for a year or two. He scored 26 points and grabbed 20 rebounds per game as a sophomore at UMass and averaged 27 points and 19 boards as a junior.

Erving left Massachusetts after his junior year and took his game to the ABA, which, lacking a TV contract and a significant fan base, was definitely a sideshow to the more glamorous NBA. Still, the legend of Dr. J grew as tales of his sensational slams and swooping finger rolls for the Virginia Squires trickled back to the outside world. Traded to the New York Nets, he won the ABA Most Valuable Player award three years in a row (1974–76).

When the ABA dissolved after the '76 season, sending four of its teams to the NBA, the Philadelphia 76ers made a $6-million deal to acquire the Doctor. An instant NBA superstar, he averaged more than 20 points per game during his first nine seasons. But the numbers fail to reflect the flair with which this doctor operated. In a move that still gets replayed during NBA telecasts, Erving once executed a reverse lay-up from behind the backboard. In 1980–81 he was the league MVP; two years later he won his only NBA championship.

Erving's play was always spectacular, but the man was dignified and quiet, as befits a doctor. When he retired following the 1986–87 season he stood third on the alltime scoring list with 18,364 points. Asked how he'd performed all those tricks, he answered, "It's easy, once you learn how to fly."

THE RECORD

YEAR	TEAM	G	FG %	FT %	REB	AST	PTS	PPG	RPG
1976–77	Phil	82	.499	.777	695	306	1,770	21.6	8.5
1977–78	Phil	74	.502	.845	481	279	1,528	20.6	6.5
1978–79	Phil	78	.491	.745	564	357	1,803	23.1	7.2
1979–80	Phil	78	.519	.787	576	355	2,100	26.9	7.4
1980–81	Phil	82	.521	.787	657	364	2,014	24.6	8.0
1981–82	Phil	81	.546	.763	557	319	1,974	24.4	6.9
1982–83	Phil	72	.517	.759	491	263	1,542	21.4	6.8
1983–84	Phil	77	.512	.754	532	309	1,727	22.4	6.9
1984–85	Phil	78	.494	.765	414	233	1,561	20.0	5.3
1985–86	Phil	74	.480	.785	370	248	1,340	18.1	5.0
1986–87	Phil	60	.471	.813	264	191	1,005	16.8	4.4
TOTAL		837	.507	.777	5,601	3,224	18,364	22.0	6.7

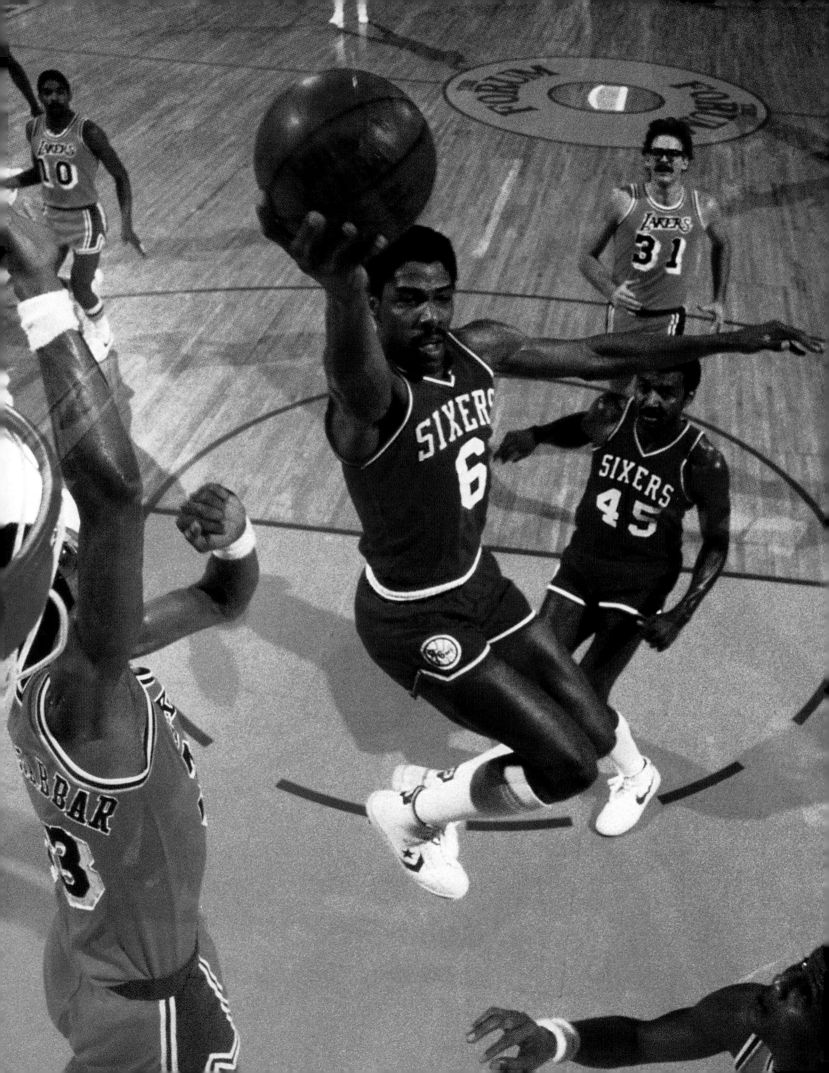

GEORGE MIKAN

George Mikan was the NBA's first dominant big man, leading the Minneapolis Lakers to five titles from 1949 to '54. Back then, when the lane was half the width it is today, the Lakers stuck to a simple plan: They had Mikan camp out in the low post, fed him the ball and watched him spin for a layup or baby hook. Primitive as that sounds, it had the inarguable virtue of working and should not persuade us that Mikan lacked other skills.

"Everyone forgets that Mikan is also the best feeder from the pivot this game has ever seen," said the great coach Joe Lapchick. "Cover him normally and he kills you with his scoring. Cover him abnormally and he murders you with passes." The only way to dilute his impact was to change the rules, which the league did in 1951, doubling the width of the lane to 12' and inventing the three-second lane violation.

Raised on a farm near Joliet, Ill., Mikan was only 5' 11" when he entered high school but was 6' 10" when he graduated. He was myopic, passive and as clumsy as any overnight giant. When a broken leg forced him to convalesce in bed for 18 months during high school, there seemed no chance he would ever become an athlete, let alone a great one.

But Mikan was lucky enough to find a mentor with the patience to transform him from a gawky giant into a tower of power. He arrived at Chicago's DePaul University the same year as legendary basketball coach Ray Meyer, who knew a godsend when it loped past him on campus. Meyer developed an imaginative regimen for Mikan that included dance, rope-skipping, shadowboxing and a drill that came to be known as "the Mikan drill," which involved taking 200 hook shots with each hand every day. "It was like watching a flower bloom," marveled Meyer. Mikan was named College Player of the Year in both his junior and senior seasons at DePaul.

A star from the moment he entered the NBA, Mikan won three straight scoring titles and averaged 23.1 points per game during his nine-year career. He went to law school in the off-seasons and later used his knowledge of contracts as the first commissioner of the ABA. Indeed, it was Mikan who developed the distinctive red, white and blue ball that the league used to set itself apart, much as Mikan himself had stood out in the early years of professional basketball.

THE RECORD

YEAR	TEAM	G	FG %	FT %	REB	AST	PTS	PPG	RPG
1946–47*	Chi	25	—	.726	—	—	413	16.5	—
1947–48*	Minn	56	—	.752	—	—	1,195	21.3	—
1948–49†	Minn	60	.416	.772	—	218	1,698	28.3	—
1949–50	Minn	68	.407	.779	—	197	1,865	27.4	—
1950–51	Minn	68	.428	.803	958	208	1,932	28.4	14.1
1951–52	Minn	64	.385	.780	866	194	1,523	23.8	13.5
1952–53	Minn	70	.399	.780	1,007	201	1,442	20.6	14.4
1953–54	Minn	72	.380	.777	1,028	174	1,306	18.1	14.3
1955–56	Minn	37	.395	.770	308	53	390	10.5	8.3
TOTAL		439	.404	.782	4,167	1,245	10,156	23.1	13.4

* National Basketball League; † Basketball Association of America

TIMELINE

1943

Mikan (right) came to Chicago's DePaul University in 1941 as an ungainly beanpole and left in '46 as a two-time national College Player of the Year. He led DePaul to the Final Four and helped coach Ray Meyer, who came to the school the same year Mikan did, establish the Blue Demons as a perennial national power.

1949

Air George: Mikan (left, with ball), who topped the league in scoring (28.3 PPG) and was second in field-goal percentage (.416), was one of the few players of his era who could play above the rim. He and the Lakers soared all the way to the Basketball Association of America title, defeating Washington four games to two in the finals.

1952

Largely because of Mikan, the league widened the lane and introduced the three-second rule, which prevented any player from taking a position in the painted area under the basket for more than three seconds at a time. The new rules did bring Mikan's scoring average down by a few points, but they didn't prevent the big man from delivering Minneapolis its third title in four years: The Lakers won a seven-game classic—with Games 1 and 4 going to overtime—over the New York Knicks.

1953

Parity—and cynically physical play—enveloped the NBA as half of the 10 teams in the league won 40 or more games and the fouls-per-game average rose to 58. (A limit on the number of fouls allowed per player would be instituted two years later.) But one thing remained the same, the predominance of Mikan (right, middle) and Minneapolis, which dropped the first game of the championship series to the Knicks and then reeled off four straight victories to claim its second straight title and fourth in five years.

1954

Mikan's scoring average dipped below 20 points per game, but he still led the Lakers to another division title and a third straight NBA championship. Minneapolis outlasted Syracuse in seven games in the finals.

OSCAR ROBERTSON

Oscar Robertson was basketball's first great all-around player. Certainly he is the only player ever to average a "triple double" for an entire season, a feat Robertson achieved in his second season with the Cincinnati Royals, when he averaged 30.8 points, 12.5 rebounds and 11.4 assists per game. "He's so great he scares me," said Red Auerbach, coach of the Boston Celtics dynasty. "He can beat you all by himself, and usually does."

The Big O, whose nickname was a nod to James Thurber's popular novel *The Wonderful O*, was indeed big (6' 5") as well as strong (210 pounds). He could back smaller defenders into the post but also possessed the quickness to blow by people. Indeed, to find another player in whom so many skills were so perfectly integrated, one must leap forward 20 years, to Magic Johnson.

The great-grandson of a slave, Robertson grew up on a farm in Tennessee but attended high school in Indianapolis, where he excelled at everything he did, graduating 16th in a class of 171 and leading the basketball team to 45 consecutive wins, including two straight state titles.

Robertson could have played college ball anywhere, but he chose the University of Cincinnati, which had neither a big-time program nor a scholarship for Roberston. He supported himself by working as a meter-reader for Cincinnati Gas & Electric and became the first player to lead the country in scoring for three straight years. In his Madison Square Garden debut he electrified the crowd by scoring 56 points. How did he feel? "I was glad," said the Big O, who was never one to waste energy talking.

Drafted by the Royals, Robertson led the NBA in assists six times and was MVP of the 1963–64 season. Though he played only 14 years, Robertson still stands seventh on the alltime scoring list and third alltime in assists. He finally won a title in 1971 after getting traded to Milwaukee, where, in rookie Lew Alcindor, he found a center to complement his outside game.

THE RECORD

YEAR	TEAM	G	FG %	FT %	REB	AST	PTS	PPG	RPG
1960–61	Cin	71	.473	.822	716	690	2,165	30.5	10.1
1961–62	Cin	79	.478	.803	985	899	2,432	30.8	12.5
1962–63	Cin	80	.518	.810	835	758	2,264	28.3	10.4
1963–64	Cin	79	.483	.853	783	868	2,480	31.4	9.9
1964–65	Cin	75	.480	.839	674	861	2,279	30.4	9.0
1965–66	Cin	76	.475	.842	586	847	2,378	31.3	7.7
1966–67	Cin	79	.493	873	486	845	2,412	30.5	6.2
1967–68	Cin	65	.500	873	391	633	1,896	29.2	6.0
1968–69	Cin	79	.486	.838	502	772	1,955	24.7	6.4
1969–70	Cin	69	.511	.809	422	558	1,748	25.3	6.1
1970–71	Mil	81	.496	.850	462	668	1,569	19.4	5.7
1971–72	Mil	64	.472	.836	323	491	1,114	17.4	5.0
1972–73	Mil	73	.454	.847	360	551	1,130	15.5	4.9
1973–74	Mil	70	.438	.835	279	446	888	12.7	4.0
TOTAL		**1,040**	**.485**	**.838**	**7,804**	**9,887**	**26,710**	**25.7**	**7.5**

TIMELINE

1959
On December 30, Robertson (above) scored 50 points in the final of the Holiday Festival tournament at Madison Square Garden, leading Cincinnati to a 96–83 triumph over Iowa. The Bearcats would reach the Final Four that season.

1961
Fresh from an NCAA Final Four appearance with Cincinnati and a gold-medal performance with the U.S. Olympic team in Rome, Robertson signed with the Royals of the NBA and won the Rookie of the Year award, topping the league in assists.

1962
An All-Star for the second straight year, Robertson (above, with ball) produced a season for the ages, *averaging* a "triple-double," with 30.8 points, 12.5 rebounds and 11.4 assists per game. But the Royals lacked a strong frontcourt and were bounced out of the playoffs in the first round by Detroit.

1969
Robertson was named MVP of the All-Star Game and once again led the league in assists, but Cincinnati, which never made it past the second round of the playoffs with Robertson, failed even to make the postseason, finishing with a 41–41 record.

1971
The Big O wins the Big One: With Lew Alcindor in the frontcourt and Robertson in the backcourt, the Bucks were unstoppable, going 66–16 and sweeping Baltimore for the title. Surprisingly, the Bucks' triumph was only the second such sweep in Finals history.

BILL RUSSELL

Large as he loomed in the lane, Bill Russell loomed even larger in the imaginations of his opponents, whom he moved to flights of inspired fancy. Call it the poetry of awe. Hall of Fame center Elvin Hayes called Russell the "Ghost" for the way he came out of nowhere to block shots. Tom Meschery called him the "Bearded Eagle" not only for his ability to fly but also for his fierce dignity. To Cincinnati general manager Pepper Wilson, Russell was "the world's largest eraser" for his ability to wipe away Boston mistakes.

Until Russell joined them for the 1956–57 season, the Celtics had been known as a mediocre bunch of gunners. Figuring the recently instituted 24-second clock would reward teams that controlled the boards, Boston coach Red Auerbach went all-out to get Russell, who instantly rewarded the coach's faith. The Celtics became the greatest dynasty in modern sports history, winning the NBA championship in 11 of Russell's 13 years, including eight straight from 1959 to '66. In 1966 Russell became the team's player-coach—the first African-American head coach in a major sport—and led Boston to two more titles.

THE RECORD									
YEAR	TEAM	G	FG %	FT %	REB	AST	PTS	PPG	RPG
1956–57	Bos	48	.427	.492	943	88	706	14.7	19.6
1957–58	Bos	69	.442	.519	1,564	202	1,142	16.6	22.7
1958–59	Bos	70	.457	.598	1,612	222	1,168	16.7	23.0
1959–60	Bos	74	.467	.612	1,778	277	1,350	18.2	24.0
1960–61	Bos	78	.426	.550	1,868	268	1,322	16.9	23.9
1961–62	Bos	76	.457	.595	1,790	341	1,436	18.9	23.6
1962–63	Bos	78	.432	.555	1,843	348	1,309	16.8	23.6
1963–64	Bos	78	.433	.550	1,930	370	1,168	15.0	24.7
1964–65	Bos	78	.438	.573	1,878	410	1,102	14.1	24.1
1965–66	Bos	78	.415	.551	1,779	371	1,005	12.9	22.8
1966–67	Bos	81	.454	.610	1,700	472	1,075	13.3	21.0
1967–68	Bos	78	.425	.537	1,451	357	977	12.5	18.6
1968–69	Bos	77	.433	.526	1,484	374	762	9.9	19.3
TOTAL		963	.440	.561	21,620	4,100	14,522	15.1	22.5

Blocked shots were not an official stat during the Russell era, largely because until he came along, no one had appreciated how disruptive a voracious blocker could be. "He put a new sound in the game," said Auerbach, "the sound of his own footsteps." He was also a trash-talker par excellence, who once told the Hawks' Bill Bridges to bring salt and pepper because he was going to force feed him "Wilson sandwiches."

Russell was a coach's dream—smart, industrious and totally team-oriented. As SPORTS ILLUSTRATED's Alex Wolff put it, "If there had not been a Bill Russell, some coach would have tried to invent him for his instructive value." A classic late bloomer, he was so mediocre as a high school junior that he'd had to share a uniform with the team's other third-string center. After graduating from Oakland's McClymonds High, he received just one scholarship offer, to the University of San Francisco. He accepted and fit perfectly into coach Phil Woolpert's disciplined offense, leading the Dons to 55 straight wins and back-to-back national collegiate titles. After college he joined the 1956 Olympic team and won a gold medal in Melbourne. Then it was off to the Celtic dynasty.

Though he never averaged 20 points per game for a season—never led his team in scoring—no one doubted Russell's worth. He won five league MVP awards, including three straight from 1961 to '63. Still, he insisted that those 11 Celtics championships were the only worthwhile measure of greatness. Who could argue?

TIMELINE

1955

Russell (right) exulted in the first of San Francisco's two consecutive NCAA titles. The Dons downed LaSalle 77–63 in the final, and Russell, who averaged 23.5 points and dominated the boards, was named MVP of the Final Four. He would win the same award after the Dons' second title the following season, when they defeated Iowa 83–71 in the championship game.

1957
Russell and fellow rookie Tom Heinsohn, of Holy Cross, joined Bob Cousy, Bill Sharman and Jungle Jim Loscutoff to form the foundation of the Celtic dynasty. Boston cruised to a 44–28 record and won the Eastern Division by six games. They swept Syracuse to get to the Finals, where they played the St. Louis Hawks in a classic seven-game thriller. Games 1 and 7 both went to double overtime and were settled by identical scores: 125–123. St. Louis took the opener but Boston won the decisive finale. The Hawks would be Boston's closest competitor during the early years of the Celtic dynasty.

1961
Russell (right, leaping) and Boston reached their fifth consecutive championship series and met St. Louis in the Finals for the fourth time in that span. The Hawks were eager to avenge the previous year's Game 7 loss—in which Russell had scored 22 points and grabbed 35 rebounds—but they fell even shorter this time around, getting dismissed by Boston in five games.

1968

After a one-year hiatus in which Philadelphia wore the crown, Russell (left) and the Celtics returned to the NBA throne, knocking off the Lakers in six games in the Finals. Russell had become the Celtics' player-coach by then, and he would lead them to another title—Boston's 11th in 13 years—the following season.

JERRY WEST

Jerry West grew up—much too slowly, it seemed to him—in the tiny West Virginia town of Cheylan, right next door to Cabincreek, where the West family received its mail. There wasn't much to do in Cheylan, so when a neighbor nailed a basketball hoop to the side of his garage, West became a tireless acolyte. He practiced around the clock, all year long, pounding his dribble in snow and mud, until his fingers bled.

"I think I became a basketball player because it is a game a boy can play by himself," said West, who never lost that work ethic even in the NBA. All that practice paid off, not only in a career scoring average of 27 points per game but also in the aesthetic purity of his play. For 25 years the NBA has used a silhouette of West, dribbling, as the centerpiece of its logo.

West carried East Bank High to the state championship and the University of West Virginia to the NCAA title game against Cal. In 1960 he and Oscar Robertson co-captained the gold-medal-winning U.S. team at the Rome Olympics.

The pair was taken 1–2 in the NBA draft, but that seemed to do little for West's confidence. "I didn't think I was good enough to play in the NBA," said the man his teammates nicknamed "Zeke from Cabincreek." As a rookie he averaged 17.6 points per game, far fewer than Robertson's 30.5. After spending the off-season practicing shooting and going to his left, West matched Robertson's 30.8 average the next year. They would form the starting backcourt in the All-Star game for the next six years.

From 1961–62 to '69–70 the Lakers would reach seven NBA Finals, losing to the invincible Boston Celtics six times and the New York Knicks once. Finally, after the 1971–72 season, with Wilt Chamberlain now on the team, West and the Lakers won a title, beating the Knicks in five games. "The greatest honor a man can have is the respect and friendship of his peers," said Bill Russell, saluting his old rival on Jerry West Night. "You have that more than any man I know."

THE RECORD

YEAR	TEAM	G	FG %	FT %	REB	AST	PTS	PPG	RPG
1960–61	LA	79	.419	.666	611	333	1,389	17.6	7.7
1961–62	LA	75	.445	.769	591	402	2,310	30.8	7.9
1962–63	LA	55	.461	.778	384	307	1,489	27.1	7.0
1963–64	LA	72	.484	.832	443	403	2,064	28.7	6.2
1964–65	LA	74	.497	.821	447	364	2,292	31.0	6.0
1965–66	LA	79	.473	.860	562	480	2,476	31.3	7.1
1966–67	LA	66	.464	.878	392	447	1,892	28.7	5.9
1967–68	LA	51	.514	.811	294	310	1,343	26.3	5.8
1968–69	LA	61	.471	.821	262	423	1,580	25.9	4.3
1969–70	LA	74	.497	.824	338	554	2,309	31.2	4.6
1970–71	LA	69	.494	.832	320	655	1,859	26.9	4.6
1971–72	LA	77	.477	.814	327	747	1,985	25.8	4.2
1972–73	LA	69	.479	.805	289	607	1,575	22.8	4.2
1973–74	LA	31	.447	.833	116	206	629	20.3	3.7
TOTAL		**932**	**.474**	**.814**	**5,376**	**6,238**	**25,192**	**27.0**	**5.8**

TIMELINE

1959
West led West Virginia to the NCAA finals, where the Mountaineers lost a 71–70 thriller to California. Averaging 33.0 points and 12.5 rebounds per game, West was named MVP of the Final Four.

1962
At 6' 2½" West was small for an NBA guard, even in the early '60s. But after a year in the league he had adjusted enough to become a superstar. He helped the Lakers to the NBA Finals, where his last-second steal and layup gave Game 3 to L.A. Boston rallied, though, and won the decisive seventh game in overtime.

1969
The addition of Wilt Chamberlian made the Lakers, who already boasted West (above, 25.9 PPG) and Elgin Baylor (24.8 PPG), seem unbeatable. Yet they still could not defeat the aging Celtics in the NBA Finals, falling 108–106 in Game 7.

1972
The Los Angeles juggernaut everyone had expected since '69 finally emerged as West (44), Chamberlain and the Lakers put it all together, winning a record 69 games, including 33 in a row, and dispatching Walt Frazier (10) and the Knicks in five games in the NBA Finals. At 33, West averaged 25.8 points per game.

NAISMITH MEMORIAL BASKETBALL HALL OF FAME

CEO: Don E.N. Gibson
Director of Public Relations: Kim Lee

1150 West Columbus Avenue
Springfield, MA 01105
Telephone: (413) 781-6500
www.hoophall.com

ENSHRINEES (PLAYERS ONLY)

NAME (YR. OF INDUCTION)	D.O.B. D.O.D.	POS.	CAREER SPAN
Kareem Abdul-Jabbar (1995)	b. 4-16-47	C	1969–89
Nate (Tiny) Archibald (1991)	b. 9-2-48	G	1970–84
Paul J. Arizin (1977)	b. 4-9-28	F	1950–62
Thomas B. Barlow (1980)	b. 7-9-1896 d. 9-26-83	F	1912–32
Rick Barry (1987)	b. 3-28-44	F	1965–80
Elgin Baylor (1976)	b. 9-16-34	F	1958–72
John Beckman (1972)	b. 10-22-1895 d. 6-22-68	G	1913–30
Walt Bellamy (1993)	b. 7-24-39	C	1961–75
Sergei Belov (1992)	b. 1-23-44	G	1964–80
Dave Bing (1990)	b. 11-24-43	G	1966–78
Larry Bird (1998)	b. 12-7-56	F	1979–92
Carol Blazejowski (1994)	b. 9-29-56	G	1974–81
Bennie Borgmann (1961)	b. 11-22-00 d. 11-11-78	G	1919–40
Bill Bradley (1982)	b. 7-28-43	F	1967–77
Joseph Brennan (1974)	b. 11-15-00 d. 5-10-89	G	1920–36
Al Cervi (1984)	b. 2-12-17	G	1937–53
Wilt Chamberlain (1978)	b. 8-21-36 d. 10-12-99	C	1959–73
Charles (Tarzan) Cooper (1976)	b. 8-30-07 d. 12-19-80	C	1924–44
Kresimir Cosic (1996)	b. 11-26-48 d. 5-25-95	C	1964–83
Bob Cousy (1970)	b. 8-9-28	G	1950–70
Dave Cowens (1991)	b. 10-25-48	C	1970–83
Joan Crawford (1997)	b. 8-22-37	F	1953–69
Billy Cunningham (1986)	b. 6-3-43	F	1965–76
Denise Curry (1997)	b. 8-22-59	F	1977–85
Bob Davies (1969)	b. 1-15-20 d. 4-22-90	G	1945–55
Forrest S. DeBernardi (1961)	b. 2-3-1899 d. 4-29-70	C	1918–31
Dave DeBusschere (1982)	b. 10-16-40	F	1962–74
H.G. (Dutch) Dehnert (1968)	b. 4-5-1898 d. 4-20-79	C	1917–35
Anne Donovan (1995)	b. 11-1-61	C	1979–89
Paul Endacott (1971)	b. 7-3-02 d. 1-8-77	F	1919–28
Alex English (1997)	b. 1-5-54	F	1976–91
Julius Erving (1993)	b. 2-22-50	F	1971–87
Harold (Bud) Foster (1964)	b. 5-30-06 d. 7-16-96	F	1924–30
Walter (Clyde) Frazier (1987)	b. 3-29-45	G	1967–80
Max (Marty) Friedman (1971)	b. 7-12-1889 d. 1-1-86	G	1906–27
Joe Fulks (1977)	b. 10-26-21 d. 3-21-76	F	1946–54
Lauren (Laddie) Gale (1976)	b. 4-22-17 d. 7-29-96	F	1935–40
Harry (the Horse) Gallatin (1991)	b. 4-26-27	C	1948–58
William Gates (1989)	b. 8-30-17 d. 12-1-99	F	1938–55
George Gervin (1996)	b. 4-27-52	F	1972–86
Tom Gola (1975)	b. 1-13-33	F	1955–66
Gail Goodrich (1996)	b. 4-23-43	G	1965–79
Hal Greer (1981)	b. 6-26-36	G	1958–73
Robert (Ace) Gruenig (1963)	b. 3-12-13 d. 8-11-58	C	1933–48
Clifford O. Hagan (1977)	b. 12-9-31	F	1956–70
Victor Hanson (1960)	b. 7-30-03 d. 4-10-82	G	1923–30
John Havlicek (1983)	b. 4-8-40	F/G	1962–78
Connie Hawkins (1992)	b. 7-17-42	F	1967–76
Elvin Hayes (1990)	b. 11-17-45	F/C	1968–84
Marques Haynes (1998)	b. 10-3-26	G	1946–83
Tom Heinsohn (1986)	b. 8-26-34	F	1956–65
Nat Holman (1964)	b. 10-19-1896 d. 2-12-95	G	1916–30

NAME (YR. OF INDUCTION)	D.O.B. D.O.D.	POS.	CAREER SPAN
Robert J. Houbregs (1987)	b. 3-12-32	C	1953–58
Bailey Howell (1997)	b. 1-20-37	F	1959–71
Chuck Hyatt (1959)	b. 2-28-08 d. 5-8-78	G	1926–44
Dan Issel (1993)	b. 10-25-48	C	1970–85
Harry (Buddy) Jeannette (1994)	b. 9-15-17	G	1938–50
William (Skinny) Johnson (1976)	b. 8-16-11 d. 2-5-80	C	1929–36
D. Neil Johnston (1990)	b. 2-4-29 d. 9-28-78	F	1951–59
K.C. Jones (1989)	b. 5-25-32	G	1958–67
Sam Jones (1983)	b. 6-24-33	G	1957–69
Edward (Moose) Krause (1975)	b. 2-2-13 d. n/a	C	1930–34
Bob Kurland (1961)	b. 12-23-24	C	1942–52
Bob Lanier (1992)	b. 9-10-48	C	1970–84
Joe Lapchick (1966)	b. 4-12-00	C	1921–37
Nancy Lieberman-Cline (1996)	b. 7-1-58	G	1976–98
Clyde Lovellette (1988)	b. 9-7-29	C/F	1953–64
Jerry Lucas (1979)	b. 3-30-40	F	1963–74
Angelo (Hank) Luisetti (1959)	b. 6-16-16	F	1934–44
C. Edward Macauley (1960)	b. 3-22-28	C	1949–59
Peter P. Maravich (1987)	b. 6-22-47 d. 1-5-88	G	1970–80
Slater Martin (1981)	b. 10-22-25	G	1949–60
Bob McAdoo (2000)	b. 9-15-51	F	1972–86
Branch McCracken (1960)	b. 6-9-08 d. 6-4-70	F/C/G	1926–36
Jack McCracken (1962)	b. 6-15-11 d. 1-5-58	F	1929–46
Bobby McDermott (1988)	b. 1-7-14 d. 10-3-63	G	1935–50
Dick McGuire (1993)	b. 1-25-26	G	1949–60
Kevin McHale (1999)	b. 12-19-57	F	1980–93
Ann Meyers (1993)	b. 3-26-55	G	1970–80
George L. Mikan (1959)	b. 6-18-24	C	1946–56
Vern Mikkelsen (1995)	b. 10-21-28	F	1949–59
Cheryl Miller (1995)	b. 1-3-64	F	1982–86
Earl Monroe (1990)	b. 11-21-44	G	1967–80
Calvin Murphy (1993)	b. 5-9-48	G	1970–83
Charles (Stretch) Murphy (1960)	b. 4-10-07 d. 8-19-92	C	1926–33
H. O. (Pat) Page (1962)	b. 3-20-1887 d. 11-23-65	G	1906–10
Bob Pettit (1970)	b. 12-12-32	F	1954–65
Andy Phillip (1961)	b. 3-7-22	G	1947–58
Jim Pollard (1977)	b. 7-9-22 d. 1-22-93	F	1947–55
Frank Ramsey (1981)	b. 7-13-31	G	1954–64
Willis Reed (1981)	b. 6-25-42	C	1964–74
Arnie Risen (1998)	b. 10-9-24	C/F	1945–48
Oscar Robertson (1979)	b. 11-24-38	G	1960–74
John S. Roosma (1961)	b. 9-3-00 d. 11-13-83	F	1921–26
Bill Russell (1974)	b. 2-12-34	C	1956–69
John (Honey) Russell (1964)	b. 5-31-02 d. 11-15-73	F	1919–45
Adolph Schayes (1972)	b. 5-19-28	F	1948–64
Ernest J. Schmidt (1973)	b. 2-12-11 d. 9-6-86	C	1929–36
John J. Schommer (1959)	b. 1-29-1884 d. 1-11-60	F	1906–09
Barney Sedran (1962)	b. 1-28-1891 d. 1-14-64	G	1909–38
Uljana Semjonova (1993)	b. 3-9-52	C	1967–89
Bill Sharman (1975)	b. 5-25-26	G	1950–61
Christian Steinmetz (1961)	b. 6-29-1887 d. 6-11-63	G	1902–05
Lusia Harris Stewart (1992)	b. 2-10-55	C	1973–77
Isiah Thomas (2000)	b. 4-30-61	G	1981–94
David Thompson (1996)	b. 7-13-54	G	1975–84
John A. (Cat) Thompson (1962)	n/a		
Nate Thurmond (1984)	b. 6-25-41	C	1963–77
Jack Twyman (1982)	b. 5-11-34	F	1955–66
Wes Unseld (1988)	b. 3-14-46	C	1968–81
Robert (Fuzzy) Vandivier (1974)	b. 12-26-03 d. 7-30-83	F	1922–26
Edward A. Wachter (1961)	b. 6-30-1883 d. 3-12-66	C	1900–24
Bill Walton (1993)	b. 11-5-52	C	1974–87
Robert F. Wanzer (1987)	b. 6-4-21	G	1947–57
Jerry West (1979)	b. 5-28-38	G	1960–74
Nera White (1992)	b. 11-15-35	F	1954–69
Lenny Wilkens (1989)	b. 10-28-37	G	1960–75
John R. Wooden (1960)	b. 10-14-10	G	1928–39
George (Bird) Yardley (1996)	b. 11-3-28	F	1953–60

HOCKEY

HOCKEY

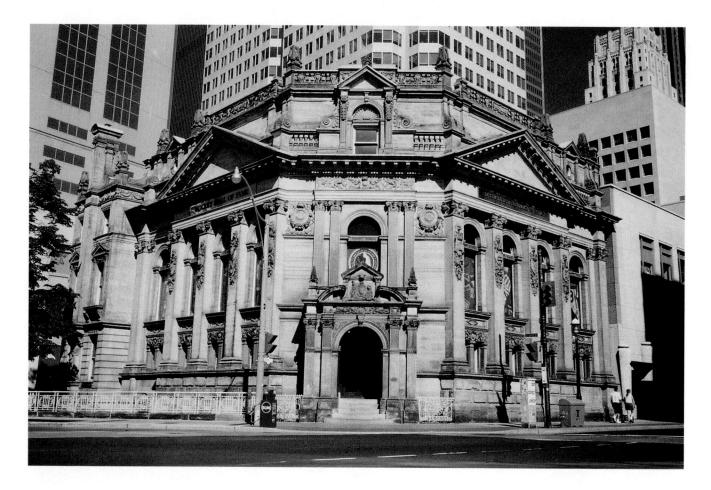

Americans love their homegrown sports with a passion that can't be denied. But Canadians, in their devotion to hockey, which seems to have been played first in Nova Scotia around 1800, leave Americans far behind. North of the border, hockey is first love and last, a reverent mania that binds all of Canada into one large puck-mad family.

That's why the curators at the Hockey Hall of Fame devote space to what they call the "Household Family Zone," the centerpiece of which is a replica of a 1950s living room. There, a wax-figure family has gathered to watch *Hockey Night in Canada,* with actual games from the '50s flickering across the ancient console. Elsewhere in the Household Zone are an "Attic Scene," which contains hockey cards and lunchboxes featuring players' faces, and a "Six A.M. Scene" that shows a family readying for an early-morning practice. Indeed, an air of family innocence pervades the entire Hall.

More than 100 years old, the Bank of Montreal building in downtown Toronto (above) became the home of the Hockey Hall of Fame in 1993. The historic building was significantly renovated for its new role as the repository for memories of Canada's national game.

Unlike the Halls for baseball, basketball and football, which are set in relatively small cities or, in the case of baseball, a bucolic town, the Hockey Hall of Fame sits in the heart of cosmopolitan downtown Toronto, at the corner of Yonge and Front streets. The Great Hall honoring members occupies part of the beautifully restored Bank of Montreal building, over a century old, while the rest of the Hockey Hall of Fame is in the modern concourse at BCE Place.

The Hall got its start in 1943, when a group of hockey supporters, led by the legendary Captain J.T. Sutherland, agreed on the need for such a tribute to the national game. The first class was elected in 1945, long before there was a building to house them. That came 16 years later, thanks largely to the work of Conn Smythe, owner of the Toronto Maple Leafs and chairman of the NHL owners' committee, who personally supervised construction on the grounds of the Canadian National

Exhibition (CNE). The Hockey Hall of Fame opened its doors on August 26, 1961, and remained on the CNE grounds for 32 years before moving to its current site. With the opening of the new Hall in 1993, floor space jumped from 6,800 square feet to more than 50,000—a good thing, since 500,000 fans visited in its first year.

Like its basketball and golf counterparts, the Hockey Hall of Fame emphasizes participation. In the Impact Zone, visitors can suit up and try to stop a foam puck traveling at full, NHL slap shot speed. Aspiring broadcasters can tape their own account of filmed action. And there's a slap shot exhibit, which permits visitors to shoot on a computerized goaltender.

Members of the Hall fall into three categories: players, of whom there are 218; builders, whose efforts have promoted the game (there are 87 of them enshrined); and referees and linesmen (14). The team with the most players in the Hall is—surprise—the Montreal Canadiens, with 45. The great Soviet goalie Vladislav Tretiak, inducted in 1989, was the first Russian. Players usually must wait three years to be eligible for the Hall, though that requirement has been waived in the case of 10 players, including, most recently, Gretzky and Mario Lemieux, whose return to the ice in December 2000 made him unique in any Hall—an active member.

Gretzky gets an area all to himself in Toronto—as well he should—much as Ruth does in Cooperstown. Among the items celebrating the Great One are the net into which he sent his record-setting 802nd goal, and the jersey, stick and puck from his NHL-record 1,851st point. And this exhibit honors not only his great feats, but also his two little feet—in the form of his first pair of skates, which he wore at age two, and bronze castings of his feet when he was an infant.

Twenty-two stars, including Gordie Howe, Bobby Orr and Maurice (Rocket) Richard, are featured in the Leg-

Roy (above), who has won more games than any other NHL goaltender, and Messier (below), who won five Stanley Cups with Edmonton and one with New York, are certain first-ballot Hall of Famers. When it's not making the rounds with the most recent NHL champion, the Stanley Cup (below) resides at the Hockey Hall of Fame.

ends of Hockey Showcase. There is a life-sized replica of the Canadiens' dressing room from the '60s. Elsewhere are exhibits of women's hockey, arenas and the evolution of equipment, part of which resembles the closet of some slasher-film villain: a collection of goalie masks.

Not all the items are so easily accomodated. Before the Boston Garden closed, officials donated the building's 1954 Zamboni ice resurfacing machine to the Hall. Getting it through the door would have required removing several pieces of the Zamboni, a sacrilege that worried Hall official Dan Hamill. "The last thing I wanted to do was screw around with the artifact," said Hill. "They asked me what to do, and I said I'd rather screw around with the building." He removed the doors to the building and in went the Zamboni.

Getting into the Hockey Hall of Fame will be a lot easier for several stars who aren't included in the following pages. Mark Messier, for example, is not profiled in this volume because he's still active and so not yet in the Hall. But there will be little suspense attending that vote, when the time comes. The same goes for goalie Patrick Roy, the alltime NHL leader in career victories.

Celebratory and family-oriented though it is, the Hockey Hall of Fame has not been without controversy. In 1993 it emerged that Gil Stein, then the league president, had rigged his election to the Hall in several ways; he resigned his enshrinement as the investigation was going forward. And in 1998, 18 members of the Hall, including Orr and Howe, threatened to resign if former players association head Alan Eagleson, who had been convicted of fraud, remained a member. Eagleson resigned.

But the disputes of the past are forgotten the moment one gets a glimpse of the Stanley Cup, which resides in the Great Hall when it's not making its annual trip among the faithful. The fabled old trophy is sure to raise goosebumps.

JEAN BELIVEAU

How often has a team purchased an entire league in order to obtain rights to one player? Well, it's happened at least once, in 1950, when the Montreal Canadiens were stirring things up around the city by threatening to snatch Jean Beliveau away from the Quebec Senior League, where the 17-year-old was earning $20,000 a year. So heated did things become that the Quebec legislature threatened to repeal the Montreal Forum's liquor license if the Canadiens went ahead with their pilfering plan. In the end, Montreal purchased the entire league just to get Beliveau.

What a deal! Known affectionately to his fans as "Le Gros Bill," or Big Bill, Beliveau played 19 seasons for the Canadiens. He led the league in scoring twice and won two Hart Trophies as the league's MVP. By the time he retired, in 1971, he had scored 507 regular-season goals, the most ever for a center at the time. More importantly, Les Canadiens had won 10 Stanley Cups, including that historic stretch of five in a row from 1956 through '60.

A brilliant skater who would just as soon set up a teammate as score himself, Beliveau led more by princely example than by shouting or other intimidation. "It was his quiet dignity," said teammate Dick Duff. "He was so unassuming for a guy of his stature. . . . He was a very unselfish player. He had great moves—that great range—and anybody playing on a line with him was certain to wind up with a lot of goals. If you got there, the puck would be there."

At 6' 3", 205 pounds, Le Gros Bill was indeed big. Hitting him, according to one who lived to tell of it, Bill Ezinicki, "was like running into an oak tree. I bounced right off the guy and landed on the seat of my pants." But Beliveau was not by nature a violent man, and it took years to persuade him that it was in his—and the team's—best interest for him to rough it up occasionally.

He was a hero to all of hockey and all of Canada, but especially to the French-Canadians. "The best thing about Beliveau is that he is in fact a paragon," wrote SPORTS ILLUSTRATED's Gary Ronberg. "Gentlemanly on the ice and off it, a miracle of modesty, a dutiful husband and a man whose loyalty to his team and its owners is unshakable, he has all the old-fashioned virtues."

THE RECORD

YEAR	TEAM	GP	G	A	PTS
1950–51	Mtl	2	1	1	2
1952–53	Mtl	3	5	0	5
1953–54	Mtl	44	13	21	34
1954–55	Mtl	70	37	36	73
1955–56	Mtl	70	47	41	88
1956–57	Mtl	69	33	51	84
1957–58	Mtl	55	27	32	59
1958–59	Mtl	64	45	46	91
1959–60	Mtl	60	34	40	74
1960–61	Mtl	69	32	58	90
1961–62	Mtl	43	18	23	41
1962–63	Mtl	69	18	49	67
1963–64	Mtl	68	28	50	78
1964–65	Mtl	58	20	23	43
1965–66	Mtl	67	29	48	77
1966–67	Mtl	53	12	26	38
1967–68	Mtl	59	31	37	68
1968–69	Mtl	69	33	49	82
1969–70	Mtl	63	19	30	49
1970–71	Mtl	70	25	51	76
TOTAL		1,125	507	712	1,219

TIMELINE

1952
The Canadiens' attempt to acquire Beliveau (below) from the Quebec Aces, for whom he scored 45 goals in '52, was nearly a source of civil unrest in Montreal.

1955
Montreal boasted the NHL's top three scorers in Boom Boom Geoffrion, Maurice Richard and Beliveau, who scored 37 goals in his first full season. But with Richard suspended for the playoffs, Les Habs lost the Cup to Detroit in seven games.

1956
Beliveau (above) paraded in Montreal with his teammates following the Canadiens' five-game triumph over Detroit in the Stanley Cup finals. Once again a first-team All-Star, Beliveau topped the NHL in scoring with 47 goals and 88 points. The Canadiens had begun their drive for five straight NHL titles, a feat unprecedented and unequaled since.

1960
Never pushed to the maximum seven games during their five-year reign of Stanley Cups, the Canadiens made quickest work of No. 5, first dispatching Chicago in four games, and then sweeping Toronto out of the way in the finals.

1968
The first year of expansion, which doubled the Original Six to 12, did nothing to faze the Canadiens, who won another Cup. Beliveau (above, after his third hat trick of the playoffs) scored 31 goals, and his 68 points placed him 11th in the NHL scoring race, which was blown wide open by the dilution of talent produced by expansion.

1978

A 17-year-old center for the Sault Ste. Marie Greyhounds of the Junior A Ontario Hockey Association, Gretzky (left) showed unmistakable signs of the brilliance to come in his pro career, scoring 70 goals and passing off for 112 assists in 64 games. He would jump to the World Hockey Association the following year.

1982

Gretzky (near right) met with Phil Esposito (far right) after breaking Esposito's single-season record of 76 goals. The Great One scored his 50th goal that season in his 39th game, shattering the old record of 50 in 50 held by Maurice Richard and Mike Bossy. Gretzky would finish with 92 goals.

1984

Gretzky and the Oilers dethroned the four-time defending Stanley Cup champion New York Islanders, knocking off Billy Smith and Co. in five games. Gretzky, who led playoff scorers with 35 points, would later rank his first Cup triumph as the greatest thrill of his incomparable career.

1988

NHL champions in 1984, '85 and '87, Gretzky and Edmonton hoisted the Stanley Cup a fourth time after dispatching the Boston Bruins in four games. Gretzky (below, with trophy) set a record with 31 assists in the postseason and won his second Conn Smythe Trophy as playoff MVP.

THE RECORD

YEAR	TEAM	GP	G	A	PTS
1979–80	Edm	79	51	86	137
1980–81	Edm	80	55	109	164
1981–82	Edm	80	92	120	212
1982–83	Edm	80	71	125	196
1983–84	Edm	74	87	118	205
1984–85	Edm	80	73	135	208
1985–86	Edm	80	52	163	215
1986–87	Edm	79	62	121	183
1987–88	Edm	64	40	109	149
1988–89	LA	78	54	114	168
1989–90	LA	73	40	102	142
1990–91	LA	78	41	122	163
1991–92	LA	74	31	90	121
1992–93	LA	45	16	49	65
1993–94	LA	81	38	92	130
1994–95	LA	48	11	37	48
1995–96	LA-StL	80	23	79	102
1996–97	NYR	82	25	72	97
1997–98	NYR	82	23	67	90
1998–99	NYR	70	9	53	62
TOTAL		**1,487**	**894**	**1,963**	**2,857**

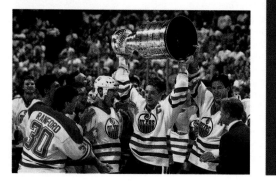

Gaudy statistics can cut both ways. How many scoring champs have been viewed more with skepticism than awe for racking up huge numbers for teams that couldn't win the big one? (Exhibit A: Wilt Chamberlain for much of his career). Wayne Gretzky may have been headed down this road at the start of his NHL career, when his goal-scoring was off the charts, but he led his Edmonton Oilers to the Stanley Cup title in his fifth season, and again in his sixth, to squelch all such skepticism. And his numbers kept getting gaudier and gaudier. Indeed, Gretzky's statistics are so enormous that, as Bill Russell said about Chamberlain's, they lose their impact.

When he retired in 1999, Gretzky held 61 NHL records, including career and season marks for scoring, goals and assists. And his margins over the runners-up are simply astounding, mind-boggling leaps forward like Babe Ruth's initial home run records were. Gretzky had 2,857 career points, more than 1,000 ahead of the second man on the list, his boyhood idol, Gordie Howe. Indeed, if you took away all of Gretzky's 894 goals and left him only his 1,963 assists, he would still top the alltime points leaders list—by 113 points.

How did he do it? Certainly, there was nothing special about Gretzky's size or strength. At 6', 185 pounds, he was lean, almost rangy, without much obvious muscle. In the Edmonton Oilers' strength tests, he invariably finished near the bottom. What he possessed were vision and imagination, which contributed to his preternatural passing skills. Tossed into the chaotic, rapidly-shifting tableau of a hockey game, somehow he always knew just how the play would develop—a gift of spatial premonition, if you will.

Growing up in Brantford, Ont., Gretzky played on a team of 10-year-olds when he was five. He was nine when people began calling him "the Great One," an accolade Gretzky immediately lived up to, scoring 378 goals in 85 games at age 10, a feat which attracted national attention in Canada. In Gretzky's first pro season, with the Indianapolis Racers and the Edmonton Oilers, both of the WHA, he exploded for 46 goals and an eye-catching 110 points. But those are WHA points, cried the skeptics. When Edmonton joined the NHL the following season, Gretzky said, "I heard a lot of talk that I'd never get 110 points like I did in the WHA." And he didn't get 110 points in the NHL—he racked up 137, on 51 goals and a league-leading 86 assists. From there, the glory years of the '80s unspooled like one endless highlight reel: He led the league in assists every season from 1980 to '92 and in points all but three of those years. He won nine Hart Trophies as the league's MVP. He led the Oilers to four Stanley Cups. In 1981–82 he scored 92 goals. In '85–86 he had 163 assists in 80 games. He took the Los Angeles Kings to the 1993 Stanley Cup by scoring a hat trick in the last game of the conference finals, including the series-winner with 3:14 remaining.

Always, he was modest and a true gentleman. As he bore down on Howe's career scoring mark of 801 goals, Gretzky said, "I wish I could stop at 800." He hated to break his idol's record, but he didn't stop. Not until 894.

1945

Howe (right) played an exhibition season with the Galt Red Wings of the Ontario Hockey Association (Junior A) before joining the big-league club in 1946. In his second year in Detroit, he and the Wings reached the Stanley Cup finals but lost to Toronto in four games. Two seasons later Howe and the Wings broke through to their first Stanley Cup title, edging the Rangers in seven games.

1963

Howe (left) posed with NHL President Clarence Campbell and the two awards Howe won after the 1962–63 season—the Hart Memorial as the league's most valuable player and the Art Ross Trophy as the NHL's top scorer. Howe, who scored 38 goals and had 48 assists, led Detroit to the Stanley Cup finals, but the Wings couldn't get past the Maple Leafs, who won in five games.

1963

Howe (right) flashed his hockey-made gaptoothed smile on November 10 after breaking Maurice Richard's career record of 544 goals, scoring No. 545 against Montreal. The 35-year-old Howe would finish the 1963–64 season

with 26 goals and 73 points in 69 games that season and help the Red Wings reach the Stanley Cup finals, where they lost to their archrival, Toronto, in seven games.

1969

The ageless Howe, who would turn 41 on March 31, produced the highest-scoring season of his endless career, firing home 44 goals and making 59 assists to finish third in the league scoring race. The Red Wings, unfortunately, finished second to last in the NHL's East Division, with a record of 33-31-12.

1980

Returning to the NHL with the Hartford Whalers after six productive seasons in the WHA (he scored more than 30 goals in four of them), Howe, who was 51 years old, proved that his comeback was no novelty act by scoring 15 goals and 41 points in 80 games. The Whalers scrapped their way into the playoffs, but Howe's greatest delight may have been passing the torch to 19-year-old league MVP Wayne Gretzky, whom Howe had met when Gretzky was 11.

GORDIE HOWE

There was something biblical about Gordie Howe's longevity. For 25 seasons he was the stubborn, unyielding backbone of the Detroit Red Wings, making the NHL All-Star team a record 21 times and winning the league's MVP award and scoring title six times each. He played through three generations of NHL players, squaring off against Maurice Richard, Bobby Orr and, eventually, Wayne Gretzky, when Howe returned, at age 52, for a final season with the Hartford Whalers. All this despite suffering a severe head injury in the 1950 Stanley Cup playoffs, which required brain surgery and left him with a permanent tic and a tactless nickname, Blinky, which he embraced with gruff humor.

Playing before sticks had curved blades, Howe was renowned for his powerful and accurate backhand. He was also the best defensive forward of his time and durable almost beyond belief: In his prime he averaged 40 minutes a game on the ice, twice the time other forwards played. From 1950 to '55 he led the Red Wings to four Stanley Cup championships. "There are two weak teams in this league and four strong ones," said the Maple Leafs' Dave Keon. "The weak ones are Boston and New York, and the strong ones are Toronto, Montreal, Chicago and Gordie Howe!"

Howe sharpened his skills during the bitterly cold winters in Saskatoon, where his father, Albert, worked in a garage. The fourth of nine children, he fashioned shin pads out of old newspapers and used tennis balls for pucks. When he was 15 Howe took the all-night train to Winnipeg, where the New York Rangers were holding their training camp. Miserably homesick, he returned to Saskatoon but was invited to try out the following year by the Red Wings. After a slow start he came into his own in the 1950–51 season and topped the league in scoring with 86 points.

THE RECORD					
YEAR	TEAM	GP	G	A	PTS
1946–47	Det	58	7	15	22
1947–48	Det	60	16	28	44
1948–49	Det	40	12	25	37
1949–50	Det	70	35	33	68
1950–51	Det	70	43	43	86
1951–52	Det	70	47	39	86
1952–53	Det	70	49	46	95
1953–54	Det	70	33	48	81
1954–55	Det	64	29	33	62
1955–56	Det	70	38	41	79
1956–57	Det	70	44	45	89
1957–58	Det	64	33	44	77
1958–59	Det	70	32	46	78
1959–60	Det	70	28	45	73
1960–61	Det	64	23	49	72
1961–62	Det	70	33	44	77
1962–63	Det	70	38	48	86
1963–64	Det	69	26	47	73
1964–65	Det	70	29	47	76
1965–66	Det	70	29	46	75
1966–67	Det	69	25	40	65
1967–68	Det	74	39	43	82
1968–69	Det	76	44	59	103
1969–70	Det	76	31	40	71
1970–71	Det	63	23	29	52
1979–80	Har	80	15	26	41
TOTAL		1,767	801	1,049	1,850

Howe "retired" in 1971, but two years later he made a comeback, enticed by the prospect of playing alongside his sons, Marty and Mark, in the new World Hockey Association. A year later, at 45, Howe was the league MVP. When the NHL added four WHA teams in 1980, he returned to the NHL, playing his final All-Star game in 1980, at age 51. "He was everything you'd expect an ideal hockey player to be," said one rival. "He's soft-spoken and thoughtful. He's also the most vicious, cruel, and meanest man I've ever met in a hockey game."

BOBBY HULL

Writers hardly knew where to start when singing the praises of the Golden Jet, Bobby Hull. Not only was he the fastest skater in the NHL, he was also ruggedly handsome, with wavy blond hair and a physique that made him look like Hercules on skates. In the words of one Chicago society columnist, Hull was like "a statue come alive from the Golden Age of Greece, incredibly handsome even without his front teeth." In addition to the glorious figure he cut on the ice, Hull possessed a world-class slapshot. Clocked at 120 miles per hour, it was easily the hardest in the business. Marveled one goalkeeper who had the misfortune to stop one of his pucks, "It felt like I had been seared by a branding iron. His shot paralyzed my arm for five minutes. It's unbelievable."

Hull developed that shot in tiny Point Anne, on the north shore of Lake Ontario, where his father worked as foreman in a cement factory to provide for his 11 children. Bobby was only 11 years old when the Chicago Blackhawks scouted him and made him an offer, proposing they pay for him to attend boarding school while he worked on his skills. He entered the NHL in 1957, but at first was hardly the superstar the Blackhawks had been expecting, scoring a respectable but not spectacular 13 goals. But in the 1959 Stanley Cup playoffs Hull was moved from center to left wing. "I felt right at home because I didn't have to do so much checking," he said. "I had something left when I went to the goal."

The next season Hull led the league with 39 goals. In the 1961–62 season, he tied the record of 50 goals shared by Rocket Richard and Bernie Geoffrion, then twice increased the mark later in his career. In his 15 NHL seasons, Hull averaged 40 goals a season and led the league in goals seven times. He won back-to-back MVP awards in 1965 and '66.

Hull was always his own man, aware of his worth and not afraid to fight to get it. In 1971, when the new World Hockey Association was formed, the two leagues began a bidding war for Hull's services. Signing with the Winnipeg Jets for a $1-million signing bonus and a $1-million, four-year contract, Hull gave the upstart league instant credibility. Then he won the new league's MVP award in his first and third seasons with the Jets— just like old times.

THE RECORD					
YEAR	TEAM	GP	G	A	PTS
1957–58	Chi	70	13	34	47
1958–59	Chi	70	18	32	50
1959–60	Chi	70	39	42	81
1960–61	Chi	67	31	25	56
1961–62	Chi	70	50	34	84
1962–63	Chi	65	31	31	62
1963–64	Chi	70	43	44	87
1964–65	Chi	61	39	32	71
1965–66	Chi	65	54	43	97
1966–67	Chi	66	52	28	80
1967–68	Chi	71	44	31	75
1968–69	Chi	74	58	49	107
1969–70	Chi	61	38	29	67
1970–71	Chi	78	44	52	96
1971–72	Chi	78	50	43	93
1979–80	Winn	18	4	6	10
	Har	9	2	5	7
TOTAL		1,063	610	560	1,170

TIMELINE

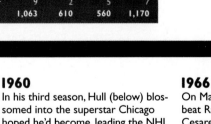

1957
The fresh-faced, 18-year-old Hull (above) was the youngest player in the NHL when he joined the Blackhawks in October. He started slowly but gradually transformed Chicago, which had been losing games, fans and money, into the most profitable franchise in the league.

1959
With Hull contributing 50 points in 70 games, the Blackhawks improved their record by 14 points over the previous season and made the playoffs for the first time since 1953. They lost to eventual champ Montreal in the first round.

1960
In his third season, Hull (below) blossomed into the superstar Chicago hoped he'd become, leading the NHL in scoring. Still, the Blackhawks' record (28-29-13) was identical to the previous year's, and they were swept by Montreal in the playoffs.

1966
On March 12, Hull beat Ranger goalie Cesare Maniago for his 51st goal of the year, breaking the record he shared with Maurice Richard and Bernie Geoffrion. He would score 54 by season's end. His 43 assists gave him 97 points, also a record.

1972
Hull (above, with wife Joanne) received a $1-million bonus for signing with the Winnipeg Jets of the upstart World Hockey Association on July 27. He would have the best season of his career with the Jets in 1974–75, when he scored a record 77 goals in 78 games and finished the season with 142 points. Hull returned to the NHL with the Jets in 1979.

1984

Playing for Laval Titan of the Quebec Major Junior Hockey League, 18-year-old Lemieux (right) generated offensive numbers that obliterated even those of the Great One, Wayne Gretzky. In 70 games, Lemieux produced an astonishing 133 goals and 149 assists, for 282 points, or an average of 4.03 points per game. Needless to say, all four totals were—and remain—records.

1989

Lemieux led the league in points for the second year in a row, and the Penguins swept the Rangers for their first playoff series victory since 1979—but were bounced out in the second round by Philadelphia.

1991

Sitting out most of the regular season to recover

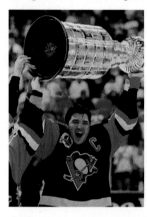

from surgery to repair a herniated disc, Lemieux (left) joined the Penguins for the final 26 games and the playoffs, in which he peaked, with 16 goals and 44 points, the second-highest postseason total in NHL history. He was named playoff MVP as the Penguins won their first Stanley Cup the hard way, losing at least the first game of every series. They rallied to defeat Minnesota in six games in the finals.

1996

Back after a one-year hiatus from hockey, Lemieux

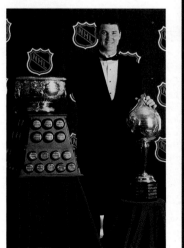

(right) posed with the Hart Trophy and the Ross Trophy, which he won as the NHL's most valuable player and leading scorer, respectively. He led the Penguins (49-29-4) to the Northeast division title and the conference finals, where they lost to the Florida Panthers.

Comebacks have a way of dealing nasty doses of reality to players and fans alike. The sports world races along far too fast to accomodate old legs and slowed reflexes. To the retired athlete on the outside looking in, this pace may look slower than it is, provoking the kind of fanciful thoughts that lead to ill-advised unretirements—think Muhammad Ali versus Larry Holmes in 1980, or Mark Spitz versus the clock or, quite literally, Father Time, in 1992.

But on December 27, 2000, when 35-year-old Mario Lemieux returned to the NHL after a hiatus of nearly four years, he made it look as if he had never been away. Playing side-by-side with Pittsburgh Penguins players whose checks he now signed as principal owner of the team, Lemieux was as dominant as ever. Only 33 seconds into the game, he set up a goal, and later he scored and added another assist. "My new nickname for Mario is Batman," said Penguins chief operating officer Tom Rooney. "A suit-wearing executive by day. At night he puts on his cape and plays." And that first game was no fluke: Lemieux finished the 2000–01 season with 76 points in 45 games.

Such heroics had been the norm for Lemieux before he retired following the 1996–97 season, citing chronic back problems and his disgust with a game marred by obstructions and slashing. He led the Penguins to Stanley Cup titles in 1991 and '92, winning back-to-back Conn Smythe Trophies as playoff MVP. In 1992–93, Lemieux won the scoring title despite sitting out a month to receive radiation therapy for Hodgkin's disease, a form of cancer. Drained by back problems and the ordeal of battling cancer, he sat out the 1994–95 season, but when he returned in '95–96 he zoomed right back to the top of the scoring leaders' list. Following his retirement in '97 the Hockey Hall of Fame waived its usual three-year waiting period, and Super Mario skated right in. Now he's back in the game and says he wants to play until 2005. There is no reason to doubt he can do it.

Lemieux's career has schooled us on the pitfalls of assigning absolute superlatives to athletes. For no sooner had people decided that Wayne Gretzky was the greatest hockey player there ever could be than along came young

THE RECORD					
YEAR	TEAM	GP	G	A	PTS
1984–85	Pitt	73	43	57	100
1985–86	Pitt	79	48	93	141
1986–87	Pitt	63	54	53	107
1987–88	Pitt	77	70	98	168
1988–89	Pitt	76	85	114	199
1989–90	Pitt	59	45	78	123
1990–91	Pitt	26	19	26	45
1991–92	Pitt	64	44	87	131
1992–93	Pitt	60	69	91	160
1993–94	Pitt	22	17	20	37
1995–96	Pitt	70	69	92	161
1996–97	Pitt	76	50	72	122
2000–01	Pitt	43	35	41	76
†TOTAL		788	648	922	1570

† Still active

Lemieux, racking up Gretzky-esque numbers: 85 goals in 1988–89, 2.67 points per game in his cancer-stricken 1992–93 season. Lemieux may end up short of Gretzky numbers, but his .822 goals- and 1.99 points-per-game averages (after the 2000–01 season) are the best ever.

And he has the chance to improve upon them, and to win another Stanley Cup, lying enticingly before him—and a Hall of Fame career behind him.

BOBBY ORR

Every sport has its pantheon of great players, men and women who score more, rebound more, get more hits than their peers. Far more rare are the players who, through some leap of the imagination, utterly transform the way their sport is played. We think of Don Hutson and the forward pass, Dick Fosbury and his high-jump flop, Babe Ruth and the home run. And of course we think of Bobby Orr who, from the moment he entered the National Hockey League in 1966 as a much-heralded 18-year-old from Parry Sound, Ont., reinvented the role of defenseman and, in so doing, made hockey a faster, more flexible game.

Before Orr came along, defensemen defended, forwards scored and each respected the other's territory and role. Orr rejected that orthodoxy. He thought nothing of rushing the puck from end to end, radically opening up the entire rink. "All Bobby did," said his teammate

Phil Esposito, "was change the face of hockey all by himself."

At 5' 11", 195 pounds, he was never the biggest man on the ice. But he was the fastest, most mobile skater—he possessed, as one rival put it, "eighteen speeds of fast." In his trademark spin move, Orr stopped and spun 360 degrees, like a figure in a table-hockey game, leaving pursuers unsure where he would go. He popularized using his feet to advance the puck and was absolutely fearless about blocking shots with his body, a trait that would contribute to his retirement after only 12 seasons, at age 30.

Orr was not just the first defense-

man to notch 100 assists in a single season, he was the first *player* to do it. He was also the first player to win the Hart Trophy as MVP three years in a row (1970–72). He led the league in scoring twice and remains the only defenseman to do so. With Orr reconfiguring the game, the Bruins, who had not made the playoffs in eight years, were suddenly a force, winning Stanley Cups in both 1970 and '72.

Despite his achievements, Orr was unfailingly modest off the ice and a consummate team player, popular with both his teammates and fans. No wonder a *Boston Globe* poll named Orr the city's alltime most popular athlete, over the likes of Ted Williams, Bob Cousy and Bill Russell. "Orr is so clearly the best in hockey," said Montreal Canadiens goalie Ken Dryden. "I don't know that there's ever been anybody that so completely dominated a team sport."

THE RECORD

YEAR	TEAM	GP	G	A	PTS
1966–67	Bos	61	13	28	41
1967–68	Bos	46	11	20	31
1968–69	Bos	67	21	43	64
1969–70	Bos	76	33	87	120
1970–71	Bos	78	37	102	139
1971–72	Bos	76	37	80	117
1972–73	Bos	63	29	72	101
1973–74	Bos	74	32	90	122
1974–75	Bos	80	46	89	135
1975–76	Bos	10	5	13	18
1976–77	Chi	20	4	19	23
1978–79	Chi	6	2	2	4
TOTAL		657	270	645	915

TIMELINE

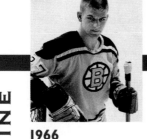

1966
After his first season, the 18-year-old Orr (above) won the Calder Trophy as rookie of the year. Bruins general manager Harry Sinden called the speedy defenseman "a star from the moment they played the national anthem in his first NHL game."

1969
With Orr in its rearguard, Boston made a steady ascent from division cellar: last in 1967, third in '68 and second in '69. Orr scored 64 points in 67 games, and the Bruins took eventual champ Montreal to OT three times before falling in the playoffs.

1970
Orr became the first player to win the Hart (MVP), Ross (scoring champ), Norris (top defenseman) and Conn Smythe (playoff MVP) trophies in one season— and ended the year with a goal (below) against St. Louis that gave the Bruins a 4–3 sudden-death overtime victory and their first Stanley Cup since 1941.

1971
The top four scorers in the NHL were Bruins, with Phil Esposito and Orr, who set a record for assists with 102, leading the way. But Montreal and goalie Ken Dryden stunned the Bruins in seven games in the first round of the playoffs.

1972
Esposito and Orr (above, left) finished 1–2 in the scoring race for the third straight year, and the Bruins ran away with the East Division, finishing 10 points ahead of the New York Rangers, whom they would defeat in six games in the Stanley Cup finals. Orr became the first man to win three straight Hart Trophies and was also named MVP of the playoffs.

1945

Scoring 15 goals in one nine-game stretch, Richard (right) terrorized NHL goalies for a record 50 goals in 50 games, leading the Canadiens to a 38-8-4 record and the regular-season title. But Montreal was upset in the first round of the playoffs by Toronto.

1953

Richard (below, facing camera) finished third in scoring with 28 goals and 33 assists. His teammate Bert Olmstead chipped in 17 goals and 28 assists, and Montreal, after two straight losing appearances in the Stanley Cup finals, downed Boston in five games for the title.

1956

With his brother, Henri, the Pocket Rocket, joining him in Montreal, Richard finished third in the NHL scoring race with 38 goals and 33 assists in 70 games, and Montreal (45-15-10) ran away with the regular-season title. The Rocket took off in the playoffs, helping the Canadiens dispatch the Rangers and the Red Wings, each in five games, to win their first Stanley Cup in 10 years.

1960

Capping his legendary 18-year career in style, the 38-year-old Richard (below, with NHL president Clarence Campbell and the Stanley Cup) scored 19 goals and made 16 assists to help the Canadiens (40-18-12) win the regular-season title by 13 points over Toronto. In the playoffs, Montreal and Richard steamrolled to a record fifth consecutive Stanley Cup title, in the minimum eight games, sweeping Chicago and then the Maple Leafs for the championship. After

the Cup, Richard ended an era in Montreal by announcing his retirement. He left the NHL after 978 games and 544 goals, a career record. The Canadiens' record of five straight NHL titles still stands.

MAURICE RICHARD

Other sportsmen have earned the nickname Rocket, including pitcher Roger Clemens and tennis great Rod Laver. But the first Rocket of real magnitude was Maurice Richard, Montreal's speedy right wing during the 1940s and '50s, when the Canadiens won eight Stanley Cups and metamorphosed into the greatest dynasty in hockey history. "There was nobody like him for putting the puck in," said fellow Hall of Famer Gordie Howe. "He was so accurate with his shot—and determined. You could see it in those crazy eyes. They'd open right up like sockets or camera lenses as he was going in on goal."

THE RECORD					
YEAR	TEAM	GP	G	A	PTS
1942–43	Mtl	16	5	6	11
1943–44	Mtl	46	32	22	54
1944–45	Mtl	50	50	23	73
1945–46	Mtl	50	27	21	48
1946–47	Mtl	60	45	26	71
1947–48	Mtl	53	28	25	53
1948–49	Mtl	59	20	18	38
1949–50	Mtl	70	43	22	65
1950–51	Mtl	65	42	24	66
1951–52	Mtl	58	27	17	44
1952–53	Mtl	70	28	33	61
1953–54	Mtl	70	37	30	67
1954–55	Mtl	67	38	36	74
1955–56	Mtl	70	38	33	71
1956–57	Mtl	63	33	29	62
1957–58	Mtl	28	15	19	34
1958–59	Mtl	42	17	21	38
1959–60	Mtl	51	19	16	35
TOTAL		978	544	421	965

A native of Montreal, Richard played 18 seasons, all with the Canadiens. He sparked Montreal's famous "Punch Line" that included Elmer Lach and Toe Blake; the three stars scored 82 of the Canadiens' NHL-record 234 goals during the 1943–44 season. In 1955 Richard's younger brother, Henri, joined the Canadiens and quickly became known as the Pocket Rocket. The Canadiens won five straight Stanley Cups with the brothers in their lineup. The Rocket became the first player to score 500 goals. When he retired in 1960, he held the NHL record, with 544.

He was a great favorite of the Montreal Forum fans. "Gooooooal by Mau-rice Ree-chaaard!" the announcer would intone, delighting the crowd, who celebrated by inundating the ice with programs, hats and galoshes. The 1944–45 season brought a veritable deluge, for that was the year Richard breached hockey's four-minute mile, scoring 50 goals in 50 games.

Classy and quiet as he was off the ice, Richard possessed a nasty temper. He was the catalyst for one of the game's darkest moments. Late in the 1954–55 season, against the Bruins in Boston, Richard viciously slashed Bruin defenseman Hal Laycoe, who had jabbed him in the eye. When an official intervened, Richard attacked him, too. Clarence Campbell, the NHL commissioner, suspended Richard for the rest of the season, including the playoffs. In French-speaking Montreal the strong suspicion was that Richard's penalty was particularly severe because of his ethnic background. When Campbell appeared at the Canadiens' Stanley Cup playoff game against the Red Wings, the Forum erupted in a riot, with 25 civilians and 12 policemen suffering injuries.

It was a dark moment in a wonderful career that ended in 1960, with a slashed Achilles tendon. Richard never lost his love of scoring. On the morning he announced his retirement, he netted four goals in a scrimmage. Some habits die hard.

Tragedy led Terry Sawchuk to goaltending, and tragedy dogged him throughout his long, troubled career. Sawchuk was 10 years old when he inherited goalie pads from his older brother, who had died of a heart ailment, and they would bring grief to a man whose nervous disposition seemed to make him thoroughly unsuited for the sport's most stressful position.

Though his career was interrupted by injury and depression, Sawchuk played more games than any goalie in NHL history. His 447 wins stood as the NHL career record until eclipsed by Patrick Roy in 2001, and his 103 shutouts remain a record. But Sawchuk believed his finest achievement was helping the underdog Toronto Maple Leafs to the Stanley Cup title over Montreal in '67.

Sawchuk entered the league in 1950 with the Detroit Red Wings and produced a goals-against average of 1.98, with 11 shutouts, and won

the Calder Trophy as rookie of the year. He was an All-Star in each of his first five seasons, and he help the Wings to titles in 1952, '54 and '55. During that first Stanley Cup run, Sawchuk was nearly perfect: In Detroit's eight straight wins, he had four shutouts and a goals-against average of 0.63, which is still a record.

Despite the three Vezina Trophies he'd won as the league's top goalie, Sawchuk was traded to Boston in 1955 when Detroit acquired another star goalie, Glen Hall. The Wings' decision unnerved Sawchuk, who missed part of his second year with the Bruins due to mononucleosis.

Playing most of his career before 1962, when the NHL began requiring face masks for goalies, Sawchuk's face came to resemble a Frankenstein mask of scars. His body got banged up too. Thanks to an early injury to his left shoulder, Sawchuk could not lift his stick arm above his shoulder and employed a deep crouch in goal.

"He didn't move so much as he exploded into a desperate release of energy," wrote Trent Frayne. "He sometimes seemed a human pinwheel. He played the whole game in pent-up tension, shouting at his teammates, crouching, straightening, diving, scrambling, his pale face drawn and tense." When he died in 1970 following a scuffle at his house with Rangers teammate Ron Stewart, he was a physical and mental wreck.

THE RECORD

YEAR	TEAM	GP	W	L	T	GAA
1949–50	Det	7	4	3	0	2.29
1950–51	Det	70	44	13	13	1.99
1951–52	Det	70	44	14	12	1.90
1952–53	Det	63	32	15	16	1.90
1953–54	Det	67	35	19	13	1.93
1954–55	Det	68	40	17	11	1.94
1955–56	Bos	68	22	33	13	2.66
1956–57	Bos	34	18	10	6	2.38
1957–58	Det	70	29	29	12	2.96
1958–59	Det	67	23	36	8	3.12
1959–60	Det	58	24	20	14	2.69
1960–61	Det	37	12	16	8	3.17
1961–62	Det	43	14	21	8	3.33
1962–63	Det	48	22	16	7	2.57
1963–64	Det	53	25	20	7	2.64
1964–65	Tor	36	17	13	6	2.56
1965–66	Tor	27	10	11	3	3.16
1966–67	Tor	28	15	5	4	2.81
1967–68	LA	36	11	14	6	3.07
1968–69	Det	13	3	4	3	2.62
1969–70	NYR	8	3	1	2	2.91
TOTAL		**971**	**447**	**330**	**172**	**2.52**

TIMELINE

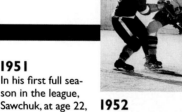

1947
The 17-year-old Sawchuk (above, front and center) played for the Galt Red Wings of the Junior A Ontario Hockey League, appearing in 30 games with a 3.13 goals-against average and four shutouts. Three seasons later he saw his first NHL action, appearing in seven games for Detroit.

1951
In his first full season in the league, Sawchuk, at age 22, topped NHL goaltenders in games, victories, minutes and shutouts (11) and helped Detroit (44-13-13) top the regular-season standings. Montreal upset the Wings in the first round of the playoffs.

1952
Sawchuk (above, in goal) produced 12 shutouts and again led the NHL in all major goaltending statistics. And this time the Wings of Gordie Howe, Ted Lindsay and Red Kelly were not to be denied, sweeping to the Stanley Cup with eight consecutive playoff victories. Sawchuk blanked Montreal twice in the finals, giving him four shutouts in the playoffs and a gold-plated goals-against average of 0.63.

1965
Sawchuk and his Toronto backup Johnny Bower won the Vezina Trophy as the top goalies in the NHL. Sawchuk's fourth Vezina, it came 10 years after his third. But the Leafs' run of three straight Cups came to an end in a brutal semifinal loss to Montreal.

1967
On March 4 Sawchuk (below, in goal) shut out the Chicago Blackhawks for the 100th blanking of his career. He would retire with 103, still the most alltime. His nearest competitor, George Hainsworth, finished with 94, and no active goalie has more than 57.

Just as Rocket Richard will forever be a Montreal Canadien, so Vladislav Tretiak, whom many consider to be the greatest goaltender of all time, will always be remembered as a member of the Soviet National Team, the fabled hockey juggernaut of the 1970s and '80s. Of course, things were much simpler for Richard in the capitalist West than for Tretiak. Much as he loved his visits to North America, Tretiak, a proud product of the Soviet system, was not pleased to spend half his time answering questions about his desire to rush into the golden embrace of the West. Addressing the rumors that swirled after the Canadiens drafted him in 1983, Tretiak wrote, "The Canadiens were selling the bearskin before the bear. I never for a moment considered playing in the NHL. It wouldn't suit me, as an officer and a Soviet citizen."

His legend may have been burnished slightly by his inaccessibility, but not much. He was flexible, athletic and quick. "A goalie must be a virtuoso on skates," he wrote in his autobiography, *The Hockey I Love.* "He does not stand in the crease, he plays in the crease." With Tretiak playing in the crease for 15 years, the Soviet National Team won 10 world championships as well as three Olympic gold medals and one silver. His one great disappointment came in the 1980 "Miracle on Ice," when he left the rebound of a shot in front of the goal, where Mark Johnson of the U.S. picked it up to tie the game at 2–2. Tretiak was replaced in the game by Vladimir Myshkin, who allowed two more goals in the U.S.'s stunning 4–3 upset.

Nothing boosted his fame more than the Summit Series of 1972, which gave new meaning to the phrase cold war. The Canadian players and fans alike expected little from these ragtag invaders, with their antiquated equipment. The Soviets went 3-1-1 in the first five games of the eight-game series, and though Team Canada came roaring back to win in historic fashion, Tretiak & Co. opened the eyes of their NHL counterparts to the wealth of untapped talent in the East.

Tretiak made his brilliance sound simple. "I followed the eyes of the player who was handling the puck," he said. "If, at the last moment, he looked first at me and then at the puck, I knew he would shoot himself. But if he looked for a moment at a teammate and then at the puck, I knew he would pass the puck to his partner." And he knew how to stop the partner's shot, too.

THE RECORD

YEAR	TEAM	GP	MIN	GA	GAA
1968–69	CSKA	3	180	2	0.67
1969–70	CSKA	34	2,040	76	2.24
1970–71	CSKA	40	2,400	81	2.03
1971–72	CSKA	30	1,800	78	2.60
1972–73	CSKA	30	1,800	80	2.67
1973–74	CSKA	27	1,620	94	3.48
1974–75	CSKA	35	2,100	104	2.97
1975–76	CSKA	33	1,980	100	3.03
1976–77	CSKA	35	2,100	98	2.80
1977–78	CSKA	29	1,740	72	2.48
1978–79	CSKA	40	2,400	111	2.78
1979–80	CSKA	36	2,160	85	2.36
1980–81	CSKA	18	1,080	32	1.78
1981–82	CSKA	41	2,460	65	1.59
1982–83	CSKA	29	1,740	40	1.38
1983–84	CSKA	22	1,320	40	1.82
†TOTAL		482	28,920	1,158	2.40

†All statistics from the Soviet League.

TIMELINE

1972
In the epic Summit Series, which is a milestone in Canadian culture, Tretiak (above) and the Soviets gave Team Canada a world-class scare before losing three games, and the series, in Moscow.

1974
Tretiak and the Soviets, who had won the world championships the previous year without losing a game, almost ran the table again, going 9–1 to win their second straight. The USSR won seven world and two Olympic titles beween 1963 and '71.

1975
At the Montreal Forum on New Year's Eve, the rangy Tretiak (above) made save after save in a classic 3–3 tie with the Montreal Canadiens, who outshot the Soviets 38–13. For his many brilliant performances there, Tretiak was as revered in Montreal as he was in Moscow. When the Soviets shut out Les Habs 5–0 at the Forum in 1982, Tretiak received a five-minute standing ovation.

1980
The single lowlight of Tretiak's legendary career came at the Lake Placid Olympics, when he was pulled—perhaps rashly—by Soviet coach Viktor Tikhonov after giving up the second goal in the U.S.'s stunning 4–3 upset of the Soviets.

1989
With Montreal legend Guy Lafleur (below, rear) looking on, Tretiak became the first Soviet player elected to the Hockey Hall of Fame. In 98 world championship games, Tretiak had a 1.78 goals-against average. He retired in '85 without ever playing in the NHL.

HOCKEY HALL OF FAME

Chairman: William Hay
President & COO: Jeff Denomme
VP of Marketing and Communications: Craig Baines

30 Yonge Street BCE Place
Toronto, Ontario Canada M5E 1X8
Telephone: (416) 360-7735
www.hhof.com

ENSHRINEES (PLAYERS ONLY)

NAME POS. (YR. OF INDUCTION)	D.O.B. D.O.D.	CAREER SPAN
Sid Abel C (1969)	b. 2-22-18	1938–54
Jack Adams C (1959)	b. 6-14-1895 d. 5-1-68	1917–27
Charles (Syl) Apps C (1961)	b. 1-18-15	1936–48
George Armstrong C/RW (1975)	b. 7-6-30	1950–71
Irvine (Ace) Bailey RW (1975)	b. 7-3-03 d. 4-7-92	1926–34
Donald H. (Dan) Bain C (1945)	b. 8-15-1874 d. 8-15-62	1895–1902
Hobey Baker C (1945)	b. 1-15-1892 d. 12-21-18	1912–14
Bill Barber LW (1990)	b. 7-11-52	1972–84
Marty Barry C (1965)	b. 12-8-05 d. 8-20-69	1927–40
Andy Bathgate C (1978)	b. 8-28-32	1952–71
Bobby Bauer RW (1996)	b. 2-16-15 d. 9-16-64	1936–52
Jean Beliveau C (1972)	b. 8-31-31	1950–71
Clint Benedict G (1965)	b. 9-26-1892 d. 11-12-76	1917–30
Douglas Bentley LW (1964)	b. 9-3-16 d. 11-24-72	1939–54
Max Bentley C (1966)	b. 3-1-20 d. 1-19-84	1941–54
Hector (Toe) Blake LW (1966)	b. 8-21-12 d. 5-17-95	1934–48
Leo Boivin D (1986)	b. 8-2-32	1951–70
Dickie Boon D (1952)	b. 1-10-1878 d. 5-3-61	1899–1906
Mike Bossy RW (1991)	b. 1-22-57	1977–87
Emile (Butch) Bouchard D (1966)	b. 9-11-20	1941–56
Frank Boucher C (1958)	b. 10-7-01 d. 12-12-77	1921–44
George (Buck) Boucher D (1960)	b. 8-19-1896 d. 10-17-60	1917–34
Johnny Bower G (1976)	b. 11-8-24	1953–70
Russell Bowie LW (1945)	b. 8-24-1880 d. 4-8-59	1898–1908
Frank Brimsek G (1966)	b. 9-26-15	1938–50
Harry L. (Punch) Broadbent RW (1962)	b. 7-13-1892 d. 3-6-71	1918–29
Walter (Turk) Broda G (1967)	b. 5-15-14 d. 10-17-72	1936–52
John Bucyk LW (1981)	b. 5-12-35	1955–78
Billy Burch C/LW (1974)	b. 11-20-00 d. 1-30-50	1922–33
Harry Cameron D (1962)	b. 2-6-1890 d. 10-20-53	1917–23
Gerry Cheevers G (1985)	b. 12-7-40	1961–80
Francis (King) Clancy D (1958)	b. 2-23-03 d. 11-8-86	1921–37
Aubrey (Dit) Clapper RW (1947)	b. 2-9-07 d. 1-21-78	1927–47
Bobby Clarke C (1987)	b. 8-13-49	1969–84
Sprague Cleghorn D (1958)	b. 1890 d. 7-11-56	1910–28
Neil Colville RW/D (1967)	b. 8-4-14 d. 12-26-87	1935–49
Charlie Conacher RW (1961)	b. 12-20-09 d. 12-30-67	1929–41
Lionel Conacher D (1994)	b. 5-29-00 d. 5-26-54	1925–37
Roy Conacher LW (1998)	b. 10-5-16 d. 12-29-84	1938–52
Alex Connell G (1958)	b. 2-8-02 d. 5-10-58	1924–37
Bill Cook RW (1952)	b. 10-9-1896 d. 4-6-86	1926–37
Fred (Bun) Cook LW (1995)	b. 9-18-03 d. 3-19-88	1926–37
Arthur Coulter D (1974)	b. 5-31-09 d. 10-14-2000	1931–42
Yvan Cournoyer RW (1982)	b. 11-22-43	1963–79
Bill Cowley C (1968)	b. 6-12-12 d. 12-31-93	1934–47
Samuel (Rusty) Crawford LW (1962)	b. 11-7-1885 d. 12-19-71	1917–19
Jack Darragh RW (1962)	b. 12-4-1890 d. 6-25-24	1917–24
Allan M. (Scotty) Davidson RW (1950)	b. 1890 d. 6-6-15	1912–14
Clarence (Hap) Day D (1961)	b. 6-14-01 d. 2-17-90	1924–38
Alex Delvecchio C (1977)	b. 12-4-32	1950–74
Cy Denneny LW (1959)	b. 12-23-1891 d. 10-12-70	1917–29
Marcel Dionne C (1992)	b. 8-3-51	1971–89
Gordie Drillon RW (1975)	b. 10-23-14 d. 10-22-86	1936–43
Charles Drinkwater RW (1950)	b. 2-22-1875 d. 9-27-46	1892–99
Ken Dryden G (1983)	b. 8-8-47	1970–79
Woody Dumart LW (1992)	b. 12-23-16	1935–54
Thomas Dunderdale C (1974)	b. 5-6-1887 d. 12-15-60	1906–24
Bill Durnan G (1964)	b. 1-22-16 d. 10-31-72	1943–50
Mervyn A. (Red) Dutton D (1958)	b. 7-23-1898 d. 3-15-87	1926–36
Cecil (Babe) Dye RW (1970)	b. 5-13-1898 d. 1-2-62	1919–31
Phil Esposito C (1984)	b. 2-20-42	1963–81
Tony Esposito G (1988)	b. 4-23-43	1968–84
Arthur F. Farrell LW (1965)	b. 2-8-1877 d. 2-7-09	1896–1901
Ferdinand (Fern) Flaman D (1990)	b. 1-25-27	1944–61
Frank Foyston C/RW (1958)	b. 2-2-1891 d. 1-19-66	1926–28
Frank Frederickson C (1958)	b. 6-11-1895 d. 4-28-79	1926–31
Bill Gadsby D (1970)	b. 8-8-27	1946–66
Bob Gainey LW (1992)	b. 12-13-53	1973–89
Chuck Gardiner G (1945)	b. 12-31-04 d. 6-13-34	1927–34
Herb Gardiner D (1958)	b. 5-8-1891 d. 1-11-72	1926–29
Jimmy Gardner LW (1962)	b. 5-21-1881 d. 11-7-40	1900–15
Bernie (Boom Boom) Geoffrion RW (1972)	b. 2-14-31	1950–68
Eddie Gerard LW/D (1945)	b. 2-22-1890 d. 12-7-37	1917–24
Ed Giacomin G (1987)	b. 6-6-39	1965–78
Rod Gilbert RW (1982)	b. 7-1-41	1960–78
Hamilton (Billy) Gilmour RW (1962)	b. 3-21-1885 d. 3-13-59	1902–16
Frank (Moose) Goheen D (1952)	b. 2-9-1894 d. 11-13-79	n/a
Ebenezer R. (Ebbie) Goodfellow C/D (1963)	b. 4-9-07 d. 9-10-65	1929–43
Michel Goulet LW (1998)	b. 4-21-60	1979–94
Mike Grant D (1950)	b. 1874 d. 8-19-55	1893–1902
Wilfred (Shorty) Green RW (1962)	b. 7-17-1896 d. 4-19-60	1923–27
Wayne Gretzky C (1999)	b. 1-26-61	1979–99
Si Griffis D (1950)	b. 9-22-1883 d. 7-9-50	1902–19
George Hainsworth G (1961)	b. 6-26-1895 d. 10-9-50	1926–37
Glenn Hall G (1975)	b. 10-3-31	1952–71
Joe Hall D (1961)	b. 5-3-1882 d. 4-5-19	1917–19
Doug Harvey D (1973)	b. 12-19-24 d. 12-26-89	1947–69
George Hay LW (1958)	b. 1-10-1898 d. 7-13-75	1926–34
William (Riley) Hern G (1962)	b. 12-5-1880 d. 6-24-29	1904–11
Bryan Hextall RW (1969)	b. 7-31-13 d. 7-25-84	1936–48
Harry (Hap) Holmes G (1972)	b. 2-21-1892 d. 1940	1917–28
Tom Hooper C (1962)	b. 11-24-1883 d. 3-23-60	1901–08

NAME Pos. (Yr. of Induction)	D.O.B. D.O.D.	CAREER SPAN
George (Red) Horner D (1965)	b. 5-28-09	1928–40
Miles (Tim) Horton D (1977)	b. 1-12-30 d. 2-14-74	1949–74
Gordie Howe RW (1972)	b. 3-31-28	1946–80
Syd Howe C/LW (1965)	b. 9-28-11 d. 5-20-76	1929–46
Harry Howell D (1979)	b. 12-28-32	1952–73
Bobby Hull LW (1983)	b. 1-3-39	1957–80
John (Bouse) Hutton G (1962)	b. 10-24-1877 d. 10-27-62	1898–1904
Harry M. Hyland RW (1962)	b. 1-2-1889 d. 8-8-69	1917–18
James (Dick) Irvin C (1958)	b. 7-19-1892 d. 3-16-57	1926–29
Harvey (Busher) Jackson LW (1971)	b. 1-19-11 d. 6-25-66	1929–44
Ernest (Moose) Johnson D (1952)	b. 2-26-1886 d. 3-25-63	1905–31
Ivan (Ching) Johnson D (1958)	b. 12-7-1898 d. 6-17-79	1926–38
Tom Johnson D (1970)	b. 2-18-28	1947–65
Aurel Joliat LW (1947)	b. 8-29-01 d. 6-2-86	1922–38
Gordon (Duke) Keats C (1958)	b. 3-1-1895 d. 1-16-71	1926–29
Leonard (Red) Kelly D/C (1969)	b. 7-9-27	1947–68
Ted (Teeder) Kennedy C (1966)	b. 12-12-25	1942–57
Dave Keon C (1986)	b. 3-22-40	1960–82
Elmer Lach C (1966)	b. 1-22-18	1940–54
Guy Lafleur RW (1988)	b. 9-20-51	1971–91
Edouard (Newsy) Lalonde C (1950)	b. 10-31-1888 d. 11-21-71	1917–27
Jacques Laperriere D (1987)	b. 11-22-41	1962–74
Guy LaPointe D (1993)	b. 3-18-48	1968–84
Edgar Laprade C (1993)	b. 10-10-19	1945–55
Reed Larson D (1996)	b. 7-30-56	1976–90
Jean (Jack) Laviolette D/RW (1962)	b. 7-27-1897 d. 1-10-60	1917–18
Hugh Lehman G (1958)	b. 10-27-1885 d. 4-8-61	1926–28
Jacques Lemaire C (1984)	b. 9-7-45	1967–79
Mario Lemieux C (1997)	b. 10-5-65	1984–
Percy LeSueur G (1961)	b. 11-18-1881 d. 1-27-62	1905–16
Herbert A. Lewis LW (1989)	b. 4-17-06 d. 1-20-91	1928–39
Ted Lindsay LW (1966)	b. 7-29-25	1944–65
Harry Lumley G (1980)	b. 11-11-26	1943–60
Duncan (Mickey) MacKay C (1952)	b. 5-25-1894 d. 5-21-40	1926–30
Frank Mahovlich LW (1981)	b. 1-10-38	1956–74
Joe Malone C/LW (1950)	b. 2-28-1890 d. 5-15-69	1917–24
Sylvio Mantha D (1960)	b. 4-14-02 d. 8-7-74	1923–37
Jack Marshall C (1965)	b. 3-14-1877 d. 8-7-65	1900–17
Fred G. (Steamer) Maxwell C (1962)	b. 5-19-1890 d. 9-11-75	1915–19
Lanny McDonald RW (1992)	b. 2-16-53	1973–89
Frank McGee C (1945)	b. n/a d. 9-16-16	1902–06
Billy McGimsie C (1962)	b. 6-7-1880 d. 10-28-68	1902–07
George McNamara D (1958)	b. 8-26-1886 d. 3-10-52	1907–17
Stan Mikita RW (1983)	b. 5-20-40	1958–80
Dicky Moore LW (1974)	b. 1-6-31	1951–68
Patrick (Paddy) Moran G (1958)	b. 3-11-1877 d. 1-14-66	1901–17
Howie Morenz C (1945)	b. 6-21-02 d. 3-8-37	1923–37
Billy Mosienko RW (1965)	b. 11-2-21 d. 7-9-94	1941–55
Joe Mullen RW (2000)	b. 2-26-57	1979–97
Frank Nighbor C (1947)	b. 1-26-1893 d. 4-13-66	1917–30
Reg Noble C/D (1962)	b. 6-23-1896 d. 1-19-62	1917–33
Herbert (Buddy) O'Connor C (1988)	b. 6-21-16 d. 8-24-77	1941–51
Harry Oliver RW (1967)	b. 10-26-1898 d. 6-16-85	1926–37
Bert Olmstead LW (1985)	b. 9-4-26	1948–62
Bobby Orr D (1979)	b. 3-20-48	1966–79
Bernie Parent G (1984)	b. 4-3-45	1965–79
Brad Park D (1988)	b. 7-6-48	1968–85
Lester Patrick D (1947)	b. 12-31-1883 d. 6-1-60	1926–27
Lynn Patrick C/LW (1980)	b. 2-3-12 d. 1-26-80	1934–46
Gilbert Perreault C (1990)	b. 11-13-50	1970–87
Tommy Phillips LW/RW (1945)	b. 5-22-1880 d. 11-30-23	1902–12
Pierre Pilote D (1975)	b. 12-11-31	1955–69
Didier (Pit) Pitre RW/D (1962)	b. 9-1-1883 d. 7-29-34	1917–23
Jacques Plante G (1978)	b. 1-17-29 d. 2-26-86	1952–73
Denis Potvin D (1991)	b. 10-29-53	1973–88
Walter (Babe) Pratt D (1966)	b. 1-7-16 d. 12-16-88	1935–47
Joe Primeau C (1963)	b. 1-29-06 d. 5-14-89	1927–36
Marcel Pronovost D (1978)	b. 6-15-30	1949–70
Bob Pulford LW (1991)	b. 3-31-36	1956–73
Harvey Pulford D (1945)	b. 1875 d. 10-31-40	1893–1908
Hubert (Bill) Quackenbush D (1976)	b. 3-2-22	1942–56
Frank Rankin C (1961)	b. 4-1-1889 d. 7-23-32	1906–14
Jean Ratelle C (1985)	b. 10-3-40	1960–81
Claude (Chuck) Rayner G (1973)	b. 8-11-20	1940–53
Kenneth Reardon D (1966)	b. 4-1-21	1940–50
Henri Richard C (1979)	b. 2-29-36	1955–75
Maurice (Rocket) Richard RW (1961)	b. 8-4-21 d. 5-27-2000	1942–60
George Richardson n/a (1950)	b. 1887 d. 2-9-16	1906–n/a
Gordon Roberts LW (1971)	b. 9-5-1891 d. 9-2-66	1909–20
Larry Robinson D (1995)	b. 6-2-51	1972–92
Art Ross D (1945)	b. 1-13-1886 d. 8-5-64	1917–18
Blair Russel C/RW (1965)	b. 9-17-1880 d. 12-7-61	1899–1908
Ernest Russell C (1965)	b. 10-21-1883 d. 2-23-63	1904–14
Jack Ruttan n/a (1962)	b. 4-5-1889 d. 1-7-73	1905–n/a
Borje Salming D (1996)	b. 4-17-51	1973–90
Denis Savard C (2000)	b. 2-4-61	1980–97
Serge Savard D (1986)	b. 1-22-46	1966–83
Terry Sawchuk G (1971)	b. 12-28-29 d. 5-31-70	1949–70
Fred Scanlan F (1965)	b. n/a d. n/a	1897–1903
Milt Schmidt C/D (1961)	b. 3-5-18	1936–56
Dave (Sweeney) Schriner LW (1962)	b. 11-30-11 d. 7-4-90	1934–46
Earl Seibert D (1963)	b. 12-7-11 d. 5-12-90	1931–46
Oliver Seibert F (1961)	b. 3-18-1881 d. 5-15-44	1900–n/a
Eddie Shore D (1947)	b. 11-25-02 d. 3-16-85	1926–40
Steve Shutt LW (1993)	b. 7-1-52	1972–85
Albert C. (Babe) Siebert LW/D (1964)	b. 1-14-04 d. 8-25-39	1925–39
Harold (Bullet Joe) Simpson D (1962)	b. 8-13-1893 d. 12-25-73	1925–31
Daryl Sittler C (1989)	b. 9-18-50	1970–85
Alfred E. Smith RW (1962)	b. 6-3-1873 d. 8-21-53	1894–1908
Billy Smith G (1993)	b. 12-12-50	1971–89
Clint Smith C (1991)	b. 12-12-13	1936–47
Reginald (Hooley) Smith C/RW (1972)	b. 1-7-03 d. 8-24-63	1924–41
Thomas Smith C (1973)	b. 9-27-1886 d. 8-1-66	1919–20
Allan Stanley D (1981)	b. 3-1-26	1948–69
Russell (Barney) Stanley RW (1962)	b. 1-1-1893 d. 5-16-71	1927–28
Peter Stastny C (1998)	b. 9-18-56	1980–95
John (Black Jack) Stewart D (1964)	b. 5-6-17 d. 5-25-83	1938–52
Nels Stewart C (1962)	b. 12-29-02 d. 8-21-57	1925–40
Bruce Stuart F (1961)	b. 1882 d. 10-28-61	1898–1911
Hod Stuart D (1945)	b. 1879 d. 6-23-07	1898–1907
Frederic (Cyclone) (O.B.E.) Taylor C/D (1947)	b. 6-23-1883 d. 6-10-79	1907–23
Cecil R. (Tiny) Thompson G (1959)	b. 5-31-05 d. 2-11-81	1928–40
Vladislav Tretiak G (1989)	b. 4-25-52	1969–85
Harry J. Trihey F (1950)	b. 12-25-1877 d. 12-9-42	1896–1901
Bryan Trottier C (1997)	b. 7-17-56	1975–94
Norm Ullman C (1982)	b. 12-26-35	1955–75
Georges Vezina G (1945)	b. 1-21-1887 d. 3-27-26	1917–26
Jack Walker F (1960)	b. 11-29-1888 d. 12-16-50	1926–28
Marty Walsh C (1962)	b. 1883 d. 1915	1907–12
Harry Watson LW (1994)	b. 5-6-23 d.	1941–57
Harry (Moose) Watson C (1962)	b. 7-14-1898 d. 9-11-57	1919–25
Ralph (Cooney) Weiland C (1971)	b. 11-5-04 d. 7-3-85	1928–40
Harry Westwick F (1962)	b. 4-23-1876 d. 4-3-57	1894–1908
Fred Whitcroft F (1962)	b. 1882 d. 1931	1906–10
Gordon (Phat) Wilson D (1962)	b. 12-29-1895 d. 8-70	1918–33
Lorne (Gump) Worsley G (1980)	b. 5-14-29	1952–74
Roy Worters G (1969)	b. 10-19-00 d. 11-7-57	1925–37

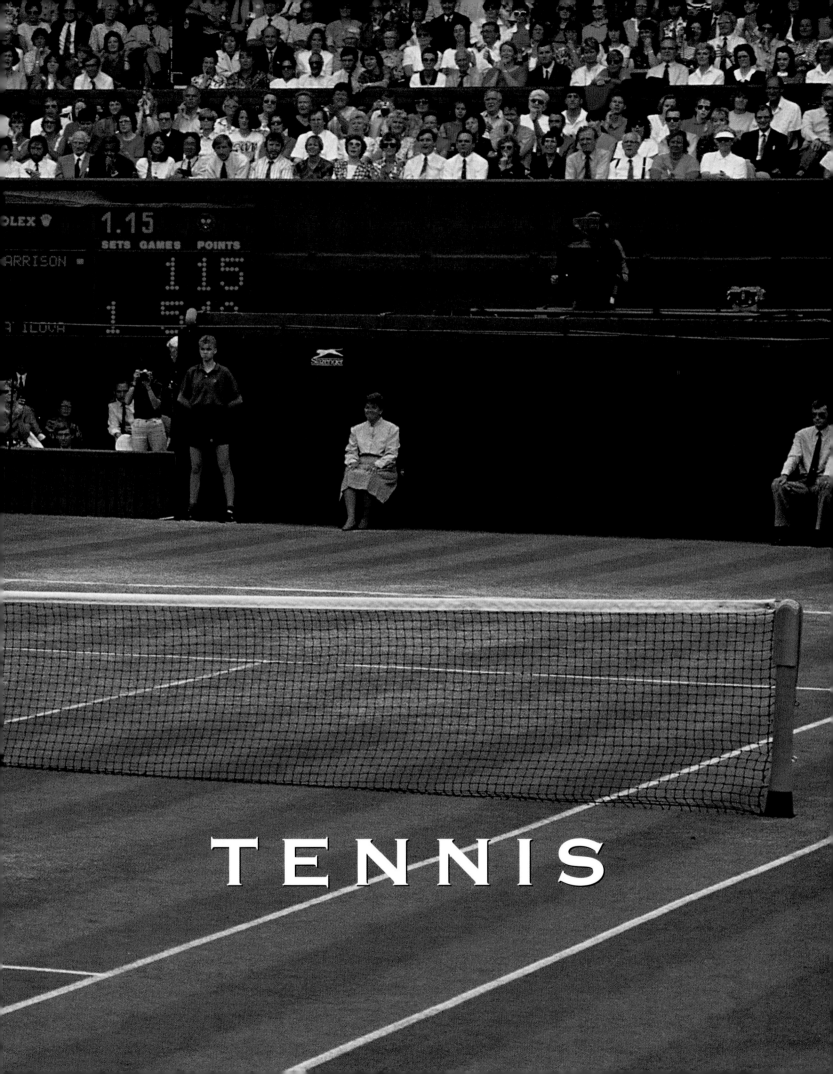

TENNIS

The story of the Tennis Hall of Fame in Newport, R.I., begins one August day in 1879, when a gentleman with the colorful name of Captain Candy decided, for reasons never fully explained, to ride his horse through the front door of the exceedingly tony Newport Reading Room club. The Captain's sudden appearance shocked the denizens of the place, though a white-coated steward is said to have had the presence of mind to chide Candy, "Sir, you cannot ride a horse in here."

Candy must have disagreed, for he rode on down the hallway, into Reading Room No. 2 and the South Room, before turning the horse, retracing his path and galloping off down the street. This, sniffed the Newport *Mercury*, was "a clear violation of the rules."

Candy's host in Newport was James Gordon Bennett Jr., the wealthy publisher of the New York *Herald*, the most important newspaper of the day. Miffed at the shabby

Designed by legendary architect Stanford White, Newport's International Tennis Hall of Fame (above) is the very picture of refinement and elegance. The stately grounds feature the United States' only competition-quality public grass courts.

treatment accorded his friend, Bennett decided to build an alternative club.

He wanted his new establishment to be nothing short of spectacular, so Bennett bought 126,000 square feet of land a quarter of a mile down the street from the Reading Room and commissioned the architectural firm of McKim, Mead and White to come up with a suitably grand design. Junior partner Stanford White was put in charge of the project and, in what would prove to be the first major commission of a great American architect, came up with a gem: The rambling two-story building, which included a prominent clocktower, a horseshoe piazza and a tennis court, stretched along Bellevue Avenue with fancy shops at pedestrian level and club rooms above. The building is wooden, with dark green trim and a shingled roof. White's design used elaborate curlicues, lattices and scrollwork.

The Casino opened to raves on July 26, 1880. Accord-

ing to the Newport *News*, "there is nothing like it in the old world or new." As you'd expect from a private club located just a lob shot away from some of the most ostentatious properties in the nation—Newport is the town that inspired the sociologist Thorstein Veblen to coin the phrase "conspicuous consumption" following a visit in 1889—no expense was spared. Mrs. Louis S. Bruguiere, a Newport grand dame whose son, James Van Alen, would become the Hall's prime mover, had a special gate built to allow her Rolls Royce right into the stadium. She liked to watch the matches without leaving her car.

Stroll through the Bellevue Avenue gate today, and you find yourself transported to an era of elegant leisure. The Casino did not offer gambling—at least not officially—but did offer a wide variety of pursuits, including archery, bowling, theater, concerts, billiards, tea parties and, of course, tennis, even though Bennett himself was not much of a player. Out back, there are now 15 grass courts, the only competition-quality grass courts in the U.S. open to the public. The Casino contains one of only 34 galleries in the world for court tennis, the funny old European forerunner of lawn tennis.

In 1881, when the newly formed U.S. Lawn Tennis Association decided to hold its first championship, Newport was the obvious first choice, partly for its cachet in rarified social circles, but also because of its first-rate facilities.

For the next 35 years, the USLTA held national championships in both singles and doubles at the Casino. The first seven singles titles would go to Richard Sears of Boston, Harvard '83. When the Hall of Fame opened in 1955, Sears was among the first inductees. The U.S. championships would be contested in old Newport until 1915, when the U.S. Lawn Tennis Association decided that Newporters considered the social side of the event more important than the tennis and decided to move the tournament to the West Side Tennis Club's new quarters in Forest Hills,

One of only five players to complete a Grand Slam, Steffi Graf (above) will soon be enshrined for eternity in Newport, as will Sampras (below), who has won more Wimbledons (seven) and more Grand Slam singles titles (13) than any modern male player. Included in the Tennis Hall of Fame's venerable collection is the patent for the game, issued in 1874.

N.Y. There it remained until its transfer to the National Tennis Center, in Flushing, N.Y. in 1978. To fill the gap, Newporters instituted the Casino Invitational for amateurs, held from 1915 to '67.

In 1954, Candy Van Alen, wife of Casino president James Van Alen, asked her husband why there was no tennis hall of fame. He began gathering memorabilia in one room of the Casino, and the collection eventually blossomed into the International Tennis Hall of Fame. A former court tennis champion affectionately known as the "Newport Bolshevik" for the revolutionary tie-break system he developed, Van Alen was elected to the Hall in 1965. In the mid-70s the Casino underwent extensive refurbishment to correct the damage from decades of neglect. Twenty years later, Van Alen estimated he'd poured $250,000 of his own money into the Hall to keep it going.

Since then the Hall has flourished. There are 175 members honored in the Enshrinement Gallery, ranging from players to writers like Bud Collins and even King Gustav V of Sweden, a tennis lover who may have saved the lives of several players, including Gottfried von Cramm, by speaking on their behalf to the Nazis.

There are galleries devoted to every period in the game's history, from the Golden Era of the 1920s, dominated by Bill Tilden, to the current big-money era, ruled by Pete Sampras, whose 13 Grand Slam singles titles make him a sure a bet for membership once the required five-year waiting period has elapsed following his distinguished career. In the equipment room one can trace the evolution of rackets, balls and shoes. There is a room dedicated to Billie Jean King, and Martina Navratilova's nine Wimbledon trophies are collected in one case. Near the entrance one can see the patent for tennis that Queen Victoria granted Major W.C. Wingfield in 1874. Nothing, alas, commemorates either Candy or Bennett, but it's hard to imagine a finer memorial than the beautiful Casino building itself.

1974

Borg (right), the tour's sensational new "Teen Angel," announced his presence among the elite by winning the Italian Open and the French Open, during which he celebrated his 18th birthday. At Roland Garros, he rallied from two sets down against Manuel Orantes to claim his first Grand Slam.

1980

Borg raised the Wimbledon trophy (left) for a modern-record fifth consecutive time, defeating John McEnroe in an epic five-set final, the fourth set of which finished 18–16 in favor of McEnroe. Borg, who had won a third straight French Open title earlier that year, recovered to win the decisive set 8–6. McEnroe would get his revenge in the U.S. Open final two months later, outlasting Borg in another five-setter, 7–6, 6–1, 6–7, 5–7, 6–4.

1981

At age 25 Borg (right) won the French Open for the sixth time, giving him 11 Grand Slam singles titles, tied with the legendary Australian Rod Laver and one short of the career leader at the time, Roy Emerson, also of Australia. In the final, Borg overcame Czechoslovakia's Ivan Lendl 6–1, 4–6, 6–2, 3–6, 6–1. An injured right shoulder had sidelined Borg for nearly two months prior to the early June tournament, and he had played in only three events since January, failng to advance past the second round in two of them.

1982

Following dispiriting four-set losses to McEnroe in the finals of both Wimbledon and the U.S. Open in 1981, Borg had announced that he would reduce his tournament schedule significantly, playing in only seven tournaments in '82—not enough, according to the rules of the Men's International Professional Tennis Council, for him to be placed in the main draw of any event. He would have to qualify for every major tournament he entered. Borg had effectively retired.

BJORN BORG

You didn't have to assume the lotus position and chant "om" to look calm and controlled in the world of men's tennis in the latter half of the 1970s. That's when bad boys like Ilie Nastase, Jimmy Connors and John McEnroe were turning the staid old game into something resembling a shouting match crossed with a hissy fit. In that hurricane of profanity and slammed rackets, Bjorn Borg was the steady, seemingly unperturbable eye. With his long dark-blond hair held in place by his trademark white headband, Borg stood out as much for his powers of concentration as for his streak of five consecutive Wimbledon victories beginning in 1976.

You want proof of icy nerves? Borg's final Wimbledon victory, over John McEnroe, was one of the great displays of high-tension tennis anyone has witnessed. After losing the first set 1–6, and winning the second and third by 7–5 and 6–3, respectively, Borg lost one of the great sets ever played, an 18–16 marathon tiebreaker in which he was stymied five times on match point and saved six set points. Somehow, Borg regrouped and came back to win the fifth set, 8–6. The following year he made it back to the Wimbledon final, with a chance to win a record sixth straight title at the All-England Club, but was finally vanquished by John McEnroe 4–6, 7–6, 7–6, 6–4.

Borg was the first in a wave of great Swedish players, opening the door for such talents as Mats Wilander and Stefan Edberg. Born in Sodertalje, Sweden, in 1956, he became interested in tennis after his father gave him a racket he'd won in a table tennis match. Using a two-handed backhand he'd borrowed from his favorite childhood sport, hockey, Borg started beating Sweden's top young players at the age of 13. Despite his unorthodox, jerky stroke, he won his first Grand Slam title at the tender age of 18, bouncing back to whip Manuel Orantes 2–6, 6–7, 6–0, 6–1, 6–1 in the 1974 French Open final. The following year he led the Swedes to their first Davis Cup final and was instrumental in their 3–2 victory over Czechoslovakia. His streak of 33 straight Davis Cup singles titles is still a record.

One strange blot on Borg's stellar résumé is that in 10 tries he never won the U.S. Open. Four times he reached the finals, coming closest to winning in 1980 when he took McEnroe to five sets. His 11th Grand Slam win came in 1981, at the French Open, where he outlasted Ivan Lendl 6–1, 4–6, 6–2, 3–6, 6–1 in the final. Borg was only 25, and many thought he was on his way to beating Roy Emerson's record of 12 Grand Slam titles. But in 1982, following a dispute with the men's tennis council over his infrequent play, Borg stunned the tennis world by retiring. He left the game a young man, but a legend all the same.

THE RECORD			
YEAR	AUS	FRENCH	WIM	U.S.
	S-D-M	S-D-M	S-D-M	S-D-M
1974	0-0-0	1-0-0	0-0-0	0-0-0
1975	0-0-0	1-0-0	0-0-0	0-0-0
1976	0-0-0	0-0-0	1-0-0	0-0-0
1977	0-0-0	0-0-0	1-0-0	0-0-0
1978	0-0-0	1-0-0	1-0-0	0-0-0
1979	0-0-0	1-0-0	1-0-0	0-0-0
1980	0-0-0	1-0-0	1-0-0	0-0-0
1981	0-0-0	1-0-0	0-0-0	0-0-0
TOTAL	0-0-0	6-0-0	5-0-0	0-0-0

DON BUDGE

In 1938 Don Budge saw to it that his name would forever be linked with tennis's Grand Slam, as the first person ever to win the sport's four major championships in a single year. While that is a superb achievement, unduplicated until 1962, when Rod Laver won his Slam, it nevertheless tends to reduce to a single fact a man who was as complete a person as he was a player. Not only was this jug-eared, red-headed young man a true sportsman who charmed people everywhere he went, he also won what is surely one of the greatest battles in tennis history, his come-from-behind defeat of Baron Gottfried von Cramm in the 1937 Davis Cup qualifier against Germany.

Born in 1915, Budge grew up in Oakland, Calif., where he excelled at every sport he tried, but at baseball especially. When his older brother Lloyd introduced him to tennis, Budge proved to be a natural there too. A lithe 6' 2", he was surprisingly agile, and his backhand, which was modeled after his left-handed baseball swing, was, according to tennis writer Allison Danzig, "probably the most potent backhand the world has ever seen."

Budge warmed up for his historic Slam by winning both Wimbledon and the U.S. Open in 1937. Still, nothing he achieved that year had as much drama as his battle with Cramm in the Davis Cup qualifying round. Coming one year after the Berlin Olympics, the match was fraught with political tension. To remind his man what was at stake, Hitler himself phoned Cramm prior to his match with Budge. Budge lost the first two sets before rallying to win the third and fourth. But the effort seemed to exhaust him and he fell behind, 1–4, in the decider. "Don't worry, Cap. I'll make it," Budge assured the U.S. captain, then rallied to tie the match, 5–5, and win, 8–6. The U.S. went on to win its first Davis Cup since 1926.

THE RECORD

YEAR	AUS	FRENCH	WIM	U.S.
	S-D-M	S-D-M	S-D-M	S-D-M
1935	0-0-0	0-0-0	0-0-0	0-0-0
1936	0-0-0	0-0-0	0-0-0	0-1-0
1937	0-0-0	0-0-0	1-1-1	1-0-1
1938	1-0-0	1-0-0	1-1-1	1-1-1
TOTAL	1-0-0	1-0-0	2-2-2	2-2-2

With the 1938 Davis Cup to be played in Philadelphia, Budge delayed turning pro in order to help the U.S. defend, which it did successfully, downing Australia 3–2. Budge knew the greatest danger in pursuing the Slam was to exhaust himself by competing too much, so he marshaled his energies. In the end, he sailed to the Slam, with only the U.S. Open final, against his doubles partner Gene Mako, reaching four sets. Here was a new standard for tennis excellence. "When he was in his prime," said 1931 Wimbledon titlist Sidney Wood, "no player, past or present, could have beaten him." Seven-time U.S. Open champ Bill Tilden seconded that, calling Budge "the finest player 365 days a year who ever lived."

TIMELINE

1938

On September 23 Budge (right) breezed past fellow American Sidney Wood in the semifinals of the U.S. Open, winning 6–3, 6–3, 6–3. In the final the next day, he defeated his best friend and doubles partner, Gene Mako, 6–3, 6–8, 6–2, 6–1 to complete the first Grand Slam in tennis history, a feat not to be repeated until 1962.

1943

Only months after downing Bobby Riggs 6–2, 6–2, 6–2 at Forest Hills for the 1942 U.S. Pro title, Budge (far left) was fingerprinted prior to being admitted to the Army. Soon after enlisting, Budge was running an obstacle course on a cool morning when he tore a muscle in his right shoulder. He served until the war's end in '45 and resumed his tennis career full time, but he never returned to his prewar form, which had seen him win his celebrated Grand Slam and numerous doubles titles, as well as producing a four-year Davis Cup record of 19–2 in singles and 6–2 in doubles.

1944

Taking time out from his home-front military duties with the Army Air Corps, Budge teamed with Bobby Riggs to win a third consecutive U.S. Pro doubles championship. The duo would win the title six straight times, and Budge, who also won national pro doubles championships with Fred Perry (1940–41), Frank Kovacs (1949) and Pancho Gonzales (1953), would win 10 in his legendary career.

1945

Budge (below, left) congratulated his frequent doubles partner, Bobby Riggs, after Riggs defeated him 9–11, 6–3, 6–3, 6–0 in the final of the $5,000 world pro hard court championship at the Los Angeles Tennis Club. Then past the age of 30, Budge was far from finished, his chronic shoulder problems notwithstanding. He reached the U.S. pro final the following year, as well as in 1947, 1949 and, at the age of 38, in 1953—the same year he partnered with 25-year-old Pancho Gonzales to win the U.S. Pro doubles championship. Budge, who was elected to the International Tennis Hall of Fame in 1964, retired from the game in 1954, with 14 major titles. He died on January 26, 2000, from injuries sustained in a car accident.

MARGARET SMITH COURT

Margaret Smith spent the last half of her career as Mrs. Court. While there could be no better name for the woman who won a record 62 Grand Slam titles, including a coveted single-year Slam in 1970, it also points to her divided loyalties. Smith Court probably would have won even more titles, but she retired briefly in 1967 when she married Barry Court and again, for longer, after the birth of their first child in 1972. She lost the 1971 Wimbledon final while pregnant. Before she retired for good in 1977, Smith Court had amassed a record 24 Grand Slam singles titles, 11 of them in the Australian Open.

At 5' 9", Smith Court was taller than most of her opponents, and she knew how to use her reach. Billie Jean King called her "the Arm." A natural lefty who was taught to play tennis right-handed, she was primarily an attacker who hit the ball harder than any woman of her generation. And she was fast enough to have been offered a berth on the Australian Olympic team in the 400- and 800-meter runs.

Smith Court was born in the country town of Albury, New South Wales, in 1942. At first she used a piece of wood for a racket, because her family could not afford a proper one. She quit school at 15 to concentrate on tennis and was lucky to attract the notice of a wealthy Melbourne businessman, who paid for lessons and charm school. She was 17 when she won her first major, the 1960 Australian Open. For the next 13 years, she would own the Australian, winning 11 of 14 singles titles and becoming a national hero.

She nearly won the Grand Slam in 1969, taking every major but Wimbledon, and when she did accomplish the sweep in '70, certifying her legend, it was in particularly grueling fashion. Smith Court had played every other week that season, winning 21 of 27 tournaments. In the Wimbledon final against the other most dominant player of the '60s, Billie Jean King, Smith Court overcame a severe ankle injury to defeat King, who was also hobbled, 14–12, 11–9. Compared to that grueling marathon, her three-set triumph over Rosie Casals in the U.S. Open final was a breeze.

Smith Court enjoyed another spectacular season in '73, winning 18 of the 25 events she entered, including three majors. She entered the Hall of Fame in 1979.

THE RECORD

YEAR	AUS	FRENCH	WIM	U.S.
	S-D-M	S-D-M	S-D-M	S-D-M
1959	0-0-0	0-0-0	0-0-0	0-0-0
1960	1-0-0	0-0-0	0-0-0	0-0-0
1961	1-1-0	0-0-0	0-0-0	0-0-1
1962	1-1-0	1-0-0	0-0-0	1-0-1
1963	1-1-1	0-0-1	1-0-1	0-1-1
1964	1-0-1	1-1-1	0-1-0	0-0-1
1965	1-1-0	0-1-1	1-0-1	1-0-1
1966	1-0-0	0-1-0	0-0-1	0-0-0
1967	0-0-0	0-0-0	0-0-0	0-0-0
1968	0-0-0	0-0-0	0-0-1	0-1-0
1969	1-1-0	1-0-1	0-1-0	1-0-1
1970	1-1-0	1-0-0	1-0-0	1-1-1
1971	1-1-0	0-0-0	0-0-0	0-0-0
1972	0-0-0	0-0-0	0-0-0	0-0-1
1973	1-1-0	1-1-0	0-0-0	1-1-0
1974	0-0-0	0-0-0	0-0-0	0-0-0
1975	0-0-0	0-0-0	0-0-1	0-1-0
1976	0-0-0	0-0-0	0-0-0	0-0-0
1977	0-0-0	0-0-0	0-0-0	0-0-0
TOTAL	11-8-2	5-4-4	3-2-5	5-5-8

TIMELINE

1960
At age 17 Smith (below) seized her first major, defeating Jan Lehane 7–5, 6–2 in the Australian final. She would win the next six as well.

1962
If anyone doubted Smith's potential after she reeled off two straight Australian Open championships, they had their doubts laid to rest in '62, when she nearly became the first woman since Maureen Connolly in 1953 to win the Grand Slam. Smith won her third straight Australian, as well as the French Open (where she defeated Lesley Turner 6–3, 3–6, 7–5 in the final) and the U.S. Open (where she downed Darlene Hard 9–7, 6–4 in the final).

1963
Collecting the only major title she failed to win the previous year, Smith (below) won Wimbledon with a 6–3, 6–4 win over Billie Jean Moffitt.

1970
Having fallen one major short of a Grand Slam in 1962, '65 and '69, Smith Court put it all together to sweep the Australian, French, Wimbledon and U.S. finals. The feat was not repeated until 1988, when Steffi Graf pulled it off.

1973
Smith Court (above, left) outlasted Chris Evert (above, right) 6–7, 7–6, 6–4 in the French Open final. Having already defeated Evonne Goolagong for the Australian Open title, Smith Court went on to win the U.S. Open (again over Goolagong) to make this the fourth year of her career in which she won three of the four Grand Slams.

1956

The 20-year-old Emerson (right) was already a three-year veteran of Australia's formidable Davis Cup team, which he helped win eight of nine Davis Cup titles between 1959 and '67. He won 22 of 24 singles matches and 13 of 15 doubles matches during that span.

1961

Emerson (left) won the U.S. Open singles title with a 7–5, 6–3, 6–2 trouncing of countryman Rod Laver in the final. In a breakout year, Emerson also won the Australian singles title and the French and Wimbledon doubles championships. He would return to the final at Forest Hills the following year but would lose to Laver 6–2, 6–4, 5–7, 6–4.

1963

Emerson won his second Australian Open championship with a 6–3, 6–3, 6–1 pasting of fellow Australian Ken Fletcher in the final. He would go on to win the French Open singles and doubles titles, defeating Pierre Darmon 3–6, 6–1, 6–4, 6–4 in the singles final and teaming with Manuel Santana to win 6–2, 6–4, 6–4 over Gordon Forbes and Abe Segal in the doubles championship.

1964

Reeling off 55 consecutive singles victories during one stretch, Emerson (below, at Wimbledon) produced the best year of his superb career. He nearly completed a Grand Slam, beating countryman Fred Stolle in the finals of the Australian Open, Wimbledon and the U.S. Open. His loss to Nicki Pietrangeli in the quarters of the French Open left him three matches short of sweeping the majors. Emmo won each of his majors in

straight sets except for the Wimbledon final, which went to four sets and featured a 12–10 slugfest in the second set. Emerson also spearheaded Australia's run to the Davis Cup, which returned Down Under from the U.S. after the Aussies downed the Yanks 3–2 in Cleveland.

ROY EMERSON

For the quarter-century from 1950 to 1975, Australia ruled tennis the way the New York Yankees lorded over major league baseball, the Montreal Canadiens owned the National Hockey League and the east Africans dominated distance running. These were the glory years of Lew Hoad, Ken Rosewall, John Newcombe and Rod Laver, as well as Margaret Smith Court and Evonne Goolagong, when that broad Aussie accent, flat as the orange earth around Ayers Rock, was sure to be accompanied by a walloping serve and a topspin-heavy forehand.

Despite tremendous competition for the distinction, the Australian man with the most overall Grand Slam titles—indeed, the man of any nationality with the most—was Roy Emerson, that paragon of consistency and toughness. Emerson won 28 Grand Slam titles, including 12 in singles. He won the Australian Open singles crown six times. He was also an exceptional doubles player. He won 16 Grand Slam titles in men's doubles with five different partners, then a record. He was known for his incredible fitness, no surprise in a man who won Grand Slam championships in three decades and claimed the U.S. Pro title in 1978, at the age of 42.

"Emmo," as Emerson was known on tour, grew up on a cattle station in a tiny Queensland town with a curious name, Black Butt. One of his chores was to milk the family's 160 cows, and all that squeezing and pulling left Emerson with powerful wrists for tennis. He was also a talented track and field athlete, who clocked 10 seconds for 100 yards and

THE RECORD			
YEAR	AUS	FRENCH	WIM	U.S.
	S-D-M	S-D-M	S-D-M	S-D-M
1959	0-0-0	0-0-0	0-1-0	0-1-0
1960	0-0-0	0-1-0	0-0-0	0-1-0
1961	1-0-0	0-1-0	0-1-0	1-0-0
1962	0-1-0	0-1-0	0-0-0	0-0-0
1963	1-0-0	1-1-0	0-0-0	0-0-0
1964	1-0-0	0-1-0	1-0-0	1-0-0
1965	1-0-0	0-1-0	1-0-0	0-1-0
1966	1-1-0	0-0-0	0-0-0	0-1-0
1967	1-0-0	1-0-0	0-0-0	0-0-0
1968	0-0-0	0-0-0	0-0-0	0-0-0
1969	0-1-0	0-0-0	0-0-0	0-0-0
1970	0-0-0	0-0-0	0-0-0	0-0-0
1971	0-0-0	0-0-0	0-1-0	0-0-0
TOTAL	6-3-0	2-6-0	2-3-0	2-4-0

excelled in both the long and high jumps. When it became clear to the Emersons that their son was a gifted tennis player, they moved to Brisbane, where he could get better competition and coaching. Joining the Australian Davis Cup team when he was 17, Emerson played on eight winning Australian teams in nine years, going 21–2 in singles and 13–2 in doubles.

Always one of the more gregarious and fun-loving of tour pros, Emmo could lead the singing and drink bottomless quantities of beer, seemingly without paying the price the following day. He won Wimbledon singles titles in 1964 and '65 and was favored to win again in '66, but he lost his chance when he injured himself charging the net in the quarterfinals against countryman Owen Davidson. But, said *The New York Times*, "he was too much of a champion to quit. His service weakened and he could not turn his body quickly for ground strokes, but he played on. The true worth of a champion often emerges more in a defeat than a victory."

CHRIS EVERT

She was everybody's sweetheart, pretty in a wholesome, blond, all-American way, athletic but safely within the bounds of femininity. In both respects, Chris Evert offered a clear contrast to her great rival, Martina Navratilova, who for years was considered vaguely suspect by mainstream America for her Iron Curtain roots and her unashamedly muscular physique. Yes, adoring fans always had to share Evert, first with bad-boy Jimmy Connors, and then with husbands John Lloyd and Andy Mills. But no one seemed to mind much. With "Chrissie" as the sport's glowing glamour girl, women's tennis climbed to new levels of popularity in the 1970s.

Yet Evert's appeal as a woman never obscured how good she was as a player. In all, she won 18 Grand Slam singles titles, tying her for fourth on the alltime list with—who else?—Navratilova. Evert's first Grand Slam title came in the 1974 French Open, and it was there, on the red clay of Roland Garros Stadium, that she would always look most comfortable, reaching the finals in nine of 14 years and winning seven. She won the first of three Wimbledon crowns in 1974, a year in which Connors also triumphed at Centre Court, engendering cheesy headlines that declared the Americans' victories a "love match."

Evert was not the most athletic of players. Her success came from hard work. Her father, Jimmy, had been a tournament pro who in 1943 reached No. 11 in the U.S. rankings. After retiring, he had become the teaching pro at the Holiday Park tennis complex in Fort Lauderdale. When his daughter was six, he saw her hitting a ball against a backboard and became her first and only coach. Not able to generate sufficient power with her backhand, she developed a powerful two-handed stroke, which soon became the preferred style among women pros. Evert announced her arrival among the game's elite at age 15 at the Tournament of the Carolinas, where she upset top-ranked Margaret Smith Court, who had recently completed the Grand Slam. Evert reached the semifinals of the U.S. Open at 16 and turned pro on her 18th birthday.

Early in her career, Evert earned nickames like Little Miss Cool and the Ice Maiden for her poker face and her relentless baseline game. Not particularly fast or strong, she was astoundingly consistent, if boringly so to some. Blessed with seemingly endless patience as she waited for opponents to falter, she reached the semifinals of the U.S. Open in 17 of 19 appearances and those of Wimbledon in 17 of 18, demonstrating that, if she was to be faulted for her consistency, at least she was consistently great.

THE RECORD

YEAR	AUS	FRENCH	WIM	U.S.
	S-D-M	S-D-M	S-D-M	S-D-M
1974	0-0-0	1-1-0	1-0-0	0-0-0
1975	0-0-0	1-1-0	0-0-0	1-0-0
1976	0-0-0	0-0-0	1-1-0	1-0-0
1977	0-0-0	0-0-0	0-0-0	1-0-0
1978	0-0-0	0-0-0	0-0-0	1-0-0
1979	0-0-0	1-0-0	0-0-0	0-0-0
1980	0-0-0	1-0-0	0-0-0	1-0-0
1981	0-0-0	0-0-0	1-0-0	0-0-0
1982	1-0-0	0-0-0	0-0-0	1-0-0
1983	0-0-0	1-0-0	0-0-0	0-0-0
1984	1-0-0	0-0-0	0-0-0	0-0-0
1985	0-0-0	1-0-0	0-0-0	0-0-0
1986	0-0-0	1-0-0	0-0-0	0-0-0
TOTAL	**2-0-0**	**7-2-0**	**3-1-0**	**6-0-0**

TIMELINE

1961

Evert (right, at age six), started playing tennis in earnest after her father, Jimmy, who won the Canadian Nationals in 1947, saw her practicing and decided to coach her. Raised on the clay courts of Fort Lauderdale, Evert grew up to become one of the world's premier baseline specialist.

1973
Eighteen-year-old Evert (left) reached the final of the French Open, where she fell 6–7, 7–6, 6–4 to Margaret Smith Court, who won three of the four Grand Slam events that season. Evert's game was best suited to the red clay of Roland Garros, and she would return to the French Open final the following year and win the first of her seven titles there, whipping Olga Morozova 6–1, 6–2.

1980
Though her baseline style was tailor-made for slower courts, Evert proved throughout her career that she could win with her game on any surface. In 1980, for the fourth time in her career, she won two of the four Grand Slam events, taking the French Open final 6–0, 6–3 over Virginia Ruzici, and winning the U.S. Open with a 5–7, 6–1, 6–1 triumph over Hana Mandlikova in the final.

1984
Evert (below, left) and her legendary rival Martina Navratilova (below, right) met for the second consecutive year in the U.S. Open final at Flushing Meadows. Navratilova won again, this time by 4–6, 6–4, 6–4. It was Evert's last appearance in a final at the U.S. Open, where she had enjoyed considerable success in her career. In 1978, when she defeated Pam Shriver 7–6, 6–4 in the final, Evert became the first woman since Helen Jacobs (1932–35) to win the tournament four straight times.

The perfect athlete for the radicalized 1960s, Billie Jean King came at you charging, like the serve-and-volley game she favored, determined to score points before you knew what was happening. It speaks volumes about King's impact as a crusader for equal wages for women that, a generation after her retirement, we remember her as much for her passionate activism as for the 39 Grand Slam titles she won, including six singles titles at Wimbledon and four at the U.S. Open.

Equality, fairness and logic were always the cornerstones of King's causes. Could there ever be justification for chauvinism or prejudice? She joined Rod Laver and other male stars in petitioning for actual prize money rather than the £50 gift voucher that had been her reward for winning Wimbledon in 1966. She was the driving force behind World Team Tennis, the first equal-pay pro league, and its first commissioner.

She helped found the Women's Tennis Association, the Women's Sports Foundation and *Women Sports* magazine.

King came to the silver spoon game from a much less privileged world than most tennis champions. The daughter of a Long Beach, Calif., fireman, she learned the game on the public courts of her hometown. Her mother sewed her tennis dresses, and her first racket was purchased with coins saved in a Mason jar. King was 17 when she won her first Grand Slam title, the 1961 women's doubles at Wimbledon. A relentless perfectionist, she moved to Australia in 1964 to take lessons from 1954 Australian Open champ Mervyn Rose. It paid off at Wimbledon in '66, when King won the first of 12 Grand Slam singles titles.

In 1973 King was given the perfect stage on which to promote her feminism when former player Bobby Riggs challenged her to what became known as the Battle of the Sexes. Riggs, 55, had already beaten Margaret Smith Court. But King whipped him 6–4, 6–3, 6–3 in front of 30,000 fans in the Astrodome. "Tennis has always been reserved for the rich, the white, the males," said a triumphant King, "and I've always been pledged to change all that."

THE RECORD

YEAR	AUS S-D-M	FRENCH S-D-M	WIM S-D-M	U.S. S-D-M
1961	0-0-0	0-0-0	0-1-0	0-0-0
1962	0-0-0	0-0-0	0-1-0	0-0-0
1963	0-0-0	0-0-0	0-0-0	0-0-0
1964	0-0-0	0-0-0	0-0-0	0-1-0
1965	0-0-0	0-0-0	0-1-0	0-0-0
1966	0-0-0	0-0-0	1-0-0	0-0-0
1967	0-0-0	0-0-1	1-1-1	1-1-1
1968	1-0-1	0-0-0	1-1-0	0-0-0
1969	0-0-0	0-0-0	0-0-0	0-0-0
1970	0-0-0	0-0-1	0-1-0	0-0-0
1971	0-0-0	0-0-0	0-1-1	1-0-1
1972	0-0-0	1-1-0	1-1-0	1-0-0
1973	0-0-0	0-0-0	1-1-1	0-0-1
1974	0-0-0	0-0-0	0-0-1	1-1-0
1975	0-0-0	0-0-0	1-0-0	0-0-0
1976	0-0-0	0-0-0	0-0-0	0-0-1
1977	0-0-0	0-0-0	0-0-0	0-0-0
1978	0-0-0	0-0-0	0-0-0	0-1-0
1979	0-0-0	0-0-0	0-1-0	0-0-0
1980	0-0-0	0-0-0	0-0-0	0-1-0
TOTAL	**1-0-1**	**1-1-2**	**6-10-4**	**4-5-4**

1959
The 15-year-old King (above), then known as Billie Jean Moffitt, was only two years away from her first Grand Slam, the '61 Wimbledon doubles title, which she won with 18-year-old Karen Hantze. They were the youngest pair to win the championship.

1971
King became the first female athlete to earn more than $100,000 in a season, after a spectacular year in which she won 17 of 31 singles events and a record 21 of 26 doubles tournaments. Her 38 titles and 192 match wins in the year are both records as well.

1973
"He's an old man, he walks like a duck, he can't see . . . and besides, he's an idiot," Rosie Casals, friend and doubles partner to King (below, left), memorably said of 55-year-old Bobby Riggs (below right) prior to the carnivalesque Battle of the Sexes match in September.

1974
After taking her fourth Wimbledon mixed doubles crown (with Owen Davidson), King won her fourth U.S. Open singles title, beating the luckless Evonne Goolagong (who lost four straight U.S. Open finals from 1973 to '76) 3–6, 6–3, 7–5 in the final.

1975
King (left) whipped Evonne Goolagong Cawley 6–0, 6–1 to win the sixth and final Wimbledon singles title of her extraordinary career. She would win one more doubles title at Wimbledon, with Martina Navratilova in 1979, to give her 20 titles at the fabled venue, more than any other player. In 1983, at age 39½, King won at Beckenham to become the oldest woman to win a pro title.

ROD LAVER

Rod Laver was born in 1938, the year Don Budge became the first tennis player to achieve a Grand Slam. Twenty-four years later Laver would become the second, duplicating Budge's feat by winning all four of the game's top championships. But what makes Laver arguably the greatest of all tennis players is that in 1969, at the dawn of "open," or professional, tennis, he produced another Slam, winning what SPORTS ILLUSTRATED's Roy Blount Jr. dubbed the "Grandest Slam." "It looks like the sport will have to be opened considerably wider," wrote Blount Jr., "to include angels, highly trained kangaroos or something as yet unenvisaged, before anyone else will be in Laver's league."

Though his nickname, the Rocket, which was applied during his scrawny youth, was originally meant sarcastically, Laver grew into it as he developed a ferocious topspin power game. He also pos-

sessed an entire arsenal of wicked strokes and spins—dinks, overhead volleys, a slice backhand and a drop shot that performed the maddening trick of bouncing back into the net like a yoyo. "It's the basis of my game, spin," he said. "Spin keeps me excited." Relatively small at 5' 8½" and 155 pounds, Laver's body, as Bud Collins memorably described it, "seemed to dangle from a massive left arm that belonged to a gorilla." With that Popeye forearm, Laver won 11 Grand Slam singles titles.

Laver learned his wicked strokes on his family's cattle ranch in Queensland, Australia. In his teens

he was discovered by Harry Hopman, Australia's great Davis Cup captain. Hopman was demanding, even controlling, managing his charges' lives off the court as well as on it. But under his tutelage, Laver flourished, dominating junior tournaments around the world before joining his country's Davis Cup team in 1959. Australia won four straight Cups with Laver on board, and he won his first Slam, after which he made the risky decision to turn pro, entering a circuit much less prestigious than the one he was leaving.

The tennis world tilted on its axis in 1968, when the British Lawn Tennis Association voted to defy the International Lawn Tennis Federation by making Wimbledon an "open" or pro event. Back to the fray rushed many of the game's greatest stars—Ken Rosewall, Pancho Gonzalez and, of course, Laver, who won his historic second Slam the following year. No man has achieved one since.

YEAR	AUS	FRENCH	WIM	U.S.
	S-D-M	S-D-M	S-D-M	S-D-M
1959	0-1-0	0-0-0	0-0-1	0-0-0
1960	1-1-0	0-0-0	0-0-1	0-0-0
1961	0-1-0	0-1-1	1-0-0	0-0-0
1962	1-0-0	1-0-0	1-0-0	1-0-0
1963	0-0-0	0-0-0	0-0-0	0-0-0
1964	0-0-0	0-0-0	0-0-0	0-0-0
1965	0-0-0	0-0-0	0-0-0	0-0-0
1966	0-0-0	0-0-0	0-0-0	0-0-0
1967	0-0-0	0-0-0	0-0-0	0-0-0
1968	0-0-0	0-0-0	1-0-0	0-0-0
1969	1-1-0	1-0-0	1-0-0	1-0-0
1970	0-0-0	0-0-0	0-0-0	0-0-0
1971	0-0-0	0-0-0	0-1-0	0-0-0
TOTAL	**3-4-0**	**2-1-1**	**4-1-2**	**2-0-0**

TIMELINE

1959
Suffering from a bruised heel, a strained groin and an upset stomach, Laver (above) still blasted his way past NCAA men's singles champ Whitney Reed at the U.S. Open, winning their match 6–1, 6–4, 5–7, 6–4.

1960
Laver won his first major singles title, outlasting his countryman Neale Fraser 5–7, 3–6, 6–3, 8–6, 8–6 in the Australian Open final. He also teamed with Bob Mark to win the Australian doubles title 1–6, 6–2, 6–4, 6–4 over Fraser and Roy Emerson.

1962
Completing a historic season with a 6–2, 6–4, 5–7, 6–4 victory over Roy Emerson in the final of the U.S. Open, Laver (below) became the first man since Don Budge in 1938 to achieve a Grand Slam.

1968
In the first year of "open competition" between professionals and amateurs, Laver reached the final of both the French Open and Wimbledon. He fell to Ken Rosewall at Roland Garros, but he defeated Tony Roche to take Wimbledon.

1969
Only one other man has completed a single Grand Slam; when Laver (above) accomplished a second he lent considerable weight to the argument for him as the greatest player who ever lived. He beat Tony Roche 7–9, 6–1, 6–3, 6–2 in the U.S. Open final to clinch it.

In all of sport there is no more powerful embodiment of the strong, independent, triumphant woman than Martina Navratilova. Of course, we know Martina—she attained celebrity mononym status years ago—primarily because of the 18 Grand Slam singles titles she won, including a record nine Wimbledons. But the great lesson of her life, about the importance of self-determination and self-transformation, also makes her an inspiration to many. "I like the fact that she's honest," said 1990 U.S. Open titlist Gabriela Sabatini. "She is how she is and nothing else, both on and off the court. She's not hiding anything."

It was not always like that. Navratilova grew up in Czechoslovakia in the 1960s. In her autobiography she attributes her indepedent spirit to her mother, who taught her that, for girls as well as for boys, "it's good to compete, good to run, good to sweat, good to get dirty, good to feel tired and healthy and refreshed." Navratilova ran and sweat for the Czech women's singles title in 1972, at 15, and made her first trip to the U.S. the following year, when she faced the woman who would become her friend and steady rival, Chris Evert, at a tournament in Akron. The American won that first meeting, but it was close, and young Martina gained confidence.

Navratilova's love of America was not lost on the Czech authorities, who reluctantly let her travel. Soon after reaching the semifinals of the 1975 U.S. Open, Navratilova defected to the U.S. (She became a citizen in 1981 and announced she was bisexual nine days later.)

For a while, her great potential was unfulfilled. She loved American fast food, and her resulting girth prompted Bud Collins to dub her the Great Wide Hope. But in one of her inspiring demonstrations of will power, she began working out with basketball player Nancy Lieberman, lifting weights and running. She became the fittest woman on the tour. She earned her first No. 1 ranking in July 1978, the same month she first won Wimbledon. For the next 13 years she never slipped out of the world's top three. The Associated Press named her Female Athlete of the 1980s. But her influence extended far beyond tennis. Said Evert, whose record against her was 43–37, "Martina revolutionized the game by her superb athleticism and aggressiveness, not to mention her outspokenness and her candor."

THE RECORD

YEAR	AUS			FRENCH			WIM			U.S.		
	S	D	M	S	D	M	S	D	M	S	D	M
1974	0	0	0	0	0	1	0	0	0	0	0	0
1975	0	0	0	0	1	0	0	0	0	0	0	0
1976	0	0	0	0	0	0	0	1	0	0	0	0
1977	0	0	0	0	0	0	0	0	0	0	1	0
1978	0	0	0	0	0	0	1	0	0	0	1	0
1979	0	0	0	0	0	0	1	1	0	0	0	0
1980	0	1	0	0	0	0	0	0	0	0	1	0
1981	1	0	0	0	0	0	0	1	0	0	0	0
1982	0	1	0	1	1	0	1	1	0	0	0	0
1983	1	1	0	0	0	0	1	1	0	1	1	0
1984	0	1	0	1	1	0	1	1	0	1	1	0
1985	1	1	0	0	1	1	1	0	1	0	0	1
1986	0	0	0	0	1	0	1	1	0	1	1	0
1987	0	1	0	0	1	0	1	0	0	1	1	1
1988	0	1	0	0	1	0	0	0	0	0	0	0
1989	0	1	0	0	0	0	0	0	0	0	1	0
1990	0	0	0	0	0	0	1	0	0	0	1	0
TOTAL	3	8	0	2	7	2	9	7	1	4	9	2

TIMELINE

1978
After defeating Chris Evert 2–6, 6–4, 7–5 Navratilova (below) exulted in her first Wimbledon championship. She would defeat Evert in straight sets to repeat in '79.

1983
Navratilova produced arguably the most dominating year in the history of women's tennis: She went 86–1 in singles play, her only loss coming to Kathy Horvath of the U.S. in the fourth round of the French Open, and swept the other three Slams.

1984
Continuing the previous year's torrid pace, Navratilova (below) won 78 of 80 matches and took the French Open, Wimbledon and the U.S. Open. She lost in the semis in Australia, leaving her two wins short of a Grand Slam.

1987
Despite winning Wimbledon and the U.S. Open, and appearing in the final of all four majors, Navratilova was bounced from the No. 1 spot in the rankings, a position she had held since 1982, by Steffi Graf, who won the French Open and 75 of her 77 matches.

1990
With a 6–4, 6–1 victory over Zina Garrison of the U.S., Navratilova (above) won her ninth Wimbledon singles title, breaking Helen Wills Moody's record of eight. At 33 she was the oldest women's Wimbledon champ since 1914.

TIMELINE

1920

Tilden (near right) shook hands with Gerald L. Patterson after defeating Patterson 2–6, 6–3, 6–2, 6–4 to win Wimbledon, a tournament he rarely entered, for the first time. Tilden would repeat as Wimbledon champ the following year.

1925

Completing a run of eight consecutive U.S. Open finals with his sixth straight championship, Tilden defeated Bill Johnston 4–6, 11–9, 6–3, 4–6, 6–3 in a thrilling final at Forest Hills. Tilden had beaten Johnston in the previous three U.S. Open finals as well.

1929

At 36 Tilden (below, with trophy) won the seventh and final U.S. Open championship of his legendary career. His run of six titles had ended in 1926, when he failed to reach the final. He returned to the championship match in '27 but lost a tense three-setter to René Lacoste (11–9, 6–3, 11–9). His seventh title, in '29, came at the expense of Francis T. Hunter, whom Tilden vanquished in the final, 3–6, 6–3, 4–6, 6–2, 6–4. Tilden would turn pro at the end of the following year.

1930

In his last year as an amateur, Tilden (below) won his third Wimbledon singles title, 10 years after he had won his first. He blitzed Wilmer Allison 6–3, 9–7, 6–4 in the final to win the 21st Grand Slam title of his career. Earlier in the year, Tilden had reached the final of the French Open, losing 3–6, 8–6, 6–3, 6–1 to Henri Cochet. At season's end Tilden took his game on the road as a touring professional with 1932 Wimbledon champ Ellsworth Vines. An expert on the nuances of the game, Big Bill wrote a classic tennis instructional guide in 1925 called *Match Play and the Spin of the Ball.*

BILL TILDEN

In the 1920s, that decade in which Americans went temporarily insane and traded their customary rectitude for giddy good times, there was no bigger star than Bill Tilden. "Big Bill" dominated tennis the way few athletes have ever dominated a sport, winning seven U.S. Open singles titles, including six straight from 1920 to '25. He also was ranked No. 1 in the world for those six years, a feat no one has matched.

Tilden was as unlikely looking an athlete as Babe Ruth, though in a very different way. Whereas Ruth had a round barrel of a belly set atop spindly legs, Tilden looked like an exotic wading bird, with exceedingly long limbs and shoulders that were perpetually stooped, almost as if he were trying to duck out of his own body. Though his "cannonball" serve was the hardest of his generation, he preferred to stay back on the baseline and engage opponents in a chess game of spin and placement. "Tilden always seems to have a thousand means of putting the ball away from his opponent's reach," said three-time French Open champ René Lacoste. "Even when beaten, he always leaves the impression on the public mind that he was superior to the victor."

THE RECORD				
YEAR	AUS	FRENCH	WIM	U.S.
	S-D-M	S-D-M	S-D-M	S-D-M
1913	—	—	0-0-0	0-0-1
1914	—	—	0-0-0	0-0-1
1915	—	—	—	0-0-0
1916	—	—	—	0-0-0
1917	—	—	—	0-0-0
1918	—	—	—	0-1-0
1919	—	—	0-0-0	0-0-0
1920	—	—	1-0-0	1-0-0
1921	—	—	1-1-0	1-1-0
1922	—	—	0-0-0	1-1-1
1923	—	—	0-0-0	1-1-1
1924	—	—	0-0-0	1-0-0
1925	—	0-0-0	0-0-0	1-0-0
1926	—	0-0-0	0-0-0	0-0-0
1927	—	0-0-0	0-1-0	0-1-0
1928	—	0-0-0	0-0-0	0-0-0
1929	—	0-0-0	0-0-0	1-0-0
1930	—	0-0-1	1-0-0	0-0-0
TOTAL	DNP	0-0-1	3-1-0	7-5-4

Some of that hauteur was his birthright. Tilden grew up on Philadelphia's Main Line, in a world of tremendous wealth and privilege. He was seven when he won his first tournament, at the tony Onteora Club in upstate New York, but that early success did little to persuade him to take the game seriously. He smoked incessantly when off the court.

Tilden's weakness was his backhand. Indeed, the turning point in his career was an embarrassing loss to Bill Johnston at the 1919 U.S. Open, in which Johnston picked mercilessly on Tilden's backhand. Tilden retreated to a friend's house in Newport, Rhode Island, which had an indoor clay court and spent the winter developing that backhand. When he returned to the game he was an almost unstoppable force. In 1930 he retired from amateur tennis and proceeded to tour the country as a professional, with dapper young Ellsworth Vines as his foil.

Tilden was a closeted homosexual, as most everyone in tennis knew. But when he was arrested in 1946 and imprisoned for having sex with a 14-year-old boy, many friends turned from him, and his fortunes declined dramatically. In 1953 Tilden died alone and nearly penniless in Los Angeles, his bags packed for the U.S. Pro championships. He was 60.

INTERNATIONAL TENNIS
HALL OF FAME

ENSHRINEES (PLAYERS ONLY)

NAME (YR. OF INDUCTION)	D.O.B. D.O.D.	CITIZENSHIP
Fred B. Alexander (1961)	b. 8-14-1880 d. 3-3-69	United States
Wilmer L. Allison (1963)	b. 12-8-04 d. 4-20-77	United States
Manuel Alonso (1977)	b. 11-12-1895 d. 11-11-84	Spain
Malcolm Anderson (2000)	b. 3-3-35	Australia
Arthur Ashe (1985)	b. 7-10-43 d. 2-6-93	United States
Juliette Atkinson (1974)	b. 4-15-1873 d. 1-12-44	United States
H.W. Bunny Austin (1997)	b. 8-20-06	Great Britain
Tracy Austin (1992)	b. 12-12-62	United States
Maud Barger-Wallach (1958)	b. 6-15-1870 d. 4-2-54	United States
Karl Behr (1969)	b. 5-30-1885 d. 10-15-49	United States
Pauline Betz Addie (1965)	b. 8-6-19	United States
Bjorn Borg (1987)	b. 6-6-56	Sweden
Jean Borotra (1976)	b. 8-13-1898 d. 6-17-94	France
Lesley Turner Bowrey (1997)	b. 8-16-42	Australia
John Bromwich (1984)	b. 11-14-18 d. 10-22-99	Australia
Norman Everard Brookes (1977)	b. 11-14-1877 d. 9-28-68	Australia
Louise Brough (1967)	b. 3-11-23	United States
Mary K. Browne (1957)	b. 6-3-1891 d. 8-19-71	United States
Jacques Brugnon (1976)	b. 5-11-1895 d. 3-20-78	France
J. Donald Budge (1964)	b. 6-13-15 d. 1-26-2000	United States
Maria E. Bueno (1978)	b. 10-11-39	Brazil
Mabel E. Cahill (1976)	b. 4-2-1863 d. n/a	Ireland
Oliver S. Campbell (1955)	b. 2-25-1871 d. 7-11-53	United States
Rosie Casals (1996)	b. 9-16-48	United States
Malcolm Chace (1961)	b. 3-12-1875 d. 7-16-55	United States
Philippe Chatrier (1992)	b. 2-2-26 d.2000	France
Clarence Clark (1983)	b. 8-27-1859 d. 6-29-37	United States
Joseph S. Clark (1955)	b.11-30-1861 d. 4-14-56	United States
William J. Clothier (1956)	b. 9-27-1881 d. 9-4-62	United States
Henri Cochet (1976)	b. 12-14-01 d. 4-1-87	France
Maureen Connolly Brinker (1968)	b. 9-17-34 d. 6-21-69	United States
Jimmy Connors (1998)	b. 9-2-52	United States
Ashley Cooper (1991)	b. 9-15-36	Australia
Gottfried von Cramm (1977)	b. 7-7-09 d. 11-8-76	Germany
Jack Crawford (1979)	b. 3-22-08 d. 9-10-91	Australia
Dwight F. Davis (1956)	b. 7-5-1879 d. 11-28-45	United States
Charlotte Dod (1983)	b. 9-24-1871 d. 6-27-60	Great Britain
John H. Doeg (1962)	b. 12-7-08 d. 4-27-78	United States
Lawrence Doherty (1980)	b. 10-8-1875 d. 8-21-19	Great Britain
Reginald Doherty (1980)	b. 10-14-1872 d. 12-29-10	Great Britain
Dorothea Douglass Chambers (1981)	b. 9-3-1878 d. 1960	United States
Jaroslav Drobny (1983)	b. 10-12-21	Czechoslovakia/ Egypt/ Great Britain
Margaret Osborne du Pont (1967)	b. 3-4-18	United States
James Dwight (1955)	b. 7-14-1852 d. 7-13-17	United States
Roy Emerson (1982)	b. 11-3-36	Australia
Pierre Etchebaster (1978)	b. 12-8-1893 d. 3-24-80	France
Chris Evert (1995)	b. 12-21-54	United States
Robert Falkenburg (1974)	b. 1-29-26	United States/Brazil
Neale Fraser (1984)	b. 10-3-33	Australia
Shirley Fry-Irvin (1970)	b. 6-30-27	United States
Charles S. Garland (1969)	b. 10-29-1898 d. 1-28-71	United States
Althea Gibson (1971)	b. 8-25-27	United States
Richard A. (Pancho) Gonzales (1968)	b. 5-9-28 d. 7-3-95	United States
Evonne Goolagong Cawley (1988)	b. 7-31-51	Australia
Bryan M. Grant Jr. (1972)	b. 12-25-10 d. 6-5-86	United States
Clarence Griffin (1970)	b. 1-19-1888 d. 3-28-73	United States
Harold H. Hackett (1961)	b. 7-12-1878 d. 11-20-37	United States
Ellen Forde Hansell (1965)	b. 9-28-1869 d. 5-11-37	United States
Darlene R. Hard (1973)	b. 1-6-1936	United States
Doris J. Hart (1969)	b. 6-20-25	United States
Ann Haydon Jones (1985)	b. 10-7-38	Great Britain
Bob Hewitt (1992)	b. 1-12-40	Australia
Lew Hoad (1980)	b. 11-23-34 d. 7-3-94	Australia
Harry Hopman (1978)	b. 8-12-06 d. 12-27-85	Australia
Hazel Hotchkiss Wightman (1957)	b. 12-20-1886 d. 12-5-74	United States
Fred Hovey (1974)	b. 10-7-1868 d. 10-18-45	United States
Joseph R. Hunt (1966)	b. 2-17-19 d. 2-2-44	United States
Francis T. Hunter (1961)	b. 6-28-1894 d. 12-2-81	United States
Helen Hull Jacobs (1962)	b. 8-6-08 d. 6-2-97	United States
William Johnston (1958)	b. 11-2-1894 d. 5-1-46	United States
Robert Kelleher (2000)	b. 3-5-13	United States
Billie Jean King (1987)	b. 11-22-43	United States
Jan Kodes (1990)	b. 3-1-46	Czechoslovakia
John A. Kramer (1968)	b. 8-1-21	United States
Rene Lacoste (1976)	b. 7-2-04 d. 10-12-96	France
William A. Larned (1956)	b. 12-30-1872 d. 12-16-26	United States
Arthur D. Larsen (1969)	b. 4-17-25	United States
Rod G. Laver (1981)	b. 8-9-38	Australia
Suzanne Lenglen (1978)	b. 5-24-1899 d. 7-4-38	France
George M. Lott Jr. (1964)	b. 10-16-06 d. 12-2-91	United States
Gene Mako (1973)	b. 1-24-16	United States
Molla Bjurstedt Mallory (1958)	b. 3-6-1884 d. 11-22-59	Norway
Hana Mandlikova (1994)	b. 2-19-62	Czechoslovakia/ Australia
Alice Marble (1964)	b. 9-28-13 d. 12-13-90	United States
Alastair B. Martin (1973)	b. 3-11-15	United States

194 Bellevue Avenue
Newport, RI 02840
Telephone: (401) 849-3990
Executive Vice President and
Chief Operating Officer: Mark Stenning
Marketing Manager: Kat Anderson
www.tennisfame.com

NAME (YR. OF INDUCTION)	D.O.B. D.O.D.	CITIZENSHIP
Dan Maskell (1996)	b. 4-11-08 d. 12-10-92	Great Britain
John McEnroe (1999)	b. 2-16-59	United States
Ken McGregor (1999)	b. 6-2-29	Australia
Kathleen McKane Godfree (1978)	b. 5-7-1896 d. 6-19-92	Great Britain
Chuck McKinley (1986)	b. 1-5-41 d. 8-10-86	United States
Maurice McLoughlin (1957)	b. 1-7-1890 d. 12-10-57	United States
Frew McMillan (1992)	b. 5-20-42	South Africa
W. Donald McNeill (1965)	b. 4-30-18 d. 11-28-96	United States
Elisabeth H. Moore (1971)	b. 3-5-1876 d. 1-22-59	United States
Angela Mortimer Barrett (1993)	b. 4-21-32	Great Britain
Gardnar Mulloy (1972)	b. 11-22-13	United States
R. Lindley Murray (1958)	b. 11-3-1892 d. 1-17-70	United States
Ilie Nastase (1991)	b. 7-19-46	Romania
Martina Navratilova (2000)	b. 10-18-56	United States
John D. Newcombe (1986)	b. 5-23-44	Australia
Betty Nuthall Shoemaker (1977)	b. 5-23-11 d. 11-8-83	Great Britain
Alex Olmedo (1987)	b. 3-24-36	Peru
Rafael Osuna (1979)	b. 9-15-38 d. 6-6-69	Mexico
Mary Ewing Outerbridge (1981)	b. 3-9-1852 d. 5-3-86	United States
Sarah Palfrey Danzig (1963)	n/a	United States
Frank A. Parker (1966)	b. 1-31-16 d. 7-24-97	United States
Gerald Patterson (1989)	b. 12-17-1895 d. 6-13-67	Australia
Budge Patty (1977)	b. 2-11-24	United States
Theodore R. Pell (1966)	b. 5-12-1879 d. 8-18-67	United States
Fred Perry (1975)	b. 5-18-09 d. 2-2-92	Great Britain
Tom Pettitt (1982)	b. 12-19-1859 d. 10-17-46	Great Britain
Nicola Pietrangeli (1986)	b. 9-11-33	Italy
Adrian Quist (1984)	b. 8-4-13 d. 11-17-91	Australia
Dennis Ralston (1987)	b. 7-27-42	United States
Ernest Renshaw (1983)	b. 1-3-1861 d. 9-2-1899	Great Britain
William Renshaw (1983)	b. 1-3-1861 d. 8-12-04	Great Britain
Vincent Richards (1961)	b. 3-20-03 d. 9-28-59	United States
Bobby Riggs (1967)	b. 2-25-18 d. 10-10-95	United States
Anthony D. Roche (1986)	b. 5-17-45	Australia
Ellen C. Roosevelt (1975)	b. 1868 d. 9-26-54	United States
Ken Rosewall (1980)	b. 11-2-34	Australia
Dorothy Round Little (1986)	b. 7-13-08 d. 11-12-82	Great Britain
Elizabeth Ryan (1972)	b. 2-8-1892 d. 7-8-79	United States
Manuel Santana (1984)	b. 5-10-38	Spain
Richard Savitt (1976)	b. 3-4-27	United States
Frederick R. Schroeder (1966)	b. 7-20-21	United States
Eleonora Sears (1968)	b. 9-28-1881 d. 3-16-68	United States
Richard D. Sears (1955)	b. 10-16-1861 d. 4-8-43	United States
Frank Sedgman (1979)	b. 10-29-27	Australia
Pancho Segura (1984)	b. 6-20-21	Ecuador
Vic Seixas Jr. (1971)	b. 8-30-23	United States
Francis X. Shields (1964)	b. 11-18-09 d. 8-19-75	United States
Henry W. Slocum Jr. (1955)	b. 5-28-1862 d. 1-22-49	United States
Margaret Smith Court (1979)	b. 7-16-42	Australia
Stan Smith (1987)	b. 12-14-46	United States
Fred Stolle (1985)	b. 10-8-38	Australia
May Sutton Bundy (1956)	b. 9-25-1886 d. 10-4-75	United States
William F. Talbert (1967)	b. 9-4-18 d. 2-28-99	United States
Bill Tilden (1959)	b. 2-10-1893 d. 6-5-53	United States
Bertha Townsend Toulmin (1974)	b. 3-7-1869 d. 5-12-09	United States
Tony Trabert (1970)	b. 8-16-30	United States
James H. Van Alen (1965)	b. 9-19-02 d. 7-3-91	United States
John Van Ryn (1963)	b. 6-30-05 d. 1999	United States
Guillermo Vilas (1991)	b. 8-17-52	Argentina
Ellsworth Vines (1962)	b. 9-28-11 d. 3-17-94	United States
Virginia Wade (1989)	b. 7-10-45	Great Britain
Marie Wagner (1969)	b. 2-2-1883 d. 3-30-75	United States
Holcombe Ward (1956)	b. 11-23-1878 d. 1-23-67	United States
Watson Washburn (1965)	b. 6-13-1894 d. 12-2-73	United States
Malcolm D. Whitman (1955)	b. 3-15-1877 d. 12-28-32	United States
Anthony Wilding (1978)	b. 10-31-1883 d. 5-9-1915	Great Britain/ New Zealand
Richard Norris Williams II (1957)	b. 1-29-1891 d. 6-2-68	United States
Helen Wills Moody Roark (1959)	b. 10-6-05 d. 1-1-98	United States
Sidney B. Wood (1964)	b. 11-1-11	United States
Robert D. Wrenn (1955)	b. 9-20-1873 d. 11-12-25	United States
Beals C. Wright (1956)	b. 12-19-1879 d. 8-23-61	United States

GOLF

When the World Golf Hall of Fame opened as part of the new World Golf Village near St. Augustine, Fla., in May 1998, golf fans wondered whether this imposing glass edifice would succeed where a number of earlier halls—at the Augusta Country Club in Georgia, at LPGA headquarters in Sugar Land, Texas, and in Pinehurst, N.C.—had come up short. Wouldn't it be wonderful if at last golf had one all-encompassing, authoritative Hall, as other sports do? Certainly, the new World Golf Hall has one huge advantage over its predecessors: It's backed by the PGA, which wants it to succeed and has the deep pockets to see that it does.

Designed by Boston-based architect E. Verner Johnson, whose specialty is museums, aquariums and halls of fame, it's a sleek, intricately designed structure. Visitors are greeted by a vast bank of video monitors, 240 square feet of screens showing a variety of memorable golfing images, from Ben Hogan's steely eyes and

With the opening of the ultra-modern World Golf Hall of Fame (above) near St. Augustine, Fla., in May 1998, the sport finally consolidated its history and memories in one location. Previously, golf had halls of fame in Georgia, Texas and North Carolina.

Arnold Palmer's farewell wave to Jack Nicklaus and Tiger Woods hitting five irons side by side. Inside, along with whimsical artifacts such as Sam Snead's lunch box and Babe Didrikson's harmonica, the emphasis is on hi-tech participation. "The overall experience is intended to stimulate golfers and non-golfers alike through modern technology and interactive displays," says the Hall's guide. There's a computer swing analyzer; a "rules challenge," in which visitors offer their own interpretation of sticky rules situations before hearing the actual rule; and a brand new Science of Golf exhibit exploring the physics of golf ball flight. It's also one of the few Halls with outdoor exhibits, including an island green ($5 for two balls) and an 18-hole putting course.

On this side of the Atlantic, golf halls of fame have had a desultory and scattered history. At the suggestion of sportswriter Grantland Rice, the PGA began electing members to a Hall of Fame in 1940. It was a nice idea, but for many years there was no actual Hall anyone could visit.

The LPGA created a Hall of Fame in 1951, inducting an inaugural class of four (Patty Berg, Babe Zaharias, Betty Jameson and Louise Suggs). Though the Ladies' Hall would have its own ongoing controversy—more on that later—it easily trumped the men's by actually having a Hall, in the clubhouse of the Augusta Country Club, site of the Titleholders Championship, which at the time was a major.

Finally, in 1972, a bundle of energy named Bill Maurer decided to build a real shrine to the game and chose Pinehurst, that lovely old village in the sandhills of North Carolina, as his site. Sure, there was a measure of self-interest in Maurer's choice: He was president of the Diamondhead Corporation, which owned and operated the famed Pinehurst resort. But still it was hard to imagine a prettier place for the Hall than Pinehurst, where the great golf architect Donald Ross had lived and built several world-class courses. Maurer sunk $2.5 million into his World Golf Hall of Fame and got for his money a handsome building with white columns and fountains. Set amongst sweet-smelling pines and magnolias, it had ambience worthy of its membership.

Its opening, in the summer of 1974, was grand indeed, with President Ford playing the famed No. 2 course with some of the 13 original inductees, including Jack Nicklaus, Sam Snead and Arnold Palmer. Top vote-getter Ben Hogan was injured but followed in a cart. Defending himself to those who wondered what right he had to build a hall, Maurer said, "Everybody else had a shot at doing it for 600 years and nobody did. If somebody else wants to build another one, fine. But I like the score I'm in the clubhouse with."

Unfortunately, Maurer's Hall did not attract many visitors. (Perhaps it was the dearth of artifacts—or the sculpture of Bobby Jones in action with a swing form that didn't much resemble his sweet stroke.) The LPGA, which had joined the Pinehurst Hall in 1977,

Perhaps no golfer in the sport's long history can be said to have been a sure bet for the Hall of Fame as early in their career as Tiger Woods (above). With six victories and nine top 10 finishes in the 2000 season, 25-year-old Karrie Webb (below) has already earned enough points to qualify for the LPGA Hall of Fame.

moved out later that year and relocated to Sugar Land.

Now, the LPGA has its own wing in the new World Golf Hall, and its enshrinees are indeed worthy of visitors. For years it was easier to smash a one-iron through the eye of a needle than to get into the LPGA Hall of Fame. In contrast to other Halls, which seem to admit three or four athletes each year, the Ladies' Hall had such stringent entry requirements that it inducted that many each *decade*. At the start of 1999, when the criteria at last were amended, presumably because the membership was growing lonesome, the Hall had only 14 members, three fewer than the Pro Football Hall had in its inaugural class. Each of the 14 had met one of three requirements: 30 tournament victories, including two majors; or 35 wins, including one major; or 40 with no majors.

Suffering in limbo, barely short of qualifying, were a number of superb golfers: Amy Alcott, for example, won five majors but "only" 29 tournaments in all, while Beth Daniel, because she had just one major, needed three wins to reach 35. The men, by contrast, are supposed to have won two majors.

Some people applauded the LPGA Hall's high standards. They contrast the fates of Chi Chi Rodriguez (in the Hall, based largely on his personality and charity work) with Lloyd Mangrum (not in, despite having won 36 tournaments, including the 1946 U.S. Open). Others, though, have come to regret the LPGA's strict objective standards for the tyranny they impose, and the golfers they exclude.

Then, in 1999, the criteria were finally changed. The LPGA Hall now requires members to total 27 points, with a major win being worth two points, other Tour wins one, and the Vare Trophy and Player of the Year Awards also counting for one point. Daniel and Alcott immediately qualified. They were delighted, as was everyone who believed membership should be a means of celebration, not an ordeal.

PATTY BERG

Patty Berg was the great pioneering champion of women's golf, its most passionate advocate and its most successful player. But golf was just one of many sports Berg excelled at as a girl. The daughter of a Minneapolis grain merchant, the feisty, freckled redhead was a top speed skater and played quarterback for a boys' midget football team called the 50th Street Tigers, where one of her teammates was the future Hall of Fame coach Bud Wilkinson.

When Berg was 12, Bobby Jones won the third leg of his famed Grand Slam at the local Interlachen Country Club. Though she could not attend—she ran her elementary school's 30-yard dash that day, and won—Berg found inspiration in this brush with greatness. "We were so happy that he won at our club," said Berg, who persuaded her father to pay for a set of clubs and a family membership to Interlachen.

A quick study, Berg won the Minneapolis city championship at

16, reached the final of the national amateur the next year and then won it in 1938, when she won 10 of 13 tournaments. Still only 20, Berg was the most famous female golfer in the country and the Associated Press's Female Athlete of the Year.

Berg turned pro in 1940, which in those days meant giving endless clinics while playing against the handful of other pros in the three tournaments staged each year for a total purse of $500. Perhaps more than anyone else, Berg is reponsible for making the women's game the lucrative business it is today. Along with her foil and friend, Babe

Didrikson, she was instrumental in forming the LPGA and promoting its early tournaments with her delightful personality and play. Berg served as the organization's first president. Under her guidance the tour rapidly expanded to nine events and a purse of $45,000.

Before she retired in 1980, Berg won 57 LPGA tournaments and a record 15 majors. They included the first U.S. Open, in 1946, seven Titleholders victories and six Western Opens. She was the first player to reach the $100,000 mark in earnings. The 64 she shot at the Richmond Open in 1952 stood as the LPGA record for 12 years.

Herbert Warren Wind considered her a throwback to Hagen and Sarazen. "Like these champions of an earlier era," he wrote, "she is the intuitive shot-maker who expresses her full personality as she plays each shot to fit its different requirements."

THE RECORD

Major titles:
1941: Western Open
1943: Western Open
1946: U.S. Open
1948: Titleholders Championship, Western Open
1951: Western Open
1953: Titleholders Championship
1955: Titleholders Championship, Western Open
1957: Titleholders Championship, Western Open
1958: Western Open

Won 57 professional titles. One of 13 founders of the LPGA. Three-time winner of Associated Press Athlete of the Year award (1938, '43, and '55).

1938
On February 4, nine days shy of her 20th birthday, Berg (above) won the Miami Biltmore tournament, defeating Jane Jameson 4 and 3 in the finals. Later in the year, Berg would win the U.S. Amateur, an event in which she had twice finished runner-up, defeating Estelle Lawson 6 and 5.

1946
At the Spokane Country Club, Berg won the inaugural U.S. Women's Open, defeating Betty Jameson 5 and 4 in the 36-hole matchplay final to claim the winner's purse of $5,600 in bonds. She would win three other tournaments during the year.

1951
Having helped found the LPGA the previous year along with 12 of her peers, Berg (below, teeing off) was inducted into the Hall of Fame in its inaugural class of pros with Betty Jameson, Louise Suggs and Babe Didrikson.

1953
Berg seized her fifth Titleholders championship, which was a major in her era, and won the inaugural LPGA Vare Trophy as the player with the lowest scoring average (75.00). She would win two more Vare Trophies and finish her career with 15 major titles, the most alltime.

1954
On August 12, at the Tam O'Shanter Golf Course in Niles, Ill., Berg missed a putt on the 18th green (above) that would have given her a 68 and the new course record for women. No matter, she still won the $150,000 World Championship event with a 69, tying the course record set by Babe Didrikson in 1953. Berg would win two other LPGA events during the year.

BABE DIDRIKSON

"I was always determined to be the greatest athlete that ever lived," wrote Babe Didrikson in her autobiography, *This Life I've Led*. For a girl growing up in Texas in the 1920s, this was an unheard-of ambition. Yet, to a remarkable degree, Babe achieved her goal, making All-America in basketball, winning three U.S. Open titles in golf and, on the grandest stage of all, winning three medals at the 1932 Olympics in Los Angeles. Who was the greatest American athlete of the 20th century? If for a moment we can shake off our customary chauvinism, the answer may be Babe Didrikson.

Like that other Babe, Didrikson was a delightful force of nature, hungry for life and fun—"the happiest girl you ever saw, like a kid," said golfer Patty Berg. Babe was also a whirlwind of early feminist ambition who relished every chance she got to prove that girls could do all those things boys said they couldn't. Nothing intimidated her—not the era's prejudice against female athletes and not the cancer which took her life at age 45.

Babe grew up in Beaumont, Texas, and attributed her athleticism to the influence of her fitness-minded parents, who built gymnastics equipment in the backyard and insisted that Babe and her six siblings work out regularly. A born performer who played blues harmonica on a weekly radio show as a kid, Babe's leap to the big time came when she was recruited to play basketball for a Dallas insurance company team, which she led to the 1931 national title, frequently scoring 30 points a game at a time when entire teams scored 20.

Babe was an incorrigible show-off, and it was her need to flaunt her talent that led her to golf. At the Los Angeles Games, she boasted to sportswriter Grantland Rice about her athletic abilities, and Rice suggested she try golf even though she'd hardly played the game. After Rice had rounded up some friends and they played a round with Babe at Brentwood, all agreed she had talent.

Her appetite whetted, she started taking lessons in 1935 and in 1938 became the first woman to play a men's tour event, shooting 84–81 and missing the cut at the L.A. Open. It was a rare setback for Babe, who won 82 tournaments in her career, including 17 straight in 1946–47. She won the 1954 U.S. Open by a record 12 shots, only 15 months after surgery for her cancer, which proved to be the only opponent Babe couldn't whip.

THE RECORD

YEAR	EVENTS	BEST FINISH	EARNINGS ($)	AVG
1950	10	1	2,875	75.88
1951	14	1	6,812	74.92
1952	8	1	4,730	75.76
1953	10	1	5,132	75.70
1954	17	1	11,437	75.61
1955	8	1	3,398	75.60

Won the U.S. Women's Open: 1948, 1950, 1954
Won Titleholders Championship: 1947, 1950, 1952
Won Western Open: 1940, 1944, 1945, 1950
Career Earnings: $66, 237

TIMELINE

1938
On December 23 Didrikson (above, middle) married former professional wrestler George Zaharias (above, left), an energetic 296-pounder who began managing her career, arranging for Didrikson to visit Australia and New Zealand, among other exotic locales, to stage golf exhibitions.

1947
Asked during the British Amateur—which she won during her legendary streak of 17 straight victories—how she was able to hit the ball so hard, Didrikson shocked her British audience by replying, "I just loosen my girdle and let it fly."

1948
Ever the entertainer, Didrikson kissed her ball (above) in thanks after making a long putt on the 9th green at the U.S. Open. She would win the tournament, the first of her three U.S. Open championships, by eight strokes over Betty Hicks.

1950
Another typically superb year for Didrikson as she won the U.S. Open, the Title-holders Open, the Western Open and five other events. Her flamboyance and drawing power went a long way toward keeping the fledgling LPGA tour alive.

1954
Only 15 months after undergoing surgery for the cancer that would take her life in 1956, Didrikson (above) won the U.S. Open for the third time, walloping the field with a 72-71-73-75 and winning by 12 strokes over Betty Hicks.

BEN HOGAN

It has long been customary to laud Ben Hogan as the greatest ball striker in golf history. And that's true, as far as it goes. But Hogan is also the game's most fascinating, inscrutable figure. He's a special hero to a certain kind of old-school perfectionist, flinty moralists who revere him not only because he won nine majors but also because of how he won those majors—the fierce, uncompromising will that drove him to practice hours and hours, until his hands bled.

Hogan was a survivor, hanging on stubbornly through both a stretch of awful play early in his career and a terrible car crash in 1949 that sapped his strength and forced him to play with his legs wrapped in bandages. He also survived, worst of all, the experience of standing in a room at the age of nine as his manic depressive father committed suicide with a .38.

Two years after his father's death Hogan began walking seven miles to Fort Worth's Glen Garden Country Club to work for 75¢ a bag as a caddie. Entering caddie tournaments, he found he could beat most everyone but a local kid named Byron Nelson. Undeterred, he arrived on the professional tour at a time when many pros were spoiled party boys who spent their time drinking and playing cards. Hogan brought with him a new work ethic. As biographer Curt Sampson puts it, he "virtually invented practice in golf." Indeed, Hogan became the game's greatest empiricist, tirelessly using his own work on the practice tee in a quest to discover the swing's Rosetta Stone.

For years Hogan teetered on the brink of financial ruin. He survived a 1932 swing through California on hamburgers and stolen oranges. Though he shared predominance of his era with his old rival, Nelson, and Sam Snead, Hogan nevertheless won 63 PGA tournaments. He won his first major at the 1946 PGA and added eight more, including four U.S. Opens.

Hogan's last major championship came at the 1953 British Open at Carnoustie, the only time he entered golf's oldest tournament. The tough old veterans of Carnoustie fell in love with Hogan, whom they nicknamed the "wee ice mon" for his unwavering concentration. Hogan was so steady at Carnoustie that he hit a tee shot right into his own divot from the previous day. Hogan, who had already won the Masters and the U.S. Open that year, would surely have been favored to complete a single-year Grand Slam, but the trip to Scotland had sapped his strength and he didn't even enter the PGA Championship. He remained the only player to win three majors in a single year until Tiger Woods did so in 2000.

THE RECORD

Major titles:
1946: PGA Championship
1948: PGA Championship, U.S. Open
1950: U.S. Open
1951: Masters, U.S. Open
1953: Masters, U.S. Open, British Open

Four-time PGA Player of the Year (1948, '50, '51, '53). Third alltime in career PGA victories with 63. Fourth alltime in major titles with nine. Won Vardon Trophy as player with lowest scoring average in 1940, '41 and '48.

TIMELINE

1950
Seventeen months after the car carrying him and his wife collided with a Greyhound bus, and doctors told him he would never walk again, Hogan (right) was not only walking but also playing championship-caliber golf. Performing in obvious pain from his injuries, he won the U.S. Open in a playoff over Lloyd Mangrum and George Fazio.

1951
Suffering from a blood clot that developed in the wake of the injuries he sustained in his 1949 car accident, Hogan nevertheless won the Masters and the U.S. Open. Hogan would win four U.S. Opens in his career, tied for the most alltime.

1953
An unrelenting perfectionist, Hogan (left, teeing off) arrived a week early for the British Open so that he could get accustomed to both the course and the Scottish weather. He practiced every day leading up to the tournament, the only British Open he would play in his career, and then, in a performance that is still revered at Carnoustie, shot 73-71-70-68 (a course record) to finish in 282 and win the event by four strokes. The victory was his third major championship of the year, after the Masters and the U.S. Open, and made Hogan the only man until Tiger Woods in 2000 to win three of golf's four majors in a calendar year.

1954
At the Masters, Hogan (below, with club) nearly added another major tournament victory to his world-class résumé, battling Sam Snead into a playoff before falling short by one stroke. Hogan would also finish runner-up after a playoff in the 1955 U.S. Open and, at age 55, make a thrilling

run at the 1967 Masters. He retired from the tour in 1960 with nine major titles and 63 PGA victories, the third most alltime. Hogan was named player of the year in 1948, '50, '51 and '53, and he won the Vardon Trophy as the lowest scorer on Tour in 1940, 41 and '48. He died on July 25, 1997.

1916
Golf's first supernova prodigy, Jones (left) qualified for the U.S. Amateur when he was 14 years old. He reached the quarterfinals of the event, defeating 1906 champion Eben Myers, whose temper was said to rival that of the fiery young Jones, in a raucous first-round match.

1926
Producing his best season to date, Jones recovered from a second-round 79 to shoot 71–73 and win the U.S. Open by a stroke over Joe Turnesa, then he went on to win the British Open and reach the final of the U.S. Amateur.

1930
In the final of the U.S. Amateur, on September 22, Jones (right) defeated Eugene Homans 8 and 7 to complete the first, and still only, single-season Grand Slam in golf history. Earlier in the year he won the U.S. Open and the British Open,

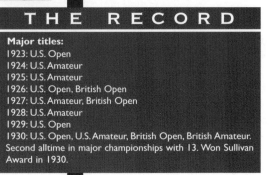

defeating Mac Smith by two strokes in both events, and rallied to take the British Amateur at St. Andrews.

1934
Jones (below) founded Augusta National Golf Club in 1933 on a course he helped design, and launched the Masters tournament the following year. Despite having retired in 1930, Jones played the tournament, shooting 76-74-72-72 to finish tied for 13th place. He continued to act as host at the Masters every year until 1967, long enough to see his tournament

become one of modern golf's Grand Slam events. In his retirement Jones practiced law and wrote, while playing the occasional exhibition, especially during World War II to raise money for the war effort. His part-memoir, part-instructional book *Down the Fairway*, remains, in the words of SPORTS ILLUSTRATED, "an incontestable classic."

BOBBY JONES

The world of sports has always had more than its share of drunks and cads but few real gentlemen and only one Bobby Jones. Blessed with as sweet a swing as ever the game has seen, Jones was golf's greatest amateur, winning 13 major championships between 1923 and 1930, including four U.S. Opens, three British Opens and the game's only single-season Grand Slam.

But as impressive as Jones was as a player, he was celebrated even more for his character and wit, for the remarkable ease with which he triumphed at every task he attempted, whether it was earning a graduate degree at Harvard, offering a witty toast or singing arias by Puccini. Many golf fans would argue that Jones's greatest legacy was the Masters tournament, which he and his friend Cliff Roberts founded in 1934 on the heavenly Augusta National course that Jones designed with Alister Mackenzie. Everyone who knew Jones agreed with the British golf writer Peter Dobereiner that Jones was the very embodiment of the English ideal of the gifted amateur.

As a boy, Jones showed exceptional talent but was undone again and again by his volcanic temper. Only 14 when he first qualified for the U.S. Amateur, he faced the 1906 champion, Eben Byers, in what soon devolved into a club-throwing derby. Jones won, he later joked, because Byers "ran out of clubs before I did." A turning point came at the British Open in 1921, when Jones stormed off the Old Course at St. Andrews in mid-round, an outburst that caused him such deep shame he vowed to control his emotions thereafter.

When he learned to control his temper, Jones was as close to invincible as a golfer has ever been. He won 13 of the 31 majors he entered, and in eight U.S. Opens he finished first four times and was runnerup four times. Everything seemed maddeningly easy for Jones, who detested practice.

In 1930 he set his sights on winning the four major championships of his day— "the Impregnable Quadrilateral" as one writer dubbed the open and amateur championships of the U.S. and Great Britain. After winning the British Amateur at St. Andrews and the Open in Hoylake, England, he sailed home to a ticker tape parade in New York City. Still exhausted he took a train to Minneapolis, where he won the U.S. Open at Interlachen. He completed golf's only Grand Slam with an 8-and-7 rout of Gene Homans in the championship match of the U.S. Amateur at Merion, Mass.

Soon thereafter, at 28, Jones retired. He made instructional films, wrote some of golf's most elegant tutorial essays and threw his heart into the Masters. He developed a sore shoulder, which turned out to be syringomyelia, a degenerative spinal disease that Jones bore with customary grace until his death in 1971. As Herbert Warren Wind put it, "As a young man he was able to stand up to just about the best that life can offer, which isn't easy, and later he stood up with equal grace to just about the worst."

THE RECORD

Major titles:
1923: U.S. Open
1924: U.S. Amateur
1925: U.S. Amateur
1926: U.S. Open, British Open
1927: U.S. Amateur, British Open
1928: U.S. Amateur
1929: U.S. Open
1930: U.S. Open, U.S. Amateur, British Open, British Amateur. Second alltime in major championships with 13. Won Sullivan Award in 1930.

Though he is famed for winning a record 11 straight tournaments in 1945, Byron Nelson is celebrated today almost as much for his courtly manner, his knack for putting other people at ease. "Lord" Byron has never betrayed a hint of imperiousness, despite his place in golf's pantheon.

Nelson and fellow Hall of Famer Ben Hogan grew up a few miles apart, in the wind-picked Texas town of Fort Worth, and were born in the same year, 1912. They often faced each other in caddie tournaments,

and while Hogan may rank a bit higher today, it was Nelson who enjoyed the most early success, dominating their early encounters and winning a major title first, the 1937 Masters. With Virginian Sam Snead, the two Texans formed one of golf's great triumvirates, dominating the game from 1938 to '50, a span in which one of the three topped the earnings list every year but two.

Renowned for his impeccable long-iron play, Nelson played his best golf during the war. A hemophiliac, he was classified 4F and contributed to the war effort by barnstorming with Bob Hope and Bing Crosby and giving exhibitions with his old pal, Jug McSpaden.

In 1944 Nelson won ten events, a great year but only a warmup for what was to come in '45,

when Nelson entered 30 tournaments, won 17 and finished runner-up in seven. His average margin of victory was 6.3 strokes. Nelson's famous streak began in mid-March, when he won the Miami Four-Ball tournament, and ended in mid-August, when he was finally beaten, finishing fourth in Memphis.

Much has been made of the fact that Nelson's streak came during the war, when some of the top golfers were off serving their country. But it must be said that Hogan came home in time to play 19 events and Snead 27. What's more, Nelson's average for those 11 wins was 67.92.

The following year Nelson stunned everyone by retiring at 34. Some believe he lost his nerve, sensing Hogan's inevitable rise. But those who have visited Nelson on his farm north of Dallas believe he wanted to spend more time there. "In his own mind," wrote SPORTS ILLUSTRATED's Sarah Ballard, "he has always been about equal parts golfer and farmer."

THE RECORD

YEAR	EVENTS	SCORING AVG.	1ST	2ND	3RD	EARNINGS($)
1933	2	—	0	0	0	NA
1934	5	—	0	2	0	741.75
1935	16	—	0	1	2	2,262
1936	22	—	1	2	4	5565
1937	17	—	2	1	1	6810
1938	19	—	2	0	5	5399
1939	21	—	4	2	1	8959
1940	17	—	3	3	2	9376
1941	25	—	3	5	0	12,151
1942	17	—	3	1	2	9,400
1943	4	—	1	1	1	NA
1944	26	—	10	5	4	38,343
1945	29	—	17	7	1	57,674
1946	21	—	6	3	3	22,987

TIMELINE

1939
Nelson (below) won his second major (after the '37 Masters), defeating Craig Wood and Denny Shute in a 36-hole playoff at the U.S. Open in Philadelphia. Nelson shot 68–70 to Wood's 68–73, while Shute fell out with a 76 after 18 holes. Nelson went on to win the Phoenix Open and the Western Open that season.

1940
In Hershey, Pa., Nelson won the matchplay PGA Championship, battling past Gene Sarazen to reach the final, where he beat Sam Snead one up. The following year Nelson beat Ben Hogan and Gene Sarazen but lost to Vic Ghezzi in the final.

1942
At the Masters, Hogan (below, left) shot 67–70 to chase down his great rival and fellow Fort Worth native Nelson (below, right)—who finished 72–73—and tie him for the lead at 280. But Nelson won the playoff, carding 69 to Hogan's 70.

1944
In a prelude to his historic season the following year, Nelson won ten PGA tournaments, including the Dallas Open (which would be renamed the Byron Nelson Classic in 1968), and led the tour in earnings, claiming $37,967 in war bonds.

1945
In July, Nelson (above, right) took the winner's trophy at the PGA championship, part of his record 11-tournament winning streak. Nelson, who ranks fifth on the alltime PGA wins list with 52, also won the Canadian Open, the Phoenix Open, and the New Orleans Open during his torrid stretch of victories.

JACK NICKLAUS

Jack Nicklaus owns the one record that Tiger Woods may never break, great as he is. That is Nicklaus's staggering total of 18 wins in golf's four major tournaments (and two more if you throw in the U.S. Amateur). For the record, Nicklaus has six wins at the Masters, four at the U.S. Open, three at the British Open and five at the PGA. And just to underscore his consistent excellence, he finished second in those four professional tournaments 19 times. When you recall that he achieved those results against the likes of Arnold Palmer, Gary Player, Lee Trevino and Tom Watson, you get some idea how great a golfer Nicklaus has been. "Jack Nicklaus," said Bobby Jones in oft-quoted awe, "plays a game with which I'm not familiar."

Nicklaus could hit the ball a mile, but it was his competitiveness that gave him such an edge. No one was more likely to make a pressure putt than Nicklaus, who began developing his extraordinary skills at the Scioto Country Club, in Columbus, Ohio. Nicklaus was a pudgy young man with a moon face and a bristling brush cut. His father was a pharmacist who expected his son to follow him into the profession but nevertheless allowed him to charge as many buckets of practice balls as he could hit.

Nicklaus was the direct descendant of golf greatness, since his first teacher, Scioto pro Jack Grout, had learned the game in Texas, playing with Ben Hogan and Byron Nelson.

Nicklaus played college golf at hometown Ohio State, winning the individual national championship in 1961 and going pro almost immediately afterward. Palmer gets credit for popularizing the game, but it was Nicklaus who solidified golf's status on the sporting landscape. From the time the pudgy, 20-year-old kid finishing runner-up to Palmer at the 1960 U.S. Open, he gave us great golf memories—of his first major, the 1962 U.S. Open; of his duel with Tom Watson at the 1977 British Open at Turnberry; and of his surprise win at the 1986 Masters, his 18th major, at age 46.

"I never thought anyone would ever put Hogan in the shadows, but he did," said Gene Sarazen. "Nicklaus has the remarkable combination of power and finesse, and he is one of the smartest guys ever to walk the fairways. And he has been an extraordinary leader. What more is there to say? Jack Nicklaus is the greatest competitor of them all."

THE RECORD

YEAR	EVENTS	SCORING AVG.	1ST	2ND	3RD	EARNINGS($)
1962	26	70.80	3	3	4	61,868
1963	25	70.42	5	2	3	100,040
1964	26	69.96	4	6	3	113,284
1965	24	70.09	5	4	2	140,752
1966	19	70.58	2	3	3	111,419
1967	23	70.23	5	2	3	188,998
1968	22	69.97	2	3	1	155,285
1969	23	71.06	3	1	0	140,167
1970	19	70.75	2	3	2	142,149
1971	18	70.08	5	3	3	244,490
1972	19	70.23	7	3	0	320,542
1973	18	69.81	7	1	1	308,362
1974	18	70.06	2	3	0	238,178
1975	16	69.87	5	1	3	298,149
1976	16	70.17	2	2	1	266,438
1977	18	70.36	3	2	1	284,509
1978	15	71.07	3	2	0	256,672
1979	12	72.49	0	0	1	59,434
1980	13	70.86	2	1	0	172,386
1981	16	70.70	0	3	0	178,213
1982	15	70.90	1	3	2	232,645
1983	16	70.88	0	3	1	256,158
1984	13	70.75	1	2	1	272,595
1985	15	71.81	0	2	1	165,456
1986	15	71.56	1	0	0	226,015
1987	11	72.89	0	0	0	64,686
1988	9	72.78	0	0	0	28,845
1989	10	72.35	0	0	0	96,594
1990*	4	68.60	2	1	1	350,000
1991*	5	69.79	3	0	0	343,734
1992*	4	71.00	0	1	1	114,547
1993*	6	71.00	1	0	0	206,028
1994*	6	70.35	1	0	0	239,278
1995*	7	69.68	1	2	1	538,800
1996*	7	70.92	2	1	0	360,861
1997*	6	71.41	0	1	0	239,932

Note: Official tour events only. *Senior Tour results.

TIMELINE

1960
Nicklaus (right) honed his game in Columbus, Ohio, and introduced it to the world as a 20-year-old amateur at the U.S. Open at Cherry Hills, where he shot 71-71-69-71 and finished second to Arnold Palmer. Said Ben Hogan, Nicklaus's playing partner, "I played 36 holes today with a kid who should have won this thing by 10 strokes." Two years later, Nicklaus would take his first professional title, defeating Palmer in a playoff at the U.S. Open in Oakmont, Pa.

1972
At Pebble Beach, site of his U.S. Amateur triumph in 1959, Nicklaus (left) won his third U.S. Open, beating Australia's Bruce Crampton by three strokes to seize the 13th major of his career, equaling Bobby Jones's esteemed record. The victory also gave Nicklaus, who had won at Augusta, the first two legs of the Grand Slam, but he would fall short of a Slam after finishing second at the British Open.

1980
The 40-year-old Nicklaus silenced the naysayers who said his best days were behind him by winning the PGA Championship and a record-tying fourth U.S. Open.

1986
To the delight of the galleries, Nicklaus (below) won his sixth Masters and his 18th major, becoming, at 46, the oldest winner at Augusta. Shooting eagle, birdie, birdie on 15, 16 and 17, Nicklaus stormed from ninth place to beat Greg Norman by one stroke.

ARNOLD PALMER

Arnold Palmer was a superb golfer, a huge hitter who won 60 PGA events, including seven majors. He was also golf's pied piper, leading the masses to embrace a game that had been the exclusive province of the upper classes.

Television certainly catalyzed this shift in golf's status, but the cameras needed a hero. They found the perfect candidate in this earthy young man from Latrobe, Pa., with a herky-jerky swing and a knack for mounting thrilling "charges." Palmer was the rare golfer ordinary people could relate to and celebrate. "His emotions—pain, pleasure, dismay, anger, and the rest—were never hidden," wrote one sportswriter, "and his followers could relive through him their own joys and frustrations."

Palmer was the son of a former steelworker who became the greenskeeper and then the golf pro at Latrobe Country Club. Schooled in the game by his dad, Palmer went to Wake Forest University on a golf scholarship but dropped out in his senior year, when his best friend was killed in a car accident. He served three years in the Coast Guard before taking up golf seriously again. He won the U.S. Amateur in 1954, turned pro the next year and won his first major, the Masters, in 1958.

But it was the 1960 season that made Palmer a national icon. At the Masters, needing two birdies on the final two holes to win, he drained putts of 27 and five feet to get them and claim the second of his four green jackets. The year's next major, the U.S. Open, was played at Cherry Hills Country Club, outside Denver. Many gripping storylines converged on the final round of the tournament: It was to be 47-year-old Ben Hogan's last shot at a major and the first for a 20-year-old amateur named Jack Nicklaus. After 54 holes Palmer appeared to be out of it, standing 15th, seven strokes behind leader Mike Souchak, four behind Hogan and Nicklaus. But Palmer birdied six of the first seven holes on Sunday and, at the end of an afternoon heavy with drama, won the tournament, beating Nicklaus, 280–282. In that one round, wrote SPORTS ILLUSTRATED's Dan Jenkins, "We witnessed the arrival of Nicklaus, the coronation of Palmer and the end of Hogan." It would be Palmer's only U.S. Open victory, but he added British Open titles in 1961 and '62 and two more Masters titles, in 1962 and '64.

In 1959 Palmer joined forces with a young go-getter named Mark McCormack. As the first superstar client for McCormack's International Management Group, Palmer was the bridge between the relatively lean early years of the PGA Tour, when players drove from tournament to tournament, and the lucrative present, when golfers are one-man business empires, piloting their own jets. Some bridge the steelworker's son built—and boy was he fun to watch doing it.

THE RECORD

YEAR	EVENTS	SCORING AVG.	1ST	2ND	3RD	EARNINGS($)
1955	31	70.99	1	0	1	7958
1956	30	71.14	2	1	0	16,145
1957	33	71.09	4	0	2	27,803
1958	32	70.66	3	5	2	42,608
1959	31	70.51	3	1	3	32,462
1960	27	69.95	8	1	2	75,263
1961	26	69.78	5	5	2	61,091
1962	21	70.27	7	1	0	81,448
1963	20	70.63	7	3	0	128,230
1964	26	70.24	2	6	4	113,203
1965	22	71.42	1	3	0	57,771
1966	22	70.69	3	2	2	110,468
1967	25	70.19	4	4	1	184,065
1968	24	70.94	2	2	0	114,602
1969	26	70.99	2	0	2	105,128
1970	22	70.89	1	3	2	128,853
1971	24	70.56	4	0	1	209,603
1972	22	71.41	0	1	2	84,181
1973	22	71.30	1	0	1	89,457
1974	20	72.45	0	1	0	36,293
1975	20	71.77	0	0	1	59,018
1976	19	72.05	0	0	0	17,018
1977	21	72.49	0	0	0	21,950
1978	15	72.87	0	0	0	27,073
1979	16	73.69	0	0	0	9,276
1980	13	71.71	0	0	0	16,589

1960
In a breakout season, Palmer (above, at Augusta) won eight tournaments, including the Masters and the U.S. Open. At the Masters, he made three clutch putts to beat Ken Venturi by a stroke, and at the U.S. Open Palmer made one of his trademark Sunday charges to overtake Jack Nicklaus. He finished second to Kel Nagle at the British Open.

1962
In April, Palmer edged Gary Player and Dow Finsterwald in a playoff to claim his third Masters title in five years and followed that up with a victory at the British Open in July, when he shot a sizzling 71-69-67-69 to win by six strokes over Kel Nagle. The British Open triumph, at Troon in Scotland, was the second in a row for Palmer, who was named player of the year.

SAM SNEAD

"Sam Snead won more PGA tournaments than anyone else: 81 at last count. The first came in 1936 and the last in 1965, when he won the Greater Greensboro Open as a spry 52-year-old. If you've watched Snead hit a ceremonial first ball at the Masters recently, you know why he won so much: No golfer has a more graceful swing than Snead's.

"For pure animal grace," wrote Grantland Rice, comparing Snead's effortless power to a tiger's, "the sight of Sam Snead murdering a tee shot; Babe Ruth swinging from the heels; and yes, Jack Dempsey raining savage destrution on a foe—these remain for me the acme of tigerish reflexes in human form."

"Slammin'" Sam was a member of one of golf's great triumvirates, dominating the game in the mid-1940s with Ben Hogan and Byron Nelson. Among Snead's 81 wins were three Masters (in 1949, '52 and '54), three PGA titles (1942, '49 and '51) and one British Open (1946).

The only gap in Snead's résumé is the absence of a U.S. Open title. Four times he was runnerup, including in 1939 when, needing only a par on the final hole to beat Byron Nelson, Snead hit into a bunker and made a triple-bogey eight.

Snead, who was famously coarse, surely cursed a blue streak after that performance.

"We were all like priests compared to Snead," said Doug Ford, the 1957 Masters champ. Born in 1912, Snead grew up in the backwoods of western Virginia. He picked up the game at the heels of his older brother, Homer, and parlayed his natural talent into jobs at the Greenbriar resort, first as caddie and then as assistant pro.

While at Greenbriar, Snead was invited to complete an all-star foursome that included two-time U.S. amateur champ Lawson Little. The young asssistant pro shot a 61. So effortless did he make it look that Greenbriar members quickly raised $300 to stake him for a shot at the pro tour. Snead won $600 in his first week and never looked back. He finished runnerup at the U.S. Open in his first try. At age 62, Snead nearly won an eighth major at the 1974 PGA, where he shot a final-round 68 to finish third, proving that a sweet swing is aprize forever.

THE RECORD

Major titles:
1942: PGA Championship
1946: British Open
1949: Masters, PGA Championship
1951: PGA Championship
1952: Masters
1954: Masters

Alltime PGA leader in victories with 81. Became oldest player to win a PGA event, when he took the Greater Greensboro Open in 1965 at the age of 52. Won Seniors Championship a record six times. Won Vardon Trophy as player with lowest scoring average in 1938, '49, '50, and '55.

TIMELINE

1937
In the U.S. Open at Oakland Hills, Snead (below) finished two strokes behind Ralph Guldahl—the first of four runner-up finishes for Snead at the Open.

1946
Snead won five tournaments, including the British Open at historic St. Andrews, where the famously unrefined Virginian reportedly said of the Old Course, "Why the hell have they built a golf course on this cow pasture?" Whatever he thought of the tournament atmosphere, it didn't distract him from the task at hand, as Snead finished 74–75 to win by four strokes over Johnny Bulla of the U.S. and Bobby Locke of South Africa.

1949
After a two-year slump, Snead (below) produced arguably the best year of his career, winning the Masters and the PGA Championship.

1950
Building on his brilliant season of the previous year, Slammin' Sam won 11 tournaments, led the tour in earnings with $35,758 and won the third Vardon Trophy of his career as the player with the best scoring average (69.23). It was the last year Snead played a full tour schedule.

1954
With tournament founder Bobby Jones (above, middle) looking on, Snead (above, left) accepted congratulations from Ben Hogan after defeating Hogan in a playoff to win the Masters. In the 18-hole playoff, Snead shot 70 to Hogan's 71 and claimed his third green jacket and seventh major. The next year Snead would win his fourth Vardon Trophy.

MICKEY WRIGHT

Thirty-one years after retiring from full-time golf at age 35, Mickey Wright remains one of the game's most mysterious figures. She stands out from her peers not only because of her otherworldly swing and the many tournaments she won with it in the early 1960s, but also because of the ease and grace with which the best player of her generation walked away from the game. Wright played only sporadically in what might have been her prime. She has not played a round of golf since 1995 and is still something of a recluse.

Her strength was the efficiency of her swing, which no less a perfectionist than Ben Hogan declared "the finest golf swing I ever saw, man or woman." Her swing mechanics gave her tremendous power. It was nothing for her to outdrive opponents by 40 yards or more or to hit the ball 220 to 250 yards from a fairway lie. With the help of the wind, Wright once drove the green of a 385-yard par-4.

Wright picked up the game when she was nine. Two years later her father gave her a set of four small clubs, and she began to play at La Jolla Country Club in her hometown of San Diego. By the time she was 13 she was shooting in the high 80s. She won her first tournament, the Southern California Girls Championship, at 14, and seized the 1952 U.S. junior girls' title at age 17.

After her freshman year at Stanford University, Wright competed in the U.S. Open, where she was the top amateur, and the U.S. Amateur, where she finished runner-up. Those performances convinced her to drop out of school to join the fledgling women's tour. One person whom Wright impressed that summer was the winner of the U.S. Open, Babe Didrikson. Even the brash Babe had to admit, "I didn't think anyone but the Babe could hit 'em like that. If I'm around five years from now, I'll have my hands full."

Alas, the great Babe died in 1956, so she missed seeing all that Wright accomplished. From 1959 until her retirement in 1970, Wright won 79 pro tournaments, including 13 majors overall and three of the four that existed in 1961—the U.S. Open, the LPGA and the Titleholders championship. She led the tour in earnings for four straight years (1961–64) and in scoring average for five consecutive years (1960–64), a record that still stands. In 1963 Wright won an unprecedented—and still unequaled—13 tournaments. In 1979, at 44 and nearly 10 years after her retirement, she entered the Coca-Cola Classic and—playing in sneakers—lost in a sudden-death playoff to Nancy Lopez.

Finally, and perhaps most importantly, Wright brought invaluable credibility to the women's game. No one could see that swing and not respect it. Pro golfer Judy Rankin put it this way: "Mickey got the outside world to take a second hard look at women golfers, and when they looked they saw the rest of us."

THE RECORD

Major titles:
1958: LPGA Championship, U.S. Open
1959: U.S. Open
1960: LPGA Championship
1961: U.S. Open, LPGA Championship, Titleholders Championship
1962: Titleholders Championship, Western Open
1963: Western Open, LPGA Championship
1964: U.S. Open
1966: Western Open

Won 82 professional events. Career earnings of $368,770. Named Associated Press female Athlete of the Year in 1963 and '64. Named Golfer of the Decade by Golf magazine (1958–67).

1961
Wright (right) blasted out of a sand trap on the 16th hole at Baltusrol en route to winning the U.S. Open—her third Open title—by six strokes over Betsy Rawls. Wright, who had already won the LPGA Championship earlier in the year, went on to take the Titleholders tournament for a sweep of the three women's majors at the time. She would win 10 tournaments that year.

1963
Wright outdid herself with a record 13 tour victories, including triumphs in the LPGA Championship and the Western Open. She led the tour in earnings, with $31,269, and won the Vare Trophy with a record 72.81 scoring average.

1964
After defeating Ruth Jessen 72–70 in an 18-hole playoff, Wright (right) hoisted the U.S. Open winner's trophy for the fourth time in her distinguished career. She was named female Athlete of the Year by the Associated Press.

1968
In Fleetwood, Pa., Wright (left) narrowly missed winning a fifth U.S. Open, finishing runner-up to Susie Berning. She won the Open in 1958, '59, '61 and '64. Citing chronic injuries, Wright reduced her LPGA schedule significantly after 1970, and she never won another major. Her 82 career LPGA wins rank her second on the alltime list, 22 victories ahead of her nearest competitor.

WORLD GOLF
HALL OF FAME

ENSHRINEES (PLAYERS ONLY)

WOMEN

NAME	INDUCTED	CAREER STATS
Amy Alcott	1999	3 Dinah Shores, 1 U.S. Open, 1 du Maurier, 29 LPGA wins (1975–91)
Patty Berg	1951	16 majors, including 1938 U.S. Open, 57 pro wins
Pat Bradley	1991	1 LPGA, 1 Dinah Shore, 1 U.S. Open, 3 du Mauriers, 31 LPGA wins (1976–95)
Donna Caponi	2001	2 U.S. Opens, 2 LPGAs, 24 LPGA wins
JoAnne Carner	1982	2 U.S. Opens (1971–76), 5 U.S. Amateurs, 43 LPGA wins
Beth Daniel	2000	1 LPGA, 32 LPGA wins (1979–95)
Sandra Haynie	1977	2 LPGAs, 42 LPGA wins
Juli Inkster	2000	2 LPGAs, 1 U.S Opens, 2 Dinah Shores, 1 du Maurier, 25 LPGA wins (1983–2000)
Betty Jameson	1951	1942 Western Open, 1947 U.S. Open, 12 pro wins
Betsy King	1995	1 LPGA, 2 U.S. Opens, 3 Dinah Shores, 33 LPGA wins (1984–2000)
Nancy Lopez	1987	3 LPGAs, 1 Dinah Shore, 48 LPGA wins (1978–1997)
Carol Mann	1977	1965 U.S. Open, 38 LPGA wins
Judy Rankin	2000	26 LPGA wins (1968–79)
Betsy Rawls	1960	2 LPGAs, 4 U.S. Opens (1951–60), 2 Western Opens, 55 LPGA wins
Patty Sheehan	1993	3 LPGAs, 2 U.S. Opens, 1 Dinah Shore, 35 LPGA wins (1981–96)
Louise Suggs	1951	13 majors, 50 LPGA victories
Joyce Wethered†	1975	4 British Amateurs (1922–29)

†Originally elected by the World Golf Hall of Fame. Never a member of the LPGA.

NAME	INDUCTED	CAREER STATS
Mickey Wright	1964	13 majors 4 LPGAs, 4 U.S. Opens, 82 LPGA wins
Kathy Whitworth	1975	3 LPGAs, 2 Titleholders, 1 Western Open, 88 LPGA wins
Babe Didrikson Zaharias	1951	12 majors (three U.S. Opens, 1948–54), 31 LPGA wins

MEN

NAME	INDUCTED	CAREER STATS
Willie Anderson	1975	4 U.S. Opens (1901–05)
Tommy Armour	1976	3 majors, including 1927 U.S. Open
John Ball	1977	8 British Amateurs, 1890 British Open
Seve Ballesteros	1997	3 British Opens, 2 Masters (1979–88)
Jim Barnes	1989	1 U.S. Open, 1 British Open, 2 PGAs (1916–25)
Julius Boros	1982	2 U.S. Opens, 1 PGA, 18 Tour wins, (1952–68)
James Braid	1976	5 British Opens (1901–10)
Jack Burke Jr.	2000	1956 Masters, 1956 PGA
Bill Campbell	1990	1964 U.S. Amateur, member of eight Walker Cup teams
Billy Casper	1978	1959 and '66 U.S. Opens, '70 Masters, 51 Tour wins
Harry Cooper	1992	31 Tour wins (1925–41)
Henry Cotton	1980	3 British Opens (1934–48)
Jimmy Demaret	1983	3 Masters (1940–50), 31 Tour wins
Roberto DeVicenzo	1989	1967 British Open
Chick Evans	1975	1916 U.S. Open, U.S. Amateur
Nick Faldo	1997	3 British Opens, 3 Masters (1987–96)

21 World Golf Drive
St. Augustine, Florida 32092
(904) 940-4000
www.wgv.com

NAME	INDUCTED	CAREER STATS	NAME	INDUCTED	CAREER STATS
Raymond Floyd	1989	1 Masters, 1 U.S. Open, 2 PGAs (1969–86)	Arnold Palmer	1974	4 Masters, 2 British Opens, 1 U.S. Open (1960), 60 Tour wins
Ralph Guldahl	1981	2 U.S. Opens, 1 Masters (1937–39)	Gary Player	1974	3 Masters, 1 U.S. Open, 2 British Opens, 3 PGAs, 21 Tour wins
Walter Hagen	1974	2 U.S. Opens, 4 British Opens, 5 PGAs (1914–29), 40 Tour wins	Chi Chi Rodriguez	1992	8 Tour wins (1963–79)
Harold Hilton	1978	1892 and '97 British Opens, 1 U.S. Amateur, 4 British Amateurs	Paul Runyan	1990	2 PGAs (1934–38), 28 Tour wins (1930–41)
Ben Hogan	1974	2 Masters, 4 U.S. Opens, 1 British Open, 2 PGAs, 63 Tour wins	Gene Sarazen	1974	1935 Masters, 2 U.S. Opens, 1932 British Open, 3 PGAs, 38 Tour wins
Hale Irwin	1992	3 U.S. Opens (1974–90)	Horton Smith	1990	2 Masters, 32 Tour wins (1934–36)
Bobby Jones	1974	5 U.S. Amateurs, 4 U.S. Opens, 3 British Opens, 1 British Amateur, including 1930 Grand Slam	Sam Snead	1974	3 Masters, 1946 British Open, 3 PGAs, 81 Tour wins
Lawson Little	1980	2 U.S. Amateurs, 2 British Amateurs, 1940 U.S. Open	John H. Taylor	1975	5 British Opens (1894–1913)
Gene Littler	1990	1953 U.S. Amateur, '61 U.S. Open, 29 Tour wins	Peter Thomson	1988	5 British Opens (1954–65)
Bobby Locke	1977	4 British Opens (1949–57)	Jerome Travers	1976	5 U.S. Amateurs, 1915 U.S. Open
Lloyd Mangrum	1999	1946 U.S. Open, 36 Tour wins	Walter Travis	1979	3 U.S. Amateurs, 1904 British Amateur
Cary Middlecoff	1986	2 U.S. Opens, 1 Masters, 40 Tour wins (1949–56)	Lee Trevino	1981	2 U.S. Opens, 2 British Opens, 2 PGAs (1968–84), 27 Tour wins
Johnny Miller	1996	1 U.S. Open, 1 British Open, 24 Tour wins	Harry Vardon	1974	7 majors, including 6 British Opens (1896–1914)
"Young" Tom Morris	1975	4 straight British Opens (1868–72)	Tom Watson	1988	5 British Opens, 1 U.S. Open, 2 Masters, 34 Tour wins (1975–83)
"Old" Tom Morris	1976	4 British Opens (1861–67)			
Byron Nelson	1974	2 Masters, 2 PGAs and 1 Masters, plus 11 straight PGA tournaments (1945), 52 Tour wins			
Jack Nicklaus	1974	6 Masters, 4 U.S. Opens, 3 British Opens, 5 PGAs, 70 Tour wins			
Francis Ouimet	1974	upset legends to win 1913 U.S. Open, plus two US Amateurs			

BEST OF
THE REST

Once upon a time, the ancient sport of boxing had its Hall of Fame at Madison Square Garden—in the storied *old* Garden at 50th Street and Eighth Avenue. But when that building was razed and the new one built above Penn Station in 1968, the collection was moved a few blocks away, to the offices of *Ring* magazine, where it languished in dusty obscurity. "At the moment," Bert Sugar, editor of *Ring*, lamented in 1982, "it's more the box Hall of Fame."

There was talk of spending $1 million to build another Hall in the new Garden, and in 1983 a rumor surfaced of a $34 million hall and museum on the Las Vegas strip—a suggestion dismissed by Sugar. "Las Vegas is an inappropriate site," he said. "Atlantic City is, too. Neither has a historic link to boxing."

Boxing does have a Hall now. It's roughly 300 miles northwest of the Garden, in the small, upstate New York town of Canastota, or "Titletown," as the sign at the city limit reads. And as is often the case with halls of fame in

In addition to an Olympic-sized swimming pool, the International Swimming Hall of Fame in Fort Lauderdale, Fla. (above), showcases Johnny Weissmuller's medals, a bronze figure of a diver dating to 480 B.C. and information about Ben Franklin's passion for swimming.

sports that do not have a single, well-funded governing body, the International Boxing Hall of Fame had rather humble beginnings. Its local precursor was something called the Boxing Showcase, a small glass-and-brick building on the edge of a McDonald's parking lot, built in 1984 to honor Canastota's two former champions, Carmen Basilio, who beat Sugar Ray Robinson to win the middleweight title in 1957, and Basilio's nephew, Billy Backus, who was welterweight champ in 1970 and '71. While chomping a Big Mac, visitors could gaze upon lifesize bronze statues of Basilio and Backus and watch footage of their fights. Encouraged by interest in the Showcase, Canastota officials decided to build a proper Hall of Fame, which opened in 1990 and, against all odds, has become a worthy reliquary for the sport, with its displays of old gloves, championship belts and thousands of issues of *Ring*.

"Here," said former light heavyweight champ Jose Torres at the opening ceremony in 1990, "I get the *smell* of boxing."

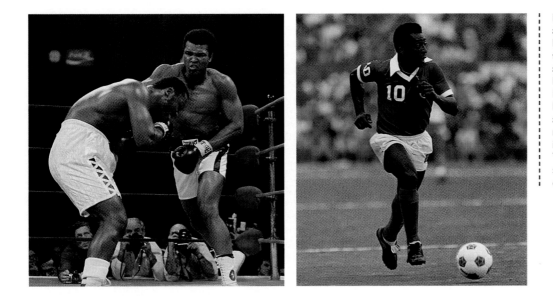

Both Joe Frazier (far left, all-white trunks) and Muhammad Ali (white trunks with black trim) are in Canastota's National Boxing Hall of Fame, while the legendary Pelé (left), star for Brazil and the New York Cosmos of the NASL, is immortalized in the New York hamlet of Oneonta, site of the National Soccer Hall of Fame.

Chlorine is what you'll smell at the International Swimming Hall of Fame in Fort Lauderdale, Fla., since the Hall is adjacent to an Olympic-sized pool. Founded in 1965 by Buck Dawson, a mischievous, born promoter in a black eye patch, the Hall reminds visitors in a variety of ways that swimming is not just a modern Olympic sport but an ancient, practical undertaking. So along with Johnny Weissmuller's medal collection, there's a miniature bronze figure of a diver dating from 480 B.C. unearthed in Italy plus more recent sculptures of noted swimmers from history, such as John F. Kennedy (a member of the first Harvard swim team to defeat Yale) and Lord Byron (who swam the Hellespont). Ben Franklin, it turns out, was America's first famous swimmer and even wrote a book on the activity, which he performed naked. For a time, the Hall's mascot was a dog, a spitz.

Motor Sports features several circuits for different types of racing, and these are reflected in the number of motor sports halls in existence—in Indianapolis; Darlington, S.C.; Novi, Mich.; Knoxville, Iowa; and Talladega, Ala., where the International Motor Sports Hall of Fame contains a variety of smaller halls, including the Quarter Midgets of America and the Western Auto Mechanics Hall of Fame. A number of drivers are members of multiple halls, including Barney Oldfield, who is in four.

The National Soccer Hall of Fame, in Oneonta, N.Y., home of perennial college soccer power Hartwick, contains the oldest known soccer ball in the U.S., dating to 1863. The Hall honors mostly Americans, which, given the sport's history in this country, limits the choices primarily to the early part of the 20th Century. But the powers that be have extended membership to anyone who played in U.S. leagues, and so Pelé and Franz Beckenbauer, who played for the legendary New York Cosmos, are members.

The Track and Field Hall of Fame got its start when an optometrist from Charleston, W.Va., Don Cohen, visited the Canadian Runners' Hall of Fame—no jokes, please—only to discover that his own country, the land of Jesse Owens, Al Oerter and Jim Thorpe, had no such shrine. Raising $900,000 in government grants, Cohen opened his hall in 1974 in a mansion overlooking the Kanawha River in Charleston. The collection, which moved to the Hoosier Dome in Indianapolis in 1983 and is now awaiting installation at the 168th Street Armory in New York City, asks each inductee to make a meaningful donation. Included are a discus from four-time Olympic champ Al Oerter, the white golf cap Dave Wottle wore while winning the 1972 Olympic 800, Tommie Smith's sunglasses, and Cornelius Warmerdam's bamboo pole-vaulting poles.

The oldest of the bunch is the National Museum of Racing and Hall of Fame, in Saratoga Springs, N.Y., which was founded in 1950 then redesigned in 1988 and again in 2000. Honorees here fall into three categories—horses, trainers and jockeys—with the four-footed members represented by the likes of Man o' War, Citation and Kelso, winner of a record five Jockey Club Gold Cup Awards.

There is a strong sense of the past in this shrine in pretty Saratoga Springs, especially in the stellar collection of oil paintings, some dating back to the 18th century. The collection also contains Steve Cauthen's duffle bag and riding gear; the silks Julie Krone wore for her historic win in the 1993 Belmont; and the whip that jockey Ron Turcotte carried but never used on Secretariat, who is represented by a full-sized bronze statue. Saratoga has a number of claims on the Hall, including the fact that the oldest continually run stakes race in America is staged right across the street. Like Cooperstown, Saratoga offers that perfect Hall of Fame combination—with past and present thrillingly at hand.

INTERNATIONAL BOXING HALL OF FAME

1 Hall of Fame Drive
Canastota, NY 13032
Telephone: (315) 697-7095
President: Donald Ackerman
Executive Director: Edward Brophy
www.ibhof.com

ENSHRINEES
(BOXERS ONLY)

MODERN

NAME (YR. OF INDUCTION)	D.O.B. D.O.D.	RECORD (KO'S)
Muhammad Ali (1990)	b. 1-17-42	56-5-0 (37)
Sammy Angott (1998)	b. 1-17-15 d. 10-22-80	99-28-8 (23)
Alexis Arguello (1992)	b. 1952	80-8-0 (64)
Henry Armstrong (1990)	b. 12-12-12 d. 10-24-88	151-21-9 (101)
Carmen Basilio (1990)	b. 4-2-27	56-16-7 (27)
Wilfred Benitez (1996)	b. 9-12-58	53-8-1 (31)
Nino Benvenuti (1992)	b. 4-26-38	82-7-1 (35)
Jackie (Kid) Berg (1994)	b. 6-28-09 d. 4-22-91	157-26-9 (57)
Jimmy Bivins (1999)	b. 12-6-19	86-25-1 (31)
Joe Brown (1996)	b. 5-18-25	103-43-13 (47)
Ken Buchanan (2000)	b. 6-28-45	62-8-0 (28)
Charley Burley (1992)	b. 9-6-17 d. 10-16-92	84-11-2 (50)
Miguel Canto (1998)	b. 1-30-49	61-9-0 (15)
Jimmy Carter (2000)	b. 12-15-23 d. 9-21-94	81-30-9 (31)
Marcel Cerdan (1991)	b. 7-22-16 d. 10-27-49	106-4-0 (61)
Antonio Cervantes (1998)	b. 12-23-45	66-12-1 (37)
Jeff Chandler (2000)	b. 9-3-56	33-2-2 (18)
Ezzard Charles (1990)	b. 1921 d. 1975	96-25-1 (59)
Billy Conn (1990)	b. 10-8-17 d. 5-29-93	63-11-1 n/a
Flash Elorde (1993)	b. 3-22-35 d. 1-2-85	88-27-2 (33)
Bob Foster (1990)	b. 12-15-38	56-8-1 (46)
Joe Frazier (1990)	b. 1-12-44	32-4-1 (27)
Gene Fullmer (1991)	b. 7-21-31	55-6-3 (24)
Khaosai Galaxy (1999)	b. 5-15-59	49-1-0 (43)
Kid Gavilan (1990)	b. 1-6-26	107-30-6 (28)
Joey Giardello (1993)	b. 7-16-30	100-25-7 (32)
Wilfredo Gomez (1995)	b. 10-29-56	44-3-1 (42)
Billy Graham (1992)	b. 9-9-22 d. 1-22-92	102-15-9 (26)
Rocky Graziano (1991)	b. 6-6-22 d. 5-22-90	66-10-6 (52)
Emile Griffith (1990)	b. 2-3-38	85-24-2 (23)
Marvin Hagler (1993)	b. 5-23-54	62-3-2 (52)
"Fighting" Harada (1995)	b. 4-5-43	55-7-0 (22)
Beau Jack (1991)	b. 4-1-21 d. 2-9-2000	83-24-5 (40)
Lew Jenkins (1999)	b. 12-4-16	65-39-5 (47)
Eder Jofre (1992)	b. 3-26-36	72-2-4 (50)
Harold Johnson (1993)	b. 8-9-28	76-11-0 (32)

NAME (YR. OF INDUCTION)	D.O.B. D.O.D.	RECORD (KO'S)
Jake LaMotta (1990)	b. 7-10-21	83-19-4 (30)
Sugar Ray Leonard (1997)	b. 1952	36-3-1 (25)
Sonny Liston (1991)	b. 5-8-32 d. 12-30-70	50-4-0 (39)
Joe Louis (1990)	b. 5-13-14 d. 4-12-81	68-3-0 (54)
Rocky Marciano (1990)	b. 9-1-23 d. 8-31-69	49-0-0 (43)
Joey Maxim (1994)	b. 3-28-22	82-29-4 (21)
Bob Montgomery (1995)	b. 2-10-19	75-19-3 (37)
Carlos Monzon (1990)	b. 8-7-42 d. 1-8-95	87-3-9 (59)
Archie Moore (1990)	b. 12-13-13 d. 12-9-98	194-26-8 (141)
Jose Napoles (1990)	b. 4-13-40	77-7-0 (54)
Ken Norton (1992)	b. 8-9-43	42-7-1 (33)
Ruben Olivares (1991)	b. 1-14-47	88-13-3 (78)
Bobo Olson (1990)	n/a	n/a
Carlos Ortiz (1991)	b. 9-9-36	61-7-1 (30)
Manuel Ortiz (1996)	b. 7-2-16 d. 5-31-70	97-28-3 (49)
Floyd Patterson (1991)	b. 1-4-35	55-8-1 (40)
Eusebio Pedroza (1999)	b. 3-2-53	42-6-1 (25)
Willie Pep (1990)	b. 9-19-22	230-11-1 (65)
Pascual Perez (1995)	b. 3-4-26 d. 1-22-77	84-7-1 (57)
Aaron Pryor (1996)	b. 10-20-55	39-1-0 (35)
Luis Rodriguez (1997)	b. 1937 d. 1996	107-13-0 (49)
Sugar Ray Robinson (1990)	b. 5-3-21 d. 4-12-89	175-19-6 (109)
Matthew Saad Muhammad (1998)	b. 8-5-54	39-16-3 (29)
Sandy Saddler (1990)	b. 1926	144-16-2 (103)
Vicente Saldivar (1999)	b. 5-3-43	37-3-0 (26)
Salvador Sanchez (1991)	b. 1-26-59 d. 8-12-82	44-1-1 (32)
Max Schmeling (1992)	b. 9-28-05	56-10-4 (39)
Michael Spinks (1994)	b. 7-13-56	32-1-0 (21)
Dick Tiger (1991)	b. 8-14-29 d. 12-14-71	61-17-3 (26)
Jose Torres (1997)	b. 1936	41-3-1 (29)
Jersey Joe Walcott (1990)	b. 1-31-14 d. 2-25-94	53-18-1 (33)
Ike Williams (1990)	b. 8-2-23 d. 9-5-94	125-24-5 (60)
Chalky Wright (1997)	b. 1912 d. 1957	145-39-16 (74)
Tony Zale (1991)	b. 5-29-13 d. 3-20-97	67-18-2 (45)
Carlos Zarate (1994)	b. 5-23-51	61-4-0 (58)
Fritzie Zivic (1993)	b. 5-8-13 d. 5-16-84	159-64-9 (80)

OLD TIMERS

NAME (YR. OF INDUCTION)	D.O.B. D.O.D.	RECORD (KO'S)
Lou Ambers	n/a	n/a
Abe Attell (1990)	b. 2-22-1884 d. 2-7-70	92-10-18 (51)
Max Baer	n/a	n/a
Jim Barry (2000)	b. 3-7-1870 d. 4-4-43	58-0-11 (40)
Jack Britton	n/a	n/a
Panama Al Brown	n/a	n/a
Tommy Burns	n/a	n/a
Tony Canzoneri (1990)	b. 1908 d. 1959	141-24-10 (44)
Georges Carpentier	n/a	n/a
Kid Chocolate	n/a	n/a
Joe Choynski (1990)	b. 11-8-1868 d. 1-25-43	52-14-6 (22)
James J. Corbett (1990)	b. 9-1-1866 d. 2-18-33	11-4-2 (7)
Johnny Coulon (1999)	b. 2-12-1889 d. 10-29-73	56-4-4 (24)
Les Darcey	n/a	n/a
Jack Delaney	n/a	n/a
"Nonpareil" Dempsey	n/a	n/a

NAME (YR. OF INDUCTION)	D.O.B. / D.O.D.	RECORD (KO'S)
Jack Dempsey (1990)	b. 6-24-1895 d. 5-31-83	60-6-8 (50)
Jack Dillon	n/a	n/a
George Dixon	n/a	n/a
Jim Driscoll	n/a	n/a
Johnny Dundee (1991)	b. 11-20-1893 d. 4-22-65	210-56-31 (22)
Bob Fitzsimmons	n/a	n/a
Tiger Flowers	n/a	n/a
Joe Gans	n/a	n/a
Frankie Genaro (1998)	b. 8-26-01 d. 12-27-66	94-22-8 (21)
Mike Gibbons	n/a	n/a
Tommy Gibbons	n/a	n/a
Harry Greb (1990)	b. 6-6-1894 d. 10-22-26	105-8-3 (48)
Young Griffo	n/a	n/a
Pete Herman (1997)	b. 1896 d. 1973	69-11-8 (19)
Peter Jackson	n/a	n/a
Joe Jeanette	n/a	n/a
James J. Jeffries	n/a	n/a
Jack Johnson	n/a	n/a
Stanley Ketchel	n/a	n/a
Johnny Kilbane	n/a	n/a
Fidel La Barba	n/a	n/a
Sam Langford	n/a	n/a
Kid Lavigne (1998)	b. 12-6-1869 d. 3-9-28	35-6-10 (19)
Benny Leonard	n/a	n/a
Battling Levinsky	n/a	n/a
John Henry Lewis	n/a	n/a
Ted (Kid) Lewis	n/a	n/a
Tommy Loughran (1991)	b. 11-29-02 d. 7-7-82	94-23-9 (17)
Benny Lynch (1998)	b. 4-12-13 d. 8-6-46	77-10-15
Sammy Mandell (1998)	b. 2-5-04 d. 11-7-67	147-26-13 (33)
Jack McAuliffe (1995)	b. 3-24-1866 d. 1937	31-0-6 (22)
Charles (Kid) McCoy (1991)	b. 10-13-1872 d. 4-18-40	86-6-6 (64)
Packey McFarland	n/a	n/a
Terry McGovern	n/a	n/a
Jimmy McLarnin (1991)	b. 12-19-06	62-11-3 (20)
Sam McVey (1999)	b. 1885 d. 1921	63-15-12 (46)
Freddie Miller (1997)	b. 1911 d. 1962	212-27-6 (44)
Battling Nelson	n/a	n/a
Phila. Jack O'Brien	n/a	n/a
Billy Petrolle	n/a	n/a
Maxie Rosenbloom	n/a	n/a
Barney Ross (1990)	b. 12-23-09 d. 1-17-67	72-4-3 (22)
Tommy Ryan	n/a	n/a
Jack Sharkey (1994)	b. 10-26-02 d. 8-17-94	38-13-3 (14)
Freddie Steele (1999)	b. 1912 d. 1984	124-6-8 (62)
Young Stribling	n/a	n/a
Lew Tendler (1999)	b. 9-28-1898 d. 11-15-70	59-11-2 (37)
Gene Tunney	n/a	n/a
Pancho Villa	n/a	n/a
"Barbados" Joe Walcott	n/a	n/a
Mickey Walker (1990)	b. 7-13-01 d. 4-28-81	93-19-4 (60)
Freddie Welsh (1997)	b. 1886 d. 1927	120-27-16 (30)
Jimmy Wilde	n/a	n/a
Kid Williams	n/a	n/a
Harry Wills (1992)	b. 5-15-1889 d. 12-21-58	65-8-2 (47)
Ad Wolgast	n/a	n/a

NATIONAL MUSEUM OF RACING HALL OF FAME

191 Union Avenue
Saratoga Springs, NY 12866
Telephone: (518) 584-0400

ENSHRINEES
(JOCKEYS/HORSES ONLY)

JOCKEY (YR. OF INDUCTION)	JOCKEY (YR. OF INDUCTION)
John Adams (1965)	John Eric Longden (1958)
Frank D. Adams (1970)	Daniel A. Maher (1955)
Joe Aitcheson Jr. (1978)	J. Linus McAtee (1956)
G. Edward Arcaro (1958)	Chris McCarron (1989)
Ted F. Atkinson (1957)	Conn McCreary (1975)
Braulio Baeza (1976)	Rigan McKinney (1968)
Jerry Bailey (1995)	James McLaughlin (1955)
George Barbee (1996)	Walter Miller (1955)
Caroll K. Bassett (1972)	Isaac B. Murphy (1955)
Russell Baze (1999)	Ralph Neves (1960)
Walter Blum (1987)	Joe Notter (1963)
George Bostwick (1968)	Winfield O'Conner (1956)
Sam Boulmetis Sr. (1973)	George M. Odom (1955)
Steve Brooks (1963)	Frank O'Neill (1956)
Don Brumfield (1996)	Ivan H. Parke (1978)
Thomas H. Burns (1983)	Gilbert W. Patrick (1970)
James H. Butwell (1984)	Laffit Pincay, Jr. (1975)
J. Dallett Byers (1967)	Samuel Purdy (1970)
Steve Cauthen (1994)	John Reiff (1956)
Frank Coltiletti (1970)	Alfred Robertson (1971)
Angel Cordero Jr. (1988)	John L. Rotz (1983)
Robert H. Crawford (1973)	Earl Sande (1955)
Pat Day (1991)	Carroll H. Shilling (1970)
Eddie Delahoussaye (1993)	William Shoemaker (1958)
Lavelle Ensor (1962)	Willie Simms (1977)
Laverne Fator (1955)	Tod Sloan (1955)
Jerry Fishback (1992)	Alfred P. Smithwick (1973)
Mack Garner (1969)	Gary Stevens (1997)
Edward Garrison (1955)	James Stout (1968)
Avelino Gomez (1982)	Fred Taral (1955)
Henry F. Griffin (1956)	Bayard Tuckerman Jr. (1973)
O. Eric Guerin (1972)	Ron Turcotte (1979)
William J. Hartack (1959)	Nash Turner (1955)
Sandy Hawley (1992)	Robert N. Ussery (1980)
Albert Johnson (1971)	Jacinto Vasquez (1998)
William J. Knapp (1969)	Jorge Velasquez (1990)
Julie Krone (2000)	George M. Woolf (1955)
Clarence Kummer (1972)	Raymond Workman (1956)
Charles Kurtsinger (1967)	Manuel Ycaza (1977)
John P. Loftus (1959)	

HORSE
(YR. OF ELECTION, YR. OF FOALING)

Ack Ack (1986, 1966)
Affectionately (1989, 1960)
Affirmed (1980, 1975)
All Along (1990, 1979)
Alsab (1976, 1939)
Alydar (1989, 1975)
Alysheba (1993, 1984)
American Eclipse (1970, 1814)
A.P. Indy (2000, 1989)
Armed (1963, 1941)
Artful (1956, 1902)
Arts and Letters (1994, 1966)
Assault (1964, 1943)
Battleship (1969, 1927)
Bayakoa (1998, 1984)
Bed o' Roses (1976, 1947)
Beldame (1956, 1901)
Ben Brush (1955, 1893)
Bewitch (1977, 1945)
Bimelech (1990, 1937)
Black Gold (1989, 1921)
Black Helen (1991, 1932)
Blue Larkspur (1957, 1926)
Bold 'n Determined (1997, 1977)
Bold Ruler (1973, 1954)
Bon Nouvel (1976, 1960)
Boston (1955, 1833)
Broomstick (1956, 1901)
Buckpasser (1970, 1963)
Busher (1964, 1942)
Bushranger (1967, 1930)
Cafe Prince (1985, 1970)
Carry Back (1975, 1958)
Cavalcade (1993, 1931)
Challedon (1977, 1936)
Chris Evert (1988, 1971)
Cicada (1967, 1959)
Citation (1959, 1945)
Coaltown (1983, 1945)
Colin (1956, 1905)
Commando (1956, 1898)
Count Fleet (1961, 1940)
Crusader (1995, 1923)
Dahlia (1981, 1970)
Damascus (1974, 1964)
Dark Mirage (1974, 1965)
Davona Dale (1985, 1976)
Desert Vixen (1979, 1970)
Devil Diver (1980, 1939)
Discovery (1969, 1931)
Domino (1955, 1891)
Dr. Fager (1971, 1964)
Easy Goer (1997, 1986)
Eight Thirty (1994, 1936)
Elkridge (1966, 1938)
Emperor of Norfolk (1988, 1885)

HORSE
(YR. OF ELECTION, YR. OF FOALING)

Equipoise (1957, 1928)
Exceller (1999, 1973)
Exterminator (1957, 1915)
Fairmount (1985, 1921)
Fair Play (1956, 1905)
Fashion (1980, 1837)
Firenze (1981, 1884)
Flatterer (1994, 1979)
Foolish Pleasure (1995, 1972)
Forego (1979, 1970)
Fort Marcy (1998, 1964)
Gallant Bloom (1977, 1966)
Gallant Fox (1957, 1927)
Gallant Man (1987, 1954)
Gallorette (1962, 1942)
Gamely (1980, 1964)
Genuine Risk (1986, 1977)
Go For Wand (1996, 1987)
Good and Plenty (1956, 1900)
Grandville (1997, 1933)
Grey Lag (1957, 1918)
Gun Bow (1999, 1960)
Hamburg (1986, 1895)
Hanover (1955, 1884)
Henry of Navarre (1985, 1891)
Hill Prince (1991, 1947)
Hindoo (1955, 1878)
Imp (1965, 1894)
Jay Trump (1971, 1957)
John Henry (1990, 1975)
Johnstown (1992, 1936)
Jolly Roger (1965, 1922)
Kelso (1967, 1957)
Kentucky (1983, 1861)
Kingston (1955, 1884)
Lady's Secret (1992, 1982)
La Prevoyante (1995, 1970)
L'Escargot (1977, 1963)
Lexington (1955, 1850)
Longfellow (1971, 1867)
Luke Blackburn (1956, 1877)
Majestic Prince (1988, 1966)
Man O' War (1957, 1917)
Miesque (1999, 1984)
Miss Woodford (1967, 1880)
Myrtlewood (1979, 1932)
Nashua (1965, 1952)
Native Dancer (1963, 1950)
Native Diver (1978, 1959)
Needles (2000, 1953)
Neji (1966, 1950)
Northern Dancer (1976, 1961)
Oedipus (1978, 1946)
Old Rosebud (1968, 1911)
Omaha (1965, 1932)
Pan Zareta (1972, 1910)

HORSE
(YR. OF ELECTION, YR. OF FOALING)

Parole (1984, 1873)
Personal Ensign (1993, 1984)
Peter Pan (1956, 1904)
Princess Doreen (1982, 1921)
Princess Rooney (1991, 1980)
Real Delight (1987, 1949)
Regret (1957, 1912)
Reigh Count (1978, 1923)
Riva Ridge (1998, 1969)
Roamer (1981, 1911)
Roseben (1956, 1901)
Round Table (1972, 1954)
Ruffian (1976, 1972)
Ruthless (1975, 1864)
Salvator (1955, 1886)
Sarazen (1957, 1921)
Seabiscuit (1958, 1933)
Searching (1978, 1952)
Seattle Slew (1981, 1974)
Secretariat (1974, 1970)
Shuvee (1975, 1966)
Silver Spoon (1978, 1956)
Sir Archy (1955, 1805)
Sir Barton (1957, 1916)
Slew O' Gold (1992, 1980)
Spectacular Bid (1982, 1976)
Stymie (1975, 1941)
Sun Beau (1996, 1925)
Sunday Silence (1996, 1986)
Susan's Girl (1976, 1969)
Swaps (1966, 1952)
Sword Dancer (1977, 1956)
Sysonby (1956, 1902)
Ta Wee (1994, 1967)
Ten Broeck (1982, 1872)
Tim Tam (1985, 1955)
Tom Fool (1960, 1949)
Top Flight (1966, 1929)
Tosmah (1984, 1961)
Twenty Grand (1957, 1928)
Twilight Tear (1963, 1941)
Two Lea (1982, 1946)
War Admiral (1958, 1934)
Whirlaway (1959, 1938)
Whisk Broom II (1979, 1907)
Winning Colors (2000, 1985)
Zaccio (1990, 1976)
Zev (1983, 1920)

INTERNATIONAL
MOTORSPORTS HALL OF FAME

Executive Director: Jim Freeman
Event Coordinator/Public Relations: Amanda
Thomas

3198 Speedway Blvd.
Talladega, AL 35160
Telephone: (256) 362-5002

ENSHRINEES
(DRIVERS ONLY)

DRIVER (YR. OF INDUCTION)	D.O.B. D.O.D.	CIRCUIT	DRIVER (YR. OF INDUCTION)	D.O.B. D.O.D.	CIRCUIT
Bobby Allison (1993)	b. 1937	NASCAR	Rex Mays (1993)	b. 1913 d. 1949	CART
Davey Allison (1998)	b. 1961 d. 1993	NASCAR	Bruce McLaren (1991)	b. 1937 d. 1970	Formula One
Mario Andretti (2000)	b. 1940	CART	Rick Mears (1997)	b. 1951	CART
Alberto Ascari (1992)	b. 1918 d. 1955	CART	Louis Meyer (1992)	b. 1904	CART
Buck Baker (1990)	b. 1919	NASCAR	Stirling Moss (1990)	b. 1929	Formula One
Buddy Baker (1997)	b. 1941	NASCAR	Tazio Nuvolari (1998)	b. 1892 d. 1953	Formula One
Tony Bettenhausen (1991)	b. 1916 d. 1961	CART	Barney Oldfield (1990)	b. 1878 d. 1946	Match Racing
Craig Breedlove (2000)	b. 1937	speed records	Benny Parsons (1994)	b. 1941	NASCAR
Jack Brabham (1990)	b. 1926	Formula One	David Pearson (1993)	b. 1934	NASCAR
Sir Malcolm Campbell (1990)	b. 1885 d. 1948	speed records	Roger Penske (1998)	b. 1937	Sports Car Racing
Rudolph Caracciola (1998)	b. 1901 d. 1959	Formula One	Lee Petty (1990)	b. 1914 d. 2000	NASCAR
Jim Clark (1990)	b. 1936 d. 1968	Formula One	Richard Petty (1997)	b. 1937	NASCAR
Ralph DePalma (1991)	b. 1916 d. 1961	CART	Nelson Piquet (2000)	b. 1952	Formula One
Mark Donohue (1990)	b. 1937 d. 1975	CART	Alain Prost (1999)	b. 1955	Formula One
Ralph Earnhardt (1997)	b. 1928 d. 1973	NASCAR	Don Prudhomme (2000)	b. 1941	Drag Racing
Richie Evans (1996)	b. 1941 d. 1985	NASCAR	Eddie Rickenbacker (1992)	b. 1890 d. 1973	Match Racing
Juan Manuel Fangio (1990)	b. 1911 d. 1995	Formula One	Glenn "Fireball" Roberts (1990)	b. 1931 d. 1964	NASCAR
Tim Flock (1991)	b. 1924 d. 1998	NASCAR	Kenny Roberts (1992)	b. 1951	Motorcycle Racing
A.J. Foyt (2000)	b. 1935	CART	Mauri Rose (1994)	b. 1906 d. 1981	CART
Don Garlits (1997)	b. 1932	Drag Racing	Johnny Rutherford (1996)	b. 1938	CART
Peter Gregg (1992)	b. 1940 d. 1980	Sports Car Racing	Wendell Scott (1999)	b. 1921 d. 1990	NASCAR
Dan Gurney (1990)	b. 1931	Formula One/ NASCAR	Ayrton Senna (2000)	b. 1960 d. 1994	Formula One
			Wilbur Shaw (1991)	b. 1902 d. 1954	CART
Jim Hall (1997)	b. 1935	Formula One	Carroll Shelby (1991)	b. 1923	Sports Car Racing
Donald Healey (1996)	b. 1919	speed records	Louise Smith (1999)	b. 1916	NASCAR
Graham Hill (1990)	b. 1929 d. 1975	Formula One	Jackie Stewart (1990)	b. 1939	Formula One
Phil Hill (1991)	b. 1919	Formula One	John Surtees (1996)	b. 1934	Motorcycle Racing
Al Holbert (1993)	b. 1946 d. 1988	Sports Car Racing	Herb Thomas (1994)	b. 1923	NASCAR
Bobby Isaac (1996)	b. 1932 d. 1977	NASCAR	Mickey Thompson (1990)	b. 1928 d. 1988	speed records
Ned Jarrett (1991)	b. 1932	NASCAR	Curtis Turner (1992)	b. 1924 d. 1970	NASCAR
Gordon Johncock (1999)	b. 1936	CART	Al Unser Sr. (1998)	b. 1939	CART
Junior Johnson (1990)	b. 1931	NASCAR	Bobby Unser (1990)	b. 1934	CART
Parnelli Jones (1990)	b. 1933	CART	Bill Vuckovich (1991)	b. 1919 d. 1955	CART
Niki Lauda (1993)	b. 1949	Formula One	Rodger Ward (1992)	b. 1921	CART
Fred Lorenzen (1991)	b. 1934	NASCAR	Joe Weatherly (1994)	b. 1922 d. 1964	NASCAR
Tiny Lund (1994)	b. 1929 d. 1975	NASCAR	Cale Yarborough (1993)	b. 1940	NASCAR
Banjo Matthews (1998)	b. 1932 d. 1996	NASCAR			

SOCCER HALL OF FAME

President: Will Lunn

Wright Soccer Campus
18 Stadium Circle
Oneonta, NY 13820
Telephone: (607) 432-3351
www.soccerhall.org

ENSHRINEES (PLAYERS ONLY)

NAME	D.O.B. D.O.D.	YEAR INDUCTED	POS.	CAREER VITALS
Annis, Robert	b. 9-5-28 d. 3-31-95		D	Played on 1948 U.S. Olympic team, 1950 U.S. World Cup team
Auld, Andy	b. 1-26-00 d. 12-6-77	n/a	M/F	1930 U.S. World Cup team
Bahr, Walter	b. 4-1-27		M	Captain of 1950 U.S. World Cup team
Barr, George	b. 1915	1983	D	Captain of Brookhattan team that won 1945 U.S. Open Cup
Beardsworth, Fred	n/a	1965		Won American Cup medals in 1920 and '21 with Robins Drydock
Beckenbauer, Franz	b. 11-11-45	1998	D	won NASL title with N.Y. Cosmos in 1977, '78 and '80
Bernabei, Raymond	b. 11-26-25	1978	D	Captain of Harmarville (Pa.) teams that won U.S. Open Cup in 1952 and '56
Bookie, Mike	b. 9-12-04 d. 10-12-44	1986	F	Played on 1930 U.S. World Cup team
Borghi, Frank	b. 4-9-25	1976	GK	1950 U.S. World Cup team
Boulos, John	b. 6-7-21	1980	F	Won 1943 and '44 U.S. Open Cup with Brooklyn Hispano
Brittan, Harold	b. 1894 d. 1964	1951	F	Played for Fall River Marksmen, won U.S. Open Cup in 1924, '27
Brown, Davey	b. 11-18-1898 d. 9-17-70	1951	F	Scored 52 goals in 38 games with ASL N.Y. Giants, 1926–27
Brown, George		1995	F	1957 U.S. national team, 1959 U.S. Pan Am Games team
Brown, James	b. 12-31-08 d. 11-9-94	1986	F	1930 U.S. World Cup team
Carenza, Joseph		1982		Member of St. Louis Zenthoefers team that upset Germany's Eintracht Frankfurt 2–1 in 1951
Carrafi, Ralph	n/a	1959	F	Played for Bruell Insurance in 1930 U.S. Open Cup final
Chacurian, Chico	b. 2-22-24	1992	F	Played for U.S. national team in 1949
Chesney, Stanley	b. 1910 d. 11-25-84	1966	GK	N.Y. Americans, 1937 U.S. Open Cup champions
Chinaglia, Giorgio	b. 1-24-47	2000	F	1974 Italian World Cup team, won NASL titles with N.Y. Cosmos 1977, '78, 80, '82
Colombo, Charlie	b. 7-20-20 d. 5-7-86	1976	M	1950 U.S. World Cup team
Coombes, Geoff	b. 4-23-19	1976	F/M	1950 U.S. World Cup team
Craddock, Robert Jr.		1997		1950 U.S. World Cup team
Danilo, Paul		1997	F	Won 1940 U.S. Amateur Cup with Morgan (Pa.) SC
Dick, Walter	b. 9-20-05 d. 7-24-89	1989	F	1934 U.S. World Cup team
Diorio, Nick	b. 2-4-21	1974	F	1950 U.S. Word Cup team
Donelli, Aldo	b. 7-22-07 d. 8-9-94	1954	F	1934 U.S. World Cup team
Douglas, Jimmy	b. 1-12-1898 d. 3-5-72	1953	GK	1924 U.S. Olympic team, 1930 U.S. World Cup team
Duggan, Thomas	b. 9-31-1897 d. 11-30-61	1955	F	Won 1923 U.S. Open with Paterson (N.J.) FC
Dunn, Jimmy	n/a	1974	F	Won 1920 U.S. Open Cup with Ben Miller FC (Mo.)

NAME	D.O.B. D.O.D.	YEAR INDUCTED	POS.	CAREER VITALS
Ely, Alex	b. 2-9-38	1997	M	1959 U.S. Olympic/Pan Am Games team
Ferguson, Jock	b. 1887 d. 9-19-73	1950	D	Played in five U.S. Open Cup finals with Bethlehem (Pa.) Steel
Florie, Thomas	b. 9-6-1897 d. 4-26-66	1986	F	1930 and '34 U.S. World Cup teams, captain in '30
Fricker, Werner		1992		President of USSF from 1984 to '90
Fryer, William	b. 7-22-95 d. 8-29-60	1951		Won U.S. Open Cup with Paterson (N.J.) FC in 1923
Gabarra, Carin Jennings	b. 1-9-65	2000	D	1995 U.S. Women's World Cup team
Gaetjens, Joe	b. 3-19-24 d. 7-10-64	1976	F	Scored goal in U.S.'s 1–0 upset of England at 1950 World Cup
Gallagher, Jimmy	b. 6-7-01 d. 10-7-71	1986	M	1930 U.S. World Cup team
Gard, Gino	b. 11-26-22	1976	GK	1950 U.S. World Cup team
Gentle, James	b. 7-21-04 d. 5-22-86	1986	F	1930 U.S. World Cup team
Getzinger, Rudy	b. 9-4-44	1991	M	1972 U.S. national team, Chicago Sting NASL 1975–76
Glover, Teddy	b. 4-7-02 d. 2-8-93	1965	D	Won 1931 ASL title with N.Y. Giants
Gonsalves, Bill	b. 8-10-08 d. 7-17-77	1950	F	1930 U.S. World Cup team
Gormley, Bob		1989	F	1948 and '54 U.S. national team
Govier, Sheldon	b. n/a d. 1948	1950	M	Played for Pullman AC (Chicago) for 25 years
Gryzik, Joseph	n/a	1973	M	1963 U.S. Pan Am Games team
Harker, Al	b. 4-11-10	1979	M/D	1934 U.S. World Cup team
Heinrichs, April	b. 2-27-64	1998	F	Captain of 1991 U.S. Women's World Cup team
Hynes, Jack	b. 1920	1977	F	1949 U.S. national team
Jaap, John	n/a	1953	F	Won 1926 U.S. Open Cup with Bethlehem (Pa.) Steel FC
Keough, Harry	b. 11-15-27	1976	D	1950 U.S. World Cup team, 1952 and '56 Olympic teams
Kropfelder, Nick	b. 4-19-23	1996		Won ASL titles with Philadelphia Nationals in 1950 and '51
Kuntner, Rudy	b. 6-10-08 d. 12-16-82	1963	F	Won 1945 Cup, ASL title and U.S. Open Cup with Brookhattan FC (NYC)
Lang, Millard	b. 8-7-12	1950	F	Led ASL in scoring in 1934 with Baltimore Canton
Maca, Joseph	b. 9-28-20 d. 7-13-82	1976	D	1950 U.S. World Cup team
McBride, Pat	b. 11-13-43	1994	M	Played for 1968 and '74 U.S. national teams
McGhee, Bart	b. 4-30-1899 d. 1-26-79	1986	F	1930 U.S. World Cup team, scored first goal by a U.S. player in World Cup competition
McGuire, John	b. 3-3-1893 d. 11-18-62	1951	F	Won 1921 U.S. Open Cup with Robbins Dry Dock (Brooklyn) and '23 U.S. Open Cup with Paterson (N.J.) FC
McIlveney, Edward	b. 10-21-24 d. 5-18-89	1976	M	1950 U.S. World Cup team
McLaughlin, Ben	b. 4-10-28	1977	F	Played for U.S. national team from 1948 to '55
Mieth, Werner	b. 4-28-12 d. 9-28-97	1974	M	Won ASL titles with Philadelphia German-Americans in 1942, '44, '47, '48 and '52
Millar, Robert	b. 5-12-1890 d. 1967	1950	F	Won three U.S. Open Cups as player, coached 1930 U.S. World Cup team
Monsen, Lloyd	b. 5-7-31	1994		Played for U.S. national team in 1952 and '55
Moore, Johnny	b. 8-28-47	1997	F	Played for NASL's San Jose Earthquakes (1974–77) and Oakland Stompers (1978)
Moorhouse, George	b. 5-4-01 d. 10-12-43	1986	D	Captain of 1934 U.S. World Cup team
Morrison, Robert	n/a	1951	M	Won 1915 and '16 U.S. Open Cups with Bethlehem (Pa.) Steel FC

NAME	D.O.B. D.O.D.	YEAR INDUCTED	POS.	CAREER VITALS
Murphy, Ed	b. 11-6-30	1998	F	Played for U.S. national team from 1955 to '69
Nanoski, John	n/a	1993	F	Won 1939 U.S. Open Cup with Brooklyn St. Mary's Celtic, scored three goals in final
O'Brien, Shamus	b. 11-29-07 d. 11-28-81	1990	F	Won 1931 ASL title with N.Y. Giants
Olaff, Gene	b. 1920	1971	GK	Won 1943 and '44 U.S. Open Cups with Brooklyn Hispano
Oliver, Arnie	b. 5-22-07 d. 10-16-93	1907		1930 U.S. World Cup team
Oliver, Len	b. 1934	1996	M	1963 U.S. Pan Am Games team, 1964 U.S. Olympic team
Pariani, Gino	b. 2-21-28	1976	F	1948 U.S. Olympic team, 1950 U.S. World Cup team
Patenaude, Bert	b. 11-4-09 d. 11-4-74	1971	F	1930 U.S. World Cup team, first player to score hat trick in a World Cup game
Pelé	b. 10-23-40	1993	F	Soccer's great ambassador and greatest player, scored 1,281 goals in 22 years Won 1958, '62 and '70 World Cups with Brazil, won 1977 NASL title with N.Y. Cosmos
Ratican, Harry	n/a	1950		Won 1918 and '19 U.S. Open Cups with Bethlehem (Pa.) Steel FC.
Renzulli, Peter	b. 1895 d. 3-14-80	1951	GK	Won 1921 and '23 U.S. Open Cups with Robbins Dry Dock (Brooklyn) and Paterson (N.J.)
Roe, Jimmy	b. 12-27-08	1997	F	Won 1933 and '34 U.S. Open Cups with Stix, Baer and Fuller SC (St. Louis)
Roth, Werner	b. 4-4-48	1989	D	Won NASL titles with N.Y. Cosmos in 1972, '77 and '78, played for U.S. national team from 1972 to '75
Roy, Willy	b. 2-8-43	1989	F	Played for U.S. national team in 1966, '70 and '74 World Cup qualifying, coach of the year for Chicago Sting, 1981
Ryan, Francis	b. 1-10-08 d. 10-14-77	1958	F	1928 U.S. Olympic team, 1934 U.S. World Cup team, 1936 U.S. Olympic team
Schaller, Willie	b. 2-23-33	1995		Played on 1952 U.S. Olympic team as a 19-year-old, 1960 U.S. Olympic team
Slone, Philip	b. 1-20-07	1986	M	1930 U.S. World Cup team
Souza, Edward	b. 9-22-21 d. 5-19-79	1976	F	1950 U.S. World Cup team
Souza, John	b. 7-12-20	1976	F	1950 U.S. World Cup team
Spalding, Dick	n/a	1950	D	1916 U.S. national team
Stark, Archie	b. 12-21-1897 d. 5-27-85	1950	F	Top scorer in U.S. soccer history, won 1926 U.S. Open Cup with Bethlehem (Pa.) Steel FC
Swords, Thomas	n/a	1951	F	Captain of 1916 U.S. national team
Tintle, George	b. 12-24-1892 d. 1-14-75	1952	GK	1916 U.S. national team
Tracey, Ralph	b. 2-6-04 d. 3-6-75	1986	M	1930 U.S. World Cup team
Vaughn, Frank	b. 1902 d. 7-9-59	1986	D	1930 U.S. World Cup team
Wallace, Frank	b. 7-15-22 d. 11-13-79	1976	F	Won 1948 and '50 U.S. Open Cup titles with Simpkins-Ford SC (St. Louis)
Weir, Alex	b. 1911	1975	M	Played in 1938 U.S. Open Cup final with Brooklyn St. Mary's Celtic
Wilson, Peter	n/a	1950	D	Played for 25 years with Scottish-Americans, Paterson Rangers and Pawtucket
Wolanin, Adam	b. 11-13-19 d. n/a	1976	F	1950 U.S. World Cup team
Wood, Alex	b. 6-12-07 d. 7-20-87	1986	D	1930 U.S. World Cup team
Zerhusen, Al	b. 12-4-31	1978	F	Played for U.S. national team in 1958, '62 and '66 World Cup qualifying

INTERNATIONAL SWIMMING HALL OF FAME

President: Dr. Samuel J. Freas
Director of Public Relations: Colleen Wilson

1 Hall of Fame Drive
Fort Lauderdale, FL 33316
Telephone: (954) 462-6536
www.ishof.org

ENSHRINEES (SWIMMERS AND DIVERS ONLY)

NAME (YR. OF INDUCTION)	CLASS	CITIZENSHIP	NAME (YR. OF INDUCTION)	CLASS	CITIZENSHIP
Abdellatief Abouheif (1998)	Open Water Swimmer	Egypt	Brad Cooper (1994)	Swimmer	Australia
Greta Andersen (1969)	Swimmer	Denmark	Joyce M. Cooper (1996)	Pioneer Swimmer	Great Britain
Hannelore Anke (1990)	Swimmer	East Germany	Lynne Cox (2000)	Open Water Swimmer	United States
Mayumi Aoki (1989)	Swimmer	Japan	Clarence (Buster) Crabbe (1965)	Swimmer	United States
Shigeo Arai (1997)	Pioneer Swimmer	Japan	Lorraine Crapp (1972)	Swimmer	Australia
Duncan Armstrong (1996)	Swimmer	Australia	Ferenc Csik (1983)	Swimmer	Hungary
Susie Atwood (1992)	Swimmer	United States	Anne Curtis (1966)	Swimmer	United States
Shirley Babashoff (1982)	Swimmer	United States	Ellie Daniel (1997)	Swimmer	United States
Catie Ball (1976)	Swimmer	United States	C.M. (Charlie) Daniels (1965)	Swimmer	United States
Dr. Istvan Barany (1978)	Swimmer	Hungary	Tamas Darnyi (2000)	Swimmer	Hungary
Mike Barrowman (1997)	Swimmer	United States	John Davies (1984)	Swimmer	Australia
Walter Bathe (1970)	Swimmer	Germany	Victor Davis (1994)	Swimmer	Canada
Sybil Bauer (1967)	Swimmer	United States	Penny Dean (1996)	Open Water Swimmer	United States
Alex Baumann (1992)	Swimmer	Canada	Rick DeMont (1990)	Swimmer	United States
Sir Frank Beaurepaire (1967)	Swimmer	Australia	Clare Dennis (1982)	Swimmer	Australia
Melissa Belote (1983)	Swimmer	United States	Willy den Ouden (1970)	Swimmer	The Netherlands
Kevin Berry (1980)	Swimmer	Australia	Donna DeVarona (1969)	Swimmer	United States
Arno Bieberstein (1988)	Pioneer Swimmer	Germany	John Devitt (1979)	Swimmer	Australia
Matt Biondi (1997)	Swimmer	United States	Olga Dorfner (1970)	Swimmer	United States
Djurdjica Bjedov (1987)	Swimmer	Yugoslavia	Taylor Drysdale (1994)	Pioneer Swimmer	United States
Ethelda Bleibtrey (1967)	Swimmer	United States	Virginia (Ginny) Duenkel (1985)	Swimmer	United States
Gerard Blitz (1990)	Pioneer Swimmer/ Water Polo	Belgium	Barbara Dunbar (2000)	Masters Swimmer	United States
			Fanny Durack (1967)	Swimmer	Australia
Jean Boiteux (1982)	Swimmer	France	Gertrude Ederle (1965)	Swimmer	United States
Arne Borg (1966)	Swimmer	Sweden	David Edgar (1996)	Swimmer	United States
Charlotte Boyle (1988)	Pioneer Swimmer	United States	Kathy Ellis (1991)	Swimmer	United States
Walter Brack (1997)	Pioneer Swimmer	Germany	Kornelia Ender (1981)	Swimmer	East Germany
Marie Braun (1980)	Swimmer	The Netherlands	John Faricy (1990)	Pioneer Swimmer	United States
George Breen (1975)	Swimmer	United States	Jeff Farrell (1968)	Swimmer	United States
Owen Joyne Bruner (1998)	Masters Swimmer	United States	Hans Fassnacht (1992)	Swimmer	Germany
Mike Bruner (1988)	Swimmer	United States	Jane Fauntz (1991)	Pioneer Swimmer/Diver	United States
Lynn Burke (1978)	Swimmer	United States	Cathy Ferguson (1978)	Swimmer	United States
Mike Burton (1977)	Swimmer	United States	Peter Fick (1978)	Swimmer	United States
Gloria Callen (1984)	Swimmer	United States	Sharon Finneran (1985)	Swimmer	United States
Novella Calligaris (1980)	Swimmer	Italy	Ralph Flanagan (1978)	Swimmer	United States
Jeannette Campbell (1991)	Swimmer	Argentina	Jennie Fletcher (1971)	Swimmer	Great Britain
Tedford Cann (1967)	Swimmer	United States	Alan Ford (1966)	Swimmer	United States
Patty Caretto (1987)	Swimmer	United States	Michelle Ford (1994)	Swimmer	Australia
Rick Carey (1993)	Swimmer	United States	Dawn Fraser (1965)	Swimmer	Australia
Christine (Kiki) Caron (1998)	Swimmer	France	Bruce Furniss (1987)	Swimmer	United States
Cathy Carr (1988)	Swimmer	United States	Hironoshin Furuhashi (1967)	Swimmer	Japan
Tracy Caulkins (1990)	Swimmer	United States	Masaru Furukawa (1981)	Swimmer	Japan
Florence Chadwick (1970)	Swimmer	United States	Rowdy Gaines (1995)	Swimmer	United States
Andrew M. (Boy) Charlton (1972)	Swimmer	Australia	Claire Galligan (1970)	Swimmer	United States
Steve Clark (1966)	Swimmer	United States	Eleanor Garatti-Seville (1992)	Pioneer Swimmer	United States
Richard Cleveland (1991)	Swimmer	United States	Tim Garton (1997)	Masters Swimmer	United States
Tiffany Cohen (1996)	Swimmer	United States	Terry Gathercole (1985)	Swimmer	Australia
Carin Cone (1984)	Swimmer	United States	Harrison Glancy (1990)	Pioneer Swimmer	United States

NAME (YR. OF INDUCTION)	CLASS	CITIZENSHIP
Brian Goodell (1986)	Swimmer	United States
Budd Goodwin (1971)	Swimmer	United States
Shane Gould (1977)	Swimmer	Australia
Jed Graef (1988)	Swimmer	United States
Judy Grinham (1981)	Swimmer	Great Britain
Michael Gross (1995)	Swimmer	Germany
Irene Guest (1990)	Pioneer Swimmer	United States
Andrea Gyarmati (1995)	Swimmer	Hungary
Valerie Gyenge (1978)	Swimmer	Hungary
Alfred Hajos (1966)	Swimmer	Hungary
Gary Hall Sr. (1981)	Swimmer	United States
Kaye Hall (1979)	Swimmer	United States
Zoltan Halmay (1968)	Swimmer	Hungary
Tetsuo Hamuro (1990)	Swimmer	Japan
Ursula Happe (1997)	Swimmer	Germany
Phyllis Harding (1995)	Swimmer	Great Britain
Joan Harrison (1982)	Swimmer	South Africa
Karen Harup (1975)	Swimmer	Denmark
Shiro Hashizume (1992)	Swimmer	Japan
John Gatenby (Jack) Hatfield (1984)	Swimmer/Water Polo	Great Britain
Cecil Healy (1981)	Swimmer	Australia
Harry Hebner (1968)	Swimmer	United States
Jerry Heidenrich (1992)	Swimmer	United States
John Hencken (1988)	Swimmer	United States
Jan Henne (1979)	Swimmer	United States
Thor Henning (1992)	Pioneer Swimmer	Sweden
Jon Henricks (1973)	Swimmer	Australia
Charles Hickcox (1976)	Swimmer	United States
John Higgins (1971)	Swimmer	United States
George Hodgson (1968)	Swimmer	Canada
Nancy Hogshead (1994)	Swimmer	United States
Harry Holiday (1991)	Swimmer	United States
Steve Holland (1989)	Swimmer	Australia
Eleanor Holm (1966)	Swimmer	United States
Frederick Holman (1988)	Pioneer Swimmer	Great Britain
Ernst Hoppenberg (1988)	Pioneer Swimmer	Germany
Richard Hough (1970)	Swimmer	United States
Ralph Hutton (1984)	Swimmer	Canada
Ragnhild Hveger (1966)	Swimmer	Denmark
Alex Jany (1977)	Swimmer	France
John Arthur Jarvis (1968)	Swimmer	Great Britain
Chet Jastremski (1977)	Swimmer	United States
Graham Johnston (1998)	Masters Swimmer	United States
Lina Kaciusyte (1998)	Swimmer	Soviet Union
Duke Kahanamoku (1965)	Swimmer	United States
Warren Kealoha (1968)	Swimmer	United States
Adolph Kiefer (1965)	Swimmer	United States
Barney Kieran (1969)	Swimmer	Australia
Lenore Kight (1981)	Swimmer	United States
John Kinsella (1986)	Swimmer	United States
Cor Kint (1971)	Swimmer	The Netherlands
Kusuo Kitamura (1965)	Swimmer	Japan
Masaji Kiyokawa (1978)	Swimmer	Japan
Reizo Koike (1996)	Pioneer Swimmer	Japan
George Kojac (1968)	Swimmer	United States
Ada Kok (1976)	Swimmer	The Netherlands
Mary Kok (1980)	Swimmer	The Netheralands
Claudia Kolb (1975)	Swimmer	United States
Ford Konno (1972)	Swimmer	United States
John and Ilsa Konrads (1971)	Swimmers	Australia
Rosemarie Kother (1986)	Swimmer	East Germany
Barbara Krause (1988)	Swimmer	East Germany
Stubby Kruger (1986)	Pioneer Swimmer/Diver	United States
Ethel Lackie (1969)	Swimmer	United States
Frederick (Freddy) Lane (1969)	Swimmer	Australia
Ludy Langer (1988)	Pioneer Swimmer	United States

NAME (YR. OF INDUCTION)	CLASS	CITIZENSHIP
G. Harold (Gus) Langner (1995)	Masters Swimmer	United States
Lance Larson (1980)	Swimmer	United States
Gunnar Larsson (1979)	Swimmer	Sweden
Walter Laufer (1973)	Swimmer	United States
Kelley Lemmon (1999)	Masters Swimmer	United States
Harry LeMoyne (1988)	Pioneer Swimmer	United States
Maria Lenk (1988)	Swimmer	Brazil
Kim Linehan (1997)	Swimmer	United States
Anita Lonsbrough (1983)	Swimmer	Great Britain
Alice Lord Landon (1993)	Pioneer Swimmer/Contributor	United States
Steve Lundquist (1990)	Swimmer	United States
Michael (Turk) McDermott (1969)	Swimmer	United States
Perry McGillivray (1981)	Swimmer	United States
Tim McKee (1998)	Swimmer	United States
Don McKenzie (1989)	Swimmer	United States
Josephine McKim (1991)	Pioneer Swimmer	United States
Frank McKinney (1975)	Swimmer	United States
Jimmy McLane (1970)	Swimmer	United States
Helene Madison (1966)	Swimmer	United States
Hideko Maehata (1979)	Swimmer	Japan
Shozo Makino (1991)	Swimmer	Japan
Hakan Malmrot (1980)	Swimmer	Sweden
Shelley Mann (1966)	Swimmer	United States
Thompson Mann (1984)	Swimmer	United States
John Marshall (1973)	Swimmer	Australia
Hendrika Mastenbroek (1968)	Swimmer	The Netherlands
Roland Matthes (1981)	Swimmer	East Germany
Mary T. Meagher (1993)	Swimmer	United States
Jack Medica (1966)	Swimmer	United States
Maxine Merlino (1999)	Masters Swimmer	United States
Caren Metschuck (1990)	Swimmer	East Germany
Debbie Meyer (1977)	Swimmer	United States
Betsy Mitchell (1998)	Swimmer	United States
Yasuji Miyazaki (1981)	Swimmer	Japan
Karen Moe (1992)	Swimmer	United States
Jim Montgomery (1986)	Swimmer	United States
Belle Moore (1989)	Pioneer Swimmer	Great Britain
Adrian Moorhouse (1999)	Swimmer	Great Britain
Pablo Morales (1998)	Swimmer	United States
Pamela Morris (1965)	Synchro/Swimmer	United States
Lucy Morton (1988)	Pioneer Swimmer	Great Britain
Ardeth Mueller (1996)	Masters Swimmer	United States
Karen Muir (1980)	Swimmer	South Africa
Bill Mulliken (1984)	Swimmer	United States
Felipe Munoz (1991)	Swimmer	Mexico
John Naber (1982)	Swimmer	United States
Jiro Nagasawa (1993)	Swimmer	Japan
Keo Nakama (1975)	Swimmer	United States
Gail Neall (1996)	Swimmer	Australia
Sandra Neilson (1986)	Swimmer	United States
Anthony Nesty (1998)	Swimmer	Suriname
Dr. Paul Neumann (1986)	Pioneer Swimmer	Austria
Martha Norelius (1967)	Swimmer	United States
Eva and Ilona Novak (1973)	Swimmer	Hungary
Ian O'Brien (1985)	Swimmer	Australia
Albina Osipowich (1986)	Pioneer Swimmer	United States
Anne Ottenbrite (1999)	Swimmer	Canada
Kristen Otto (1993)	Swimmer	East Germany
Yoshi Oyakawa (1973)	Swimmer	United States
Sue Pedersen (1995)	Swimmer	United States
Andrea Pollack (1987)	Swimmer	East Germany
William Prew (1998)	Pioneer Swimmer	United States
Galina Prozumenshikova (1977)	Swimmer	Soviet Union
Erich Rademacher (1972)	Swimmer/Water Polo	Germany
Emil Rausch (1968)	Swimmer	Germany
Austin Rawlinson (1994)	Pioneer Swimmer	Great Britain

NAME (YR. OF INDUCTION)	CLASS	CITIZENSHIP
Katherine Rawls (1965)	Swimmer/Diver	United States
Rica Reinisch (1989)	Swimmer	East Germany
Ulrike Richter (1983)	Swimmer	East Germany
Aileen Riggin (Soule) (1967)	Swimmer/Diver	United States
Wally Ris (1966)	Swimmer	United States
Carl Robie (1976)	Swimmer	United States
Gail Roper (1997)	Masters Swimmer	United States
Murray Rose (1965)	Swimmer	Australia
Clarence Ross (1988)	Pioneer Swimmer	United States
Norman Ross (1967)	Swimmer	United States
Dick Roth (1987)	Swimmer	United States
Keena Rothhammer (1991)	Swimmer	United States
Doug Russell (1985)	Swimmer	United States
Sylvia Ruuska (1976)	Swimmer	United States
Roy Saari (1976)	Swimmer	United States
Evgeni Sadovyi (1999)	Swimmer	Hungary
Vladimir Salnikov (1993)	Swimmer	Soviet Union
Carroll E. Schaeffer (1968)	Swimmer	United States
Otto Scheff (1988)	Pioneer Swimmer	Austria
Petra Schneider (1989)	Swimmer	Germany
Clark Scholes (1980)	Swimmer	United States
Don Schollander (1965)	Swimmer	United States
Hilde Schrader (1994)	Pioneer Swimmer	Germany
Carolyn Schuler (1989)	Swimmer	United States
Nida Senff (1983)	Swimmer	The Netherlands
Tim Shaw (1989)	Swimmer/Water Polo	United States
Erwin Sietas (1992)	Pioneer Swimmer	Germany
Robert Skelton (1988)	Pioneer Swimmer	United States
Jonty Skinner (1985)	Swimmer	South Africa
Bill Smith (1966)	Swimmer	United States
Walter, Leonard and Wallace Spence (1967)	Swimmers	British Guyana
Mark Spitz (1977)	Swimmer	United States
Allen Stack (1979)	Swimmer	United States
Carrie Steinseifer (1999)	Swimmer	United States
Ted Stickles (1995)	Swimmer	United States
Tom Stock (1989)	Swimmer	United States
Sharon Stouder (1972)	Swimmer	United States
Eva Szekely (1976)	Swimmer	Hungary
Katalin Szoke (1985)	Swimmer	Hungary
Ray Taft (1996)	Masters Swimmer	United States
Nobutaka Taguchi (1987)	Swimmer	Japan
Katsuo Takaishi (1991)	Pioneer Swimmer	Japan
Satoko Tanaka (1991)	Swimmer	Japan
Elaine Tanner (1980)	Swimmer	Canada
Jean Taris (1984)	Swimmer	France
Ulrika Tauber (1988)	Swimmer	East Germany
Henry Taylor (1969)	Swimmer	Great Britain
Noboru Terada (1994)	Pioneer Swimmer	Japan
Mark Tewksbury (2000)	Swimmer	Canada
David Theile (1968)	Swimmer	Australia
Petra Thumer (1987)	Swimmer	East Germany
Mike Troy (1971)	Swimmer	United States
Yoshiyuki Tsuruta (1968)	Swimmer	Japan
Albert VandeWeghe (1990)	Swimmer	United States
Nel Van Vliet (1973)	Swimmer	The Netherlands
Jesse Vasallo (1997)	Swimmer	United States
Joe Verdeur (1966)	Swimmer	United States
Matt Vogel (1996)	Swimmer	United States
Herbert (Hal) Vollmer (1990)	Pioneer Swimmer	United States
Chris von Saltza (1966)	Swimmer	United States
Otto Wahle (1996)	Pioneer Swimmer	Austria/United States
Helen Wainwright (1972)	Swimmer/Diver	United States
Clara Lamore Walker (1995)	Masters Swimmer	United States
Lillian (Pokey) Watson (1984)	Swimmer	United States
Mary Wayte (2000)	Swimmer	United States
Captain Matthew Webb (1965)	Swimmer	Great Britain
Mariechen Wehselau (1989)	Pioneer Swimmer	United States
Johnny Weissmuller (1965)	Swimmer	United States
Michael Wenden (1979)	Swimmer	Australia
Beverly Whitfield (1995)	Swimmer	Australia
Sharon Wichman (1991)	Swimmer	United States
Tracey Wickham (1992)	Swimmer	Australia
Albert M. Wiggins (1994)	Swimmer	United States
David Wilkie (1983)	Swimmer	Great Britain
Robert Windle (1990)	Swimmer	Australia
Margaret Woodbridge (1989)	Pioneer Swimmer	United States
Cynthia Woodhead (1994)	Swimmer	United States
Mina Wylie (1975)	Swimmer	Australia
Tsuyoshi Yamanaka (1983)	Swimmer	Japan
William Yorzyk (1971)	Swimmer	United States
Masanori Yusa (1992)	Pioneer Swimmer	Japan
Alberto Zorilla (1976)	Swimmer	Argentina

NATIONAL TRACK & FIELD HALL OF FAME

1 RCA Dome, Suite 140
Indianapolis, IN 46225
Telephone: (317) 261-0500
Chief Executive Officer: Craig Masback
Director of Media Relations: Pete Cava
www.usatf.org

ENSHRINEES (ATHLETES ONLY)

NAME (YR. OF INDUCTION)	D.O.B. D.O.D.	CAREER VITALS
Dave Albritton (1980)	b. 4-13-13 d. 5-14-94	Olympic high jumper
Horace Ashenfelter (1975)	b. 1-23-23	Set world record in steeplechase (1952)
Evelyn Ashford (1997)	b. 4-15-57	Four-time Olympic sprinter
Willie Banks (1999)	b. 3-11-56	Set world record in triple jump (1985)
James Bausch (1979)	b. 3-29-06 d. 7-9-74	Won decathlon at 1932 Olympics
Bob Beamon (1977)	b. 8-29-46	Destroyed long jump w.r. at 1968 Olympics
Percy Beard (1981)	b. 1-26-08 d. 3-26-90	Silver medalist in hurdles at 1932 Olympics.
Jim Beatty (1990)	b. 10-28-34	First to break four-minute-mile barrier indoors
Dr. Greg Bell (1988)	b. 11-7-30	Won long jump at 1956 Olympics
Dee Boeckmann (1976)	b. 11-9-04 d. 4-25-89	On first U.S. women's Olympic team (1928)

NAME (YR. OF INDUCTION)	D.O.B. D.O.D.	CAREER VITALS
John Borican (2000)	b. 4-4-13 d. 1-4-43	National decathlon champion in 1941
Ralph Boston (1974)	b. 5-9-39	Won long jump at 1960 Olympics
Don Bragg (1996)	b. 5-15-35	Won pole vault at 1960 Olympics
Valerie Brisco (1995)	b. 7-6-60	Won three golds at 1984 Olympics
Doris Brown Heritage (1990)	b. 9-17-42	Five-time world cross-country champion
Lee Calhoun (1975)	b. 2-23-33 d. 6-22-89	Won hurdles at 1956 and '60 Olympics
Milt Campbell (1989)	b. 12-9-33	Won decathlon at 1956 Olympics
Henry Carr (1997)	b. 11-27-42	Sprinter, won two golds at 1964 Olympics
Chandra Cheeseborough (2000)	b. 1-10-59	Sprinter, won two golds at 1984 Olympics
Ellery Clark (1991)	b. 3-13-1874 d. 2-17-49	Won high jump and long jump at 1896 Games
Alice Coachman (Davis) (1975)	b. 11-9-23	First black woman to win an Olympic gold medal
Harold Connolly (1984)	b. 8-1-31	Won hammer throw at 1956 Olympics
Lillian Copeland (1994)	b. 11-25-04 d. 2-7-64	Won discus throw at 1932 Olympics
Tom Courtney (1978)	b. 8-17-33	Won 800-meter run at 1956 Olympics
Glenn Cunningham (1974)	b. 8-4-09 d. 3-10-88	Won two national collegiate distance titles
Willie Davenport (1982)	b. 6-8-43	Won hurdles at 1968 Olympics
Glenn Davis (1974)	b. 9-12-34	Won hurdles at 1956 and '60 Olympics
Harold Davis (1974)	b. 1-5-21	Tied world record for 100-meter dash in 1941
Mildred (Babe) Didrikson (Zaharias) (1974)	b. 6-26-14 d. 9-27-56	Won two golds at 1932 Olympics
Harrison Dillard (1974)	b. 7-8-23	Sprinter, won Olympic gold in 1948 and '52
Ken Doherty (1976)	b. 5-16-05 d. 4-17-96	Won decathlon bronze at 1928 Olympics
Charles Dumas (1990)	b. 2-12-37	First man to high jump 7'
Lee Evans (1983)	b. 2-25-47	Won 400-meter dash with w.r. at the 1968 Olympics
Norwood (Barney) Ewell (1986)	b. 2-25-18 d. 4-4-86	Won back-to-back NCAA sprint titles (1940 and '41)
Ray Ewry (1974)	b. 10-14-1873 d. 9-29-37	Won 10 gold medals, most alltime
Heriwentha (Mae) Faggs (Starr) (1976)	b. 4-10-32 d. 1-27-2000	Won gold on 4 x 100-meter relay at 1952 Olympics
Barbara Ferrell (Edmonson) (1988)	b. 7-28-47	Two-time Olympic sprinter
John Flanagan (1975)	b. 1-9-1868 d. 6-4-38	Won hammer throw in 1900, '04 and '08 Olympics
Dick Fosbury (1981)	b. 3-6-47	Won high jump at 1968 Olympics
Greg Foster (1998)	b. 4-4-58	Silver medalist in hurdles at 1984 Olympics.
Fortune Gordien (1979)	b. 9-9-22 d.4-10-90	Won two Olympic discus medals
Charles Greene (1992)	b. 3-21-44	Bronze medalist in 100 at 1968 Olympics
Florence Griffith-Joyner (1995)	b. 12-21-59 d. 9-21-98	Won three sprints at 1988 Olympics
Archie Hahn (1983)	b. 9-14-1880 d. 1-21-55	Won three sprints at 1904 Olympics
Evelyne Hall (Adams) (1988)	b. 9-10-09 d. 4-20-93	Second in 80-meter hurdles at 1932 Olympics
Brutus Hamilton (1974)	b. 7-19-00 d. 12-28-70	Silver medalist in 1920 Olympic decathlon
Glenn Hardin (1978)	b. 7-1-10 d. 3-6-75	Won hurdles at 1936 Olympics
Bob Hayes (1976)	b. 12-20-42	Won 100-meter dash at 1964 Olympics
Franklin (Bud) Held (1987)	b. 10-25-27	NCAA javelin champ in 1948, '49 and '50
Harry Hillman (1976)	b. 8-9-1881 d. 8-9-45	Won three hurdles events at 1904 Olympics
Jim Hines (1979)	b. 9-10-46	Won 100-meter dash at 1968 Olympics
Dr. Bud Houser (1979)	b. 9-25-01 d. 10-1-94	Won shot put and discus at 1924 Olympics
DeHart Hubbard (1979)	b. 11-25-03 d. 6-23-76	Won the long jump at 1924 Olympics
Charlie Jenkins (1992)	b. 1-7-34	Won 400-meter dash at 1956 Olympics
Bruce Jenner (1980)	b. 10-28-49	Won decathlon at 1976 Olympics
Cornelius Johnson (1994)	b. 8-28-13 d. 2-15-46	Won high jump at 1936 Olympics
Rafer Johnson (1974)	b. 8-18-35	Won decathlon at 1960 Olympics
Hayes Jones (1976)	b. 8-4-38	Won high hurdles at 1964 Olympics
John A. Kelley (1980)	b. 9-6-07	Marathoning career spanned eight decades
Abel Kiviat (1985)	b. 6-23-1892 d. 8-24-91	Silver medalist in 1,500 at 1912 Olympics
Dr. Alvin Kraenzlein (1974)	b. 12-12-1876 d. 1-6-28	Won four gold medals at 1900 Olympics
Ron Laird (1986)	b. 5-31-38	Four-time Olympic racewalker
Francie Larrieu (Smith) (1998)	b. 11-23-52	Five-time Olympic distance runner
Don Lash (1995)	b. 8-15-14 d. 9-19-94	Won seven straight national cross-country titles
Henry Laskau (1997)	b. 9-12-16 d. 5-7-2000	Three-time Olympic racewalker
Marty Liquori (1995)	b. 9-11-49	Won three straight NCAA mile titles
Dr. Dallas Long (1996)	b. 6-13-40	Won shot put at 1964 Olympics
Madeline Manning-Mims (1984)	b. 1-11-48	Won 800-meter run at 1968 Olympics
Bob Mathias (1974)	b. 11-19-30	Won decathlon at 1948 Olympics at age 17
Randy Matson (1984)	b. 3-5-45	Won 1968 Olympic shot put
Joe McCluskey (1996)	b. 6-11-11	Won 27 national distance titles
Mildred McDaniel (Singleton) (1983)	b. 11-3-33	Won Olympic high jump in 1956
Edith McGuire (Duvall) (1979)	b. 6-3-44	Won 200-meter dash at 1964 Olympics
Ted Meredith (1982)	b. n/a d. 11-2-57	Won 800-meter run at 1912 Olympics
Ralph Metcalfe (1975)	b. 5-29-10 d. 10-10-78	Second in the 100 at 1932 and '36 Olympics
Rod Milburn (1993)	b. 5-18-50 d. 11-11-97	Won 110-meter hurdles in 1972 Olympics
Billy Mills (1976)	b. 6-30-38	Won 10,000-meter run at 1964 Olympics.

NAME (YR. OF INDUCTION)	D.O.B. D.O.D.	CAREER VITALS
Charles Moore (1999)	b. 8-12-29	Never lost a 400-meter race in his career
Bobby Morrow (1975)	b. 10-15-35	Won 100 and 200 at 1956 Olympics
Edwin Moses (1994)	b. 8-31-55	Won 400 hurdles at 1976 and '84 Olympics.
Lon Myers (1974)	b. 2-16-1858 d. 2-15-1899	Top 440 and 880 runner of 19th Century
Renaldo Nehemiah (1997)	b. 3-24-59	Set 110 hurdles w.r. in 1981
Parry O'Brien (1974)	b. 1-28-32	Won shot put at 1952 and '56 Olympics
Al Oerter (1974)	b. 8-19-36	Won Olympic discus in 1956, '60 '64 and '68
Harold Osborn (1974)	b. 4-13-1899 d. 4-5-75	Won high jump and decathlon at 1924 Olympics
Jesse Owens (1974)	b. 9-12-13 d. 3-31-80	Won four golds at 1936 Olympics
Charlie Paddock (1976)	b. 11-8-00 d. 7-21-43	Won 100-meter dash at 1920 Games
Mel Patton (1985)	b. 11-16-24	Won 200-meter dash ay 1948 Olympics
Eulace Peacock (1987)	b. 8-27-14 d. 12-13-96	Won AAU 100-meter dash and long jump titles
Steve Prefontaine (1976)	b. 1-25-51 d. 5-30-75	Won six national collegiate distance titles
Meyer Prinstein (2000)	b. 1878 d. 3-10-25	Four-time Olympic jumping gold medalist
Joie Ray (1976)	b. 4-13-1894 d. 5-15-78	Won 13 AAU distance titles
Greg Rice (1977)	b. 1-3-16 d. 5-19-91	1940 Sullivan Award winner
Bob Richards (1975)	b. 2-20-26	Won pole vault at 1952 and '56 Olympics
Louise Ritter (1995)	b. 2-18-58	Won high jump 1988 Olympics
Arnie Robinson (2000)	b. 4-7-48	Won long jump at 1976 Olympics
Betty Robinson (Schwartz) (1977)	b. 8-23-11 d. 5-17-99	Won women's Olympic 100-meter dash in 1928
Bill Rodgers (1999)	b. 12-23-47	Won Boston and New York City Marathons four times each
Ralph Rose (1976)	b. 3-17-1885 d. 10-16-13	Won shot put at 1904 and '08 Olympics
Wilma Rudolph (1974)	b. 6-23-40 d. 11-12-94	Won 100 and 200 at 1960 Olympics
Jim Ryun (1980)	b. 4-29-47	Second in 1,500-meter race at 1968 Olympics
Kate Schmidt (1994)	b. 12-29-53	Set nine U.S. javelin records
Jackson Scholz (1977)	b. 3-15-1897 d. 10-26-86	Won 200-meter dash at 1920 Olympics
Bob Schul (1991)	b. 9-28-37	Won 5,000 and 10,000-meter races at 1964 Olympics
Bob Seagren (1986)	b. 10-17-46	1968 Olympic pole vault champ
Maren Seidler (2000)	b. 6-11-51	Four-time Olympic shot putter
Mel Sheppard (1976)	b. 9-5-1883 d. 1-4-42	800- and 1,500-meter champ at 1908 Olympics
Martin Sheridan (1988)	b. 3-28-1881 d. 3-27-18	Won nine Olympic medals (second most alltime)
Jean Shiley (Newhouse) (1993)	b. 11-20-11	High jump champ at 1932 Olympics
Frank Shorter (1989)	b. 10-31-47	Won Olympic Marathon in 1972

NAME (YR. OF INDUCTION)	D.O.B. D.O.D.	CAREER VITALS
Dr. Dave Sime (1981)	b. 7-25-36	Four-time sprint world record holder
Robert Simpson (1974)	b. 5-25-1892 d. 10-10-75	Won national AAU high hurdles in 1916
Tommie Smith (1978)	b. 6-5-44	Won 200-meter dash at 1968 Olympics
Andy Stanfield (1977)	b. 12-29-27 d. 6-15-85	Won 200-meter dash 1952 Olympics
Les Steers (1974)	b. 6-16-17	Set two high jump world records in 1941
Helen Stephens (1975)	b. 2-3-18 d. 1-17-94	Won 100-meter dash at 1936 Olympics
Dwight Stones (1998)	b. 12-6-53	Won high jump bronze at 1972 and '76 Olympics
Frederick Morgan Taylor (2000)	b. 4-17-03 d. 2-16-75	Won 400-meter hurdles at 1924 Olympics
Dr. Walter Tewksbury (1996)	b. 3-21-1876 d. 4-25-68	Won five medals at 1900 Olympics
John Thomas (1985)	b. 3-3-41	Won two Olympic high jump medals
Earl Thomson (1977)	b. 2-15-1895 d. 4-19-71	Won high hurdles at 1920 Olympics
Jim Thorpe (1975)	b. 5-28-1888 d. 2-28-53	1912 Olympic decathlon and pentathlon champ
Eddie Tolan (1982)	b. 9-29-08 d. 1-30-67	Won 100 and 200 at 1932 Olympics
Bill Toomey (1975)	b. 1-10-39	1968 Olympic decathlon champ
Forrest Towns (1976)	b. 2-6-14 d. 4-4-91	Won high hurdles at 1936 Olympics
Wyomia Tyus (1980)	b. 8-29-45	Won 100-meter dash at 1964 and '68 Olympics
Stella Walsh (1975)	b. 4-3-11 d. 12-4-80	Won 100-meter dash at 1932 Olympics
Cornelius (Dutch) Warmerdam (1974)	b. 6-22-15	Set world record in pole vault
Martha Watson (1987)	b. 8-19-46	Four-time Olympic long jumper
Willye White (1981)	b. 1-1-39	Five-time Olympic sprinter/long jumper
Mal Whitfield (1974)	b. 10-11-24	Won 800-meter race at 1948 and '52 Olympics.
Mac Wilkins (1993)	b. 11-15-50	1976 Olympic discus champ
Archie Williams (1992)	b. 5-1-15 d. 6-24-93	Won 400-meter dash at 1936 Olympics
Fred Wilt (1981)	b. 12-14-20 d. 9-5-94	Won eight AAU distance titles
Rick Wohlhuter (1990)	b. 12-23-48	Third in 800 at 1976 Olympics
John Woodruff (1978)	b. 7-5-15	Won 800 at 1936 Olympics
Dave Wottle (1982)	b. 8-7-50	Won 800 at 1972 Games
Frank Wykoff (1977)	b. 10-29-09 d. 1-1-80	Two-time Olympic sprint gold medalist
George Young (1981)	b. 7-24-37	Third in 1968 Olympic steeplechase

PHOTOGRAPHY CREDITS

FRONT COVER
Clockwise from top left: Walter Iooss Jr. (Brown); National Baseball Library (Baseball Hall of Fame bulding); Bettmann/Corbis (Thorpe); John G. Zimmerman (Nicklaus); Neil Leifer (Aaron); Baseball Hall of Fame Library (Ruth); Walter Iooss Jr. (Chamberlain and Russell).

BACK COVER
Top: Graphic Artists/Hockey Hall of Fame (Orr); Chris Cole/Allsport (Navratilova).

FRONT MATTER
1, Focus on Sports; 2-3, Bettmann/Corbis.

6, top, National Baseball Library; bottom, Walter Iooss Jr.; 7, left, Russ Adams; right, *Branford Expositer*; 8-9, Hulton Getty; 10, Transcendental Graphics; 11, top, V.J. Lovero; bottom, Paul J. Bereswill; 12, Fred Kaplan; 13, top, Hy Peskin; middle, Walter Iooss Jr. ; bottom, Neil Leifer; 14, top, AP; middle, Detroit News; bottom, Transcendental Graphics; 15, Transcendental Graphics; 16, Alfred Puhn/Archive Photos; 17, left, AP; middle, National Baseball Library; right, AP; 18, Transcendental Graphics; 19, left, Corbis; middle, AP; right, Bettmann/Corbis; 20, Culver Pictures; 21, top, *Sports Illustrated* Picture Collection; middle, Culver Picture; bottom, Corbis; 22, top, Bettmann/Corbis; middle, Walter Iooss Jr.; bottom, AP; 23, Neil Leifer.; 24, left, Daily News; middle, Bettmann/Corbis; right, John Iacono; 25, John G. Zimmerman; 26, Transcendental Graphics; 27, left, Corbis; middle, Corbis; right, Corbis; 28, top, AP; middle, AP Photo; bottom, AP; 29, Hy Peskin; 30, Brown Brothers; 31, top, National Baseball Library; middle, Culver Pictures; bottom, Transcendental Graphics; 34-35, Walter Iooss Jr.; 36, HOF/NFL Photos; 37, left, Peter Read Miller; right, Scott Wachter/TDSI; 38, Walter Iooss Jr.; 39, left, Marvin E. Newman; middle, Neil Leifer; right, Steve Schapiro/Black Star; 40, Neil Leifer.; 41, left, James Drake; middle, Bill Eppridge/TimePix; right, Neil Leifer; 42, top, Transcendental Graphics; middle, Evan Peskin; bottom, AP; 43, Hy Peskin; 44, Culver Pictures; 45, top, *The New York Times;* middle, Bettmann/Corbis; bottom, Brown Brothers; 46, Neil Leifer; 47, top, Don Uhrbrock; middle, James Drake; bottom, NFL Photos; 48, left, AP; middle, Corbis; right, AP; 49, Corbis; 50, Mike Powell/Allsport; 51,top, Bettmann/Corbis; middle, Walter Iooss Jr.; bottom, Richard Mackson; 52, Andy Hayt; 53, top, Richard Mackson; middle, Bill Smith/NFL Photos; bottom, Heinz Kluetmeier; 54, SportsChrome; 55, left, Roy Hobson; middle, Jerry Wachter; right, Damian Strohmeyer; 56, Walter Iooss Jr..; left, Bettmann/Corbis; middle, Bettmann/Corbis; right, Walter Iooss Jr.; 60-61, John G. Zimmerman; 62, Art on File/Corbis; 63, left, Scott Cunningham/NBA Photos; right, Al Messerschmidt; 64, left, Rich Clarkson; middle, Peter Read Miller/NBA Photos; right, Andy Hayt; 65, Allsport; 66, Richard Meek; 67, top, AP; middle, Fred Kaplan; bottom, Walter Iooss Jr.; 68, SportsGalleryInc/John Sandhaus; 69, left, James Drake; middle, Manny Millan; right, Andrew D. Bernstein/NBA Photos; 70, left, Transcen- dental Graphics; middle, AP; right, Heinz Kluetmeier; 71, Sheedy and Long; 72, Hy Peskin; 73, top, AP; middle, Walter Iooss Jr.; bottom, Bettmann/Corbis; 74, top, Corbis; middle; James Drake; Peter Read Miller; 75, Manny Millan; 76, Bettmann/Corbis; 77, top, AP; middle, AP; bottom, Corbis; 78, James Drake; 79, left, Bettmann/Corbis; middle, Corbis; right, Heinz Kluetmeier; 80, Robert Huntzinger; 81, top, Rich Clarkson; middle, Transcendental Graphics; bottom, Sheedy and Long; 82, James Drake; 83, left, Richard Phillips; middle, Eric Schweikardt; right, Walter Iooss Jr.; 86-87, Paul J. Bereswill; 88, Hockey Hall of Fame; 89, top, Shaun Best/Reuters/TimePix; bottom, John Biever; 90, James Drake; 91, left, Frank Prazak/Hockey Hall of Fame; middle, AP; right, Bruce Bennett Studios; 92, top, Lane Stewart; middle, Paul Kennedy; bottom, David E. Klutho; 93, Paul J. Bereswill; 94, top, *Detroit News;* middle, James McCarthy/Hockey Hall of Fame; bottom, AP; 95, Bettmann/Corbis; 96, James Drake; 97, left, AP; middle, Art Rickerby; right, AP; 98, top, Pierre Cote/La Presse; middle, Sylvia Pecota/Allsport; bottom, Reuters NewMedia Inc./Corbis; 99, David E. Klutho; 100, Graphic Artists/Hockey Hall of Fame; 101, left, Tony Triolo; middle, Brearley Collection; right, Neil Leifer; 102, top, AP; middle, Imperial Oil-Turofsky/Hockey Hall of Fame; bottom, Imperial Oil-Turofsky/Hockey Hall of Fame; 103, Richard Meek; 104, left, Hockey Hall of Fame; middle, Burt Glinn/TimePix; right, Imperial Oil-Turofsky/Hockey Hall of Fame; 105, Graphic Artists/Hockey Hall of Fame; 106, left, Melchoir DeGiacomo; middle, Tony Triolo; bottom, Doug MacLellan/Hockey Hall of Fame; 107, M. DiGiacomo/Bruce Bennett Studios; 110-111, David Walberg; 112, Bob Bowen/Progressive Image/Corbis; 113, top, Bob Martin; bottom, Clive Brunskill/Allsport; 114, top, Hulton Getty; middle, Tony Duffy; bottom, Russ Adams; 115, Walter Iooss Jr.; 116, Bettmann/Corbis; 117, top, Bettmann/Corbis; middle, Bettmann/Corbis; bottom, Bettmann/Corbis; 118, Phillip Leonian; 119, left, Central Press; middle, Hulton Getty; right, Michael Merchant; 120, top, John G. Zimmerman; middle, John Iacono; bottom, Hulton Getty; 121, Hulton Getty; 122, Manny Millan; 123, top, Courtesy of Chris Evert; middle, Michael Merchant; bottom, Manny Millan; 124, Walter Iooss Jr.; left, *Long Beach Independent Press Telegram;* middle, UPI/Corbis-Bettmann; right, Hulton Getty; 126, Sheedy and Long; 127, left, Bettmann/Corbis; middle, Bettmann/Corbis; right, Gerry Cranham; 128, Manny Millan; 129, left, Tony Duffy; middle, Manny Millan; right, Bob Martin/Allsport; 130, top, Bettmann/Corbis; middle, Culver Pictures; bottom, AP; 131, Frederic Lewis; 134-135, James Drake; 136, Courtesy of World Golf Hall of Fame; 137, top, Jeff J. Mitchell/Reuters/TimePix; bottom, J.D. Cuban; 138, Hulton Getty; 139, left, Bettmann/Corbis; middle, Bettmann/Corbis; right, Corbis; 140, AP; 141, left, Courtesy of Mrs. R.L. Bowen; middle, AP; right, AP; 142, Corbis, 143, top, Hy Peskin; middle, AP, bottom, AP; 144, top, European; middle, Bettmann/Corbis; bottom, *Atlanta Journal;* 145, Bettmann/Corbis; 146, Morse-Pix; 147, left, AP; middle, AP; right, Bettmann/Corbis; 148, Neil Leifer; 149, top, John G. Zimmerman; middle, Walter Iooss Jr.; bottom, John Iacono; 150, John G. Zimmerman; 151, top, AP; middle, John G. Zimmerman; bottom, James Drake; 152, Hy Peskin; 153, left, AP; middle, Corbis; right, AP; 154, James Drake; 155, top, Bettmann/Corbis; middle, AP; bottom, Hy Peskin; 158-159, Neil Leifer; 160, Tony Arruza/Corbis; 161, left, Tony Triolo; right, George Tiedemann.